Insurance Era

Insurance Era

Risk, Governance, and the Privatization of Security in Postwar America

CALEY HORAN

The University of Chicago Press

Chicago and London

The University of Chicago Press, Chicago 60637
The University of Chicago Press, Ltd., London
© 2021 by The University of Chicago
All rights reserved. No part of this book may be used or reproduced in any
manner whatsoever without written permission, except in the case of brief
quotations in critical articles and reviews. For more information, contact
the University of Chicago Press, 1427 E. 60th St., Chicago, IL 60637.
Published 2021
Paperback edition 2024
Printed and bound by CPI Group (UK) Ltd, Croydon, CR0 4YY

33 32 31 30 29 28 27 26 25 24   1 2 3 4 5

ISBN-13: 978-0-226-78438-0 (cloth)
ISBN-13: 978-0-226-83329-3 (paper)
ISBN-13: 978-0-226-78441-0 (e-book)
DOI: https://doi.org/10.7208/chicago/9780226784410.001.0001

Library of Congress Cataloging-in-Publication Data

Names: Horan, Caley, author.
Title: Insurance era : risk, governance, and the privatization of security in postwar
    America / Caley Horan.
Description: Chicago ; London : The University of Chicago Press, 2021. |
    Includes bibliographical references and index.
Identifiers: LCCN 2020051200 | ISBN 9780226784380 (cloth) |
    ISBN 9780226784410 (ebook)
Subjects: LCSH: Insurance—United States—History—20th century. |
    Insurance—Privatization—United States. | United States—History—1945– | United
    States—Civilization—1945–
Classification: LCC HG8531 .H67 2021 | DDC 368.00973/09045—dc23
LC record available at https://lccn.loc.gov/2020051200

♾ This paper meets the requirements of ANSI/NISO Z39.48-1992 (Permanence of Paper).

For
Jee-Yeon "Jay" Kim

Contents

Introduction

The significance of a business is not wholly an affair of its statistics.
WALLACE STEVENS, "Insurance and Social Change"

In 1937, two years after the passage of the Social Security Act and the birth of the American welfare state, Wallace Stevens contemplated the future of insurance. In "Insurance and Social Change," an essay penned for the Hartford Accident and Indemnity Company's monthly magazine, the famed modernist poet surveyed the rapidly changing social landscape in Europe and the United States and noted an upsurge in demands for social and economic security. "As the social mass seeks to maintain itself, it relies more and more on insurance," he mused. "The truth is that we may well be entering an insurance era."[1]

Though best known for his poetry, Stevens was no stranger to the world of insurance. He worked in the field of surety and fidelity claims for most of his adult life and served as executive vice president at the Hartford for more than two decades. One of only a handful of published texts in which the poet discusses his day job, "Insurance and Social Change" addresses a question that first emerged as a topic of heated debate in the United States during the 1930s, and remained so for the rest of the century: What level of social and economic security should Americans expect, and how should they attain it?

"Insurance and Social Change" begins with a vision of a world in which "insurance [has] been made perfect." In this utopian future, insurance would guarantee protection for everyone "against everything." Could such a world be possible? Was it already in the process of becoming? To answer these questions, Stevens looked abroad, to Europe, where political change and public pressure for social insurance programs had been "most acute." After surveying the state of the field in Italy, Germany, England, and Soviet Russia, Stevens concluded that perfect insurance was still a long way off. The problem, according to Stevens, was "nationalization," the replacement of private insurance providers with government programs. Demand for social and economic security had become so great in parts of Europe that governments there had begun embracing insurance to what Stevens called "a point approaching identity." Stevens viewed this development—the rise of the welfare states of Europe—with alarm.[2]

Stevens was not alone in fearing the welfare state. Many American conservatives and business leaders in the 1930s believed that New Deal programs like Social Security represented the first step toward full-scale socialization of private enterprise. Unlike most of his colleagues in the insurance industry, however, Stevens was willing to remain optimistic. In the coming "insurance era," he reckoned, public insurance programs of one sort or another would be inevitable. Social Security was but a "minor case," the leading edge of a manageable tide that, if kept in check, might lift all boats. Once Americans developed an attachment to basic coverage of the sort now offered by government "old age" and unemployment programs, new forms of insurable security would no doubt come into view. "Universal insurance, or insurance for all, is not the same thing as insurance for everything," Stevens reassured his nervous colleagues in the industry. Public welfare programs, so long as they were limited, might even serve private providers by helping to expand desire for security and new insurance products.[3]

To prevent nationalization, Stevens argued, private industry would need to collaborate with government. But collaboration would not be possible if robust public insurance schemes, of the sort that were proliferating in Europe, took root in the United States. To prevent this very real possibility, Stevens urged his colleagues in the insurance industry to work together to ensure that the American welfare state remain limited. "If private companies can continue to expand with profit and adapt to the changing needs of changing times," he declared confidently, "no question of nationalization is likely to arise under our system."[4] Stevens's appeal did not fall on deaf ears. Though not all leaders of the insurance industry shared his willingness to adapt to Social Security, nearly all agreed that a growing welfare state intent on providing security to its citizens was a serious threat. Confronted by a global trend toward socialized risk, Wallace Stevens and other leaders of the insurance industry assessed their options. The coming insurance era signaled danger, but could it also present an opportunity? By unifying, expanding, and adapting, could private insurers shape this new era, and perhaps even make it their own?

An Insurance Era

This book examines the marketing, investing, and underwriting activities of select segments of the private insurance industry in the United States as it confronted the threat of government incursion and worked to adapt to what Stevens called the "changing needs of changing times" during the mid-decades of the twentieth century. Stevens's poetic heralding of an "insurance era" provides the launching point for this study, but the poet-businessman was not the first, or last, thinker to imagine the twentieth century in these terms.

The era Stevens saw on the horizon had already begun to emerge by the 1930s. During the early years of the twentieth century, a great number of American intellectuals—from economists seeking solutions to the rise of industrial accidents, to pragmatists hoping to "tame chance" and end war—turned to the social sharing of risk as a powerful response to the uncertainties and dangers unleashed by industrial capitalism.[5] As the sociologist Jonathan Simon has argued, these thinkers imagined insurance as a blueprint for the government of industrial societies, one that offered "an almost magical solution" to the problems of an uncertain and rapidly changing modern world.[6] The promise of insurance—its ability to produce social stability by spreading risk across populations—also attracted the interest of governments. The rise of the modern welfare state, a twentieth-century development, fundamentally transformed the relationship between states and their citizens. This turn toward the socialization of risk was a process Stevens hoped to contain, as it was already well underway when he penned "Insurance and Social Change."

By the 1980s, the turn toward socialized risk had transformed many aspects of daily life in nations across the world. It had also attracted the attention of a number of social and political theorists. Among those thinkers, few have been more influential in igniting scholarly interest in insurance than the French theorist François Ewald. Inspired by Michel Foucault's late work on rationalities of government and the management of populations—an approach dubbed "governmentality"—Ewald launched into research on insurance during the late 1970s. He focused on the same development Wallace Stevens had identified with alarm in the 1930s: the embrace of insurance by the nations of Europe "to a point approaching identity." Ewald located the welfare state, and its insurance mindset, at the center of what he considered a new era of social organization. His resulting formulation, the "insurance society," described the welfare states that emerged in Europe over the course of the twentieth century, as well as the new role accorded to risk in shaping both public policy and popular understandings of responsibility and collective organization across the liberal West.[7]

The notion that insurance had ushered in a new era of social organization attracted a devoted set of international followers. Together with the anthropologist Mary Douglas and the sociologist Ulrich Beck, both of whom produced groundbreaking studies in the 1980s on the social and cultural life of risk, these thinkers helped launch an "insurance turn" in social theory.[8] By the end of the century, scholars working in diverse fields across the humanities and social sciences had begun focusing their attention on risk as a social and political technology and on insurance as a novel form of government—one that gathered knowledge about populations, shaped the behavior of groups and individuals, defined and incentivized responsibility, and helped determine the boundaries of community through the creation of pools designated to spread and share risk. Like Stevens, these scholars also saw the twentieth century as an insurance era—a period when risk spreading and risk management became central functions of government and powerful shapers of social life.[9]

At the center of Ewald's notion of the "insurance society" lies an understanding of insurance as an abstract technology that changes over time according to shifting social and historical contexts. Insurance, he explains, can take many forms—from annuities to maritime insurance to life, health, or property and casualty insurance. It can also be administered and deployed by a variety of institutions, be they state governments, private corporations, fraternal societies, or other organizations. Ewald argues that these diverse insurance forms and institutions reflect and grow out of differing "imaginaries," or visions—the social and political objectives to which insurance is put to use.[10] Each of these categories—form, institution, and imaginary—combine at different times in different ways to shape contemporary meanings of insurance. "Existing in economic, moral, and political junctures which continually alter," Ewald writes, "the practice of insurance is always reshaping its techniques."[11]

Despite this insistence on the changeable quality of insurance in differing contexts, Ewald and other theorists of the insurance era have focused their attention primarily on the welfare states of Western Europe, often overlooking the American case.[12] Yet the United States also became an "insurance society," with its own unique "insurance imaginary," by the end of the twentieth century. More private than public, and more rooted in the individualization of risk than collective risk sharing, the American insurance society was structured on different terms than those in Europe. To understand this divergence—and the unique character of the insurance era in the United States—it is necessary to examine the immense but often overlooked power exercised by the private insurance industry in America.

The Expansion of Private Insurance in the United States

Thinking of the United States as its own kind of "insurance society" means taking seriously the role played by private industry in shaping American conceptions of risk, responsibility, and collective efforts to manage uncertainty. Several historians have undertaken this project over the past three decades.

The nineteenth century looms large in American insurance history. Commercial insurers and other financial organizations first institutionalized risk during this era, turning uncertainty and hazard into profitable trade. As the historian Jonathan Levy has illustrated, the commodification of risk in the early nineteenth century shaped the development of American capitalism and forged new associations between the ownership of risk and the ownership of oneself—a crucial linkage in the era of slavery. Insurance companies, Levy argues, played a central role in introducing risk to American life by transforming it into something quantifiable and fungible, a commodity that could be bought and sold on the market.[13]

Insurance companies were not the only spreaders of risk or institutional providers of security in the nineteenth century, however. As David Beito and other scholars have shown, extended kinship networks, mutual aid organizations, fraternal societies, lodges, and other voluntary risk-sharing institutions offered crucial support for working-class and minority populations in an era when commercial insurance was available only to elites, and before the advent of the American welfare state.[14] Fraternal orders, for example, pooled the resources of members and provided aid for the sick, the elderly, and dependents of deceased providers. Members of these orders typically came from similar backgrounds. As Beito argues, "Donors and recipients [of mutual aid] often came from the same, or nearly the same, walks of life; today's recipient could be tomorrow's donor, or vice versa."[15] Participants were drawn to voluntary mutual aid organizations not only for the protection offered in the face of misfortune, but also for the sense of community and solidarity membership provided. Many lodges and fraternal groups strengthened communal bonds by combining mutual support with elaborate rituals of membership.[16] Fraternals and other forms of mutual aid differed from commercial insurance in crucial ways. Structured primarily around internal ties between members (rather than abstract classifications of risk), they embraced a risk-spreading vision—an insurance imaginary—rooted in solidarity, interdependence, and a shared commitment to mutual aid.

Historians debate the precise causes of the contraction of American fraternalism. Beito, for example, argues that federal provision of Social Security in the 1930s "crowded out" voluntary mutual aid organizations. This perspective discounts the growth of private insurance in the United States and the successful efforts made by insurance companies during the early years of the twentieth century to court the very populations that formed the base of fraternal life. These efforts centered around the sale of "industrial insurance," a form of life insurance that catered to workers by charging low, weekly rates. Though these policies did not provide long-term security (they were typically used by working-class families to cover burial expenses), they were tremendously popular.[17] By the 1910s, the three largest industrial insurers—Metropolitan, Prudential, and John Hancock—provided nearly 20 percent of the life insurance in force in the United States, insuring nearly 25 percent of the population.[18]

Industrial insurance introduced private security to large segments of the American population. It also fundamentally changed the industry itself. Insurance companies accustomed to dealing only with elites viewed this newly insured mass of American workers as a group of subpar risks in need of management and training. Eager for the premium dollars of workers but concerned about the potential for excessive claims, industrial life insurers launched a series of campaigns designed to improve the health, welfare, and insurability of their new clients. These efforts often involved invasive forms of surveillance and interventions that sought to eradicate traditional forms of medicine and healing practiced by immigrants and minority groups. Campaigns to improve the welfare of industrial workers, however, earned insurance companies a reputation for performing philanthropic "good works," and cemented associations between insurance and public service that would last into the final decades of the twentieth century.

By the 1920s, Americans seeking security could also find it in the form of group insurance plans—benefits packages sold to employers by private insurers and then distributed to workers as a condition of employment. These group plans, which eventually offered a mix of pensions, annuities, and sickness and accident insurance, launched in the 1910s and quickly became an important source of business for large insurance companies. The plans offered much-needed security to workers and their families—but it was security that came at a price. As the historian Jennifer Klein has shown, the advent of employer-sponsored group insurance plans represented a continuation of nineteenth-century "welfare capitalism," a form of employer paternalism that, once reinvigorated by group insurance plans in the early twentieth century, had profound impacts on industrial relations.[19] Tying crucial benefits, unavailable elsewhere, to the employment contract gave industry a leg up in negotiations with labor. "For employers," writes Klein, "the unilateral purchase of commercial group insurance offered one key to containing union power and union political goals."[20]

Employment-linked group plans also benefited the insurance industry. In the 1920s, selling large group plans to a single employer allowed insurance companies to save on the costs associated with sending visiting agents door-to-door to sell industrial insurance policies. As the 1920s gave way to the Depression years of the 1930s—and as demands for security from what Wallace Stevens called "the social mass" grew louder—group plans also helped insurers stave off government incursion into the insurance business. The Social Security Act, with its combination of old-age, survivors, unemployment, and disability insurance, was enormously popular among working Americans. Still, many believed that it didn't do enough. Throughout the 1930s and 1940s, a chorus of social reformers, leftists, and minority groups joined labor organizations in insisting on a nationalized health insurance program to accompany Social Security, one that would replace the employment-linked system of benefits put in place by the group insurance model.[21] Klein illustrates how large employers and large insurers became allies in a battle against these forces, fighting side by side against the nationalization of healthcare and pension programs in the 1930s and 1940s.[22] Unification of the insurance industry, of the sort Stevens called for in "Insurance and Social Change," contributed to the success of efforts to defeat nationalization. By the late 1940s, the employment-linked model for health insurance in particular had been largely secured.

This did not mean, however, that the threat to private insurers from government had passed. Leaders of nearly every field of insurance—especially forms sold on the individual market—continued to fear government encroachment via the introduction of new social insurance programs, or via unwanted regulation of the insurance business. Insurers developed a host of strategies (including advertising, public service initiatives, targeted investments, and extensive lobbying) to combat nationalization and ensure that Social Security remained what Stevens called a "minor case."

On the legal front, insurance leaders committed to a tenacious defense of the state-based, rather than federal, regulatory structure that governed the industry. The passage of the McCarran–Fergusson Act in 1945 cemented this structure, which set insurance apart from other financial institutions by creating a patchwork of laws that differed from state to state. Congress passed the act in the wake of *United States v. South-Eastern Underwriters Association*, a case brought against the South-Eastern Underwriters Association under the Sherman Antitrust Act. In this case, the government accused the insurance alliance of price-fixing, intimidation, and other coercive tactics used to maintain its regional monopoly. The United States Supreme Court decided against South-Eastern Underwriters, ruling that the federal government could regulate insurance under the commerce clause of the Constitution. This decision represented a devastating blow to the entire industry, and insurers responded with aggressive lobbying in support of the McCarran–Ferguson Act, which would allow for federal control over some antitrust abuses but leave all other regulation of insurance to the states.

The passage of the act, made possible by extensive industry lobbying, marked an important moment in the history of insurance regulation. The complexity of the state-based system it cemented made it difficult for actors outside the industry—especially those seeking large-scale change on a national level, to intervene in insurance regulation. Industry critics hoping to pass laws that prohibited discrimination in insurance underwriting, for example, were forced to mount campaigns in every state. Lack of federal oversight also allowed insurers to pit states against one another, fostering competition among state governments to pass laws favored by the industry.[23]

By 1945, leaders of the insurance business had achieved great success in following Wallace Stevens's directive to adapt to changing times and "continue to expand with profit." In fact, the industry had emerged from depression and war in surprisingly good shape.[24] The commodification of risk, launched in the early nineteenth century, continued apace as insurance companies invented and popularized new forms of coverage. Though the state still loomed as a potential threat, competition from fraternal organizations and other forms of mutual aid had been largely suppressed. The corporate group model for health insurance and pensions had been secured with the assistance of allies in manufacturing. And the state-based regulatory structure that protected the industry from federal oversight, secured by passage of the McCarran–Fergusson Act, was firmly in place.

Insurance in Postwar America

Historians of insurance in the United States have focused their studies primarily on the nineteenth and early twentieth centuries. *Insurance Era* continues this story into the second half of the twentieth century. By underscoring the social, economic, and political power wielded by private insurers in the United States, it argues that the industry played a profound but often hidden role in shaping American life. To illustrate this role, *Insurance Era* examines three crucial aspects of insurance practice. Part I examines marketing and public relations. Part II explores insurance company investments in cities and suburbs. Part III addresses underwriting and risk classification, and the industry's successful defense of these practices in the face of charges of discrimination.

PART I: SELLING "SELF-MADE" SECURITY

Insurance historians of the nineteenth and early twentieth centuries have been keen to distinguish between various forms of insurance coverage, typically focusing their studies on a single field, such as life or health. Many of the strict divisions between insurance fields began to crumble during the postwar period with the advent of "all-risk" umbrella polices like homeowners insurance (invented in 1950), and as mergers created "multiline" firms that offered numerous forms of coverage. A regulatory system that did not distinguish between various fields of insurance bolstered the industry's newfound unity. So, too, did insurance leaders, who called on companies in all segments of the industry to sell private security as a single idea. These calls culminated in the creation of powerful public relations organizations, typically run by large life insurers but committed to "speaking with one voice" for the industry writ large.[25]

As chapter 1 illustrates, these public relations organizations embraced advertising as a powerful tool through which to sell "the idea" of private security. In advertisements throughout the postwar era, industry leaders encouraged Americans to view participation in public insurance programs as a form of dependency, and to instead seek out "self-made" security through the purchase of private insurance products. This privatized vision of security emphasized individual responsibility while downplaying the importance of collective risk sharing. Industry marketing also directly confronted the state. By depicting government insurance programs as inefficient and wasteful, insurance leaders hoped to check desire for public provision and limit the growth of the welfare state.

Public service programming, the focus of chapter 2, offered insurance companies another powerful tool for encouraging "self-made" security. Industry-sponsored public health and safety initiatives helped boost esteem for the industry, associating insurance companies with an altruistic commitment to the public good. These programs also saved insurance companies millions of dollars on claims. Insurance leaders did not find these motives contradictory, and in fact believed that their "business interest" in reducing loss made the industry especially well suited to interventions into individual and social life. In speeches, conference presentations, trade journal articles, and other venues, these leaders often reflected on the power of insurance as a governing technology—one that could help prevent disease, limit automobile accidents, and reduce damage to life and property. Public service initiatives served these goals by offering outlets through which insurers could shape the conduct of Americans and encourage them to manage their own risks. These efforts helped insurance leaders position their industry as a state-like yet private actor committed to overseeing the health and safety of the nation.

PART II: INVESTING IN PRIVATIZATION

Leaders of the investment wings of insurance companies pursued their own governing programs. Barred from investing in real estate "not directly related to the business of insurance," the industry entered the postwar era flush with capital but lacking investment outlets. Insurers addressed this problem by forming new partnerships with state and local governments, and by calling for new laws that would allow them to invest in residential and commercial real estate. State insurance regulators responded to these calls in the 1940s, offering generous land grants and tax breaks to insurance companies willing to invest in much-needed housing for the nation. The resulting wave of industry investments spawned an urban form unique to the postwar era: the insurance housing complex. Chapter 3 examines the massive private housing developments life insurance companies built in cities across the nation during the early postwar years. Insurers exercised substantial control over the construction and administration of these "urban utopias," which they segregated neatly by class and race. This control allowed companies to create environments structured around the strict governance of tenants and the efficient management of risk.

Bad publicity generated by resistance to racial segregation in insurance housing developments dampened enthusiasm for such projects, however, and by the early 1950s the industry had abandoned its commitments to urban housing. Insurers turned next to the suburbs as an attractive outlet for their investment capital. Life insurance companies poured billions of dollars into the American suburbs during the 1950s and early 1960s. This expanding web of investments earned companies like Prudential (one of the more active suburban investors) a reputation as a "mighty pump," a powerful force that drove suburbanization and shaped the national economy. Advertising its investments in the postwar economy strengthened and maintained the insurance industry's beneficent image while also offering evidence that economic growth, job creation, and infrastructure development could be secured through private, and not just public, means. Insurance investors painted their business as an important nation builder, and, as chapter 4 illustrates, in many ways it was. The tremendous size and economic clout of the insurance industry assured its influence in setting and cementing trends like the absentee ownership and standardization of regional shopping centers, the movement of corporate offices from urban to suburban settings, and patterns of disinvestment in American cities that ultimately led to crisis and decline.

PART III: DEFENDING DISCRIMINATION

Private insurers in the United States have never shied away from the term *discrimination*, and in fact have embraced it, claiming to discriminate fairly using sophisticated and objective actuarial tools. This claim to fairness, and the

philanthropic image the industry worked to cultivate for most of the twentieth century, suffered a damaging blow in the late 1960s and 1970s, when civil
rights and feminist activists launched a series of highly publicized debates
over insurance discrimination. These debates centered on the industry's use
of risk classifications to determine pricing and availability of private insurance products. Insurance companies had worked throughout the postwar
period to refine their risk classification structures, a process that entailed
the collection of massive amounts of data and the production of new categories related to risk. Insurers argued that the classification and pooling of
risk helped incentivize individual responsibility, control the cost of insurance
coverage, and protect consumers classified as low-risk from subsidizing those
classified as high-risk. The refinement of risk classification structures—often
through the use of categories like place of residence, or immutable characteristics like biological sex—also helped insurance companies beat out com-
petitors. Individual companies used risk classification to identify what the industry called "bad risks" and eliminate them from coverage—a practice that
was designed to reduce claims, lower premiums, and attract more "good risk"
customers. This strategy gave private companies a competitive advantage, but
it had disastrous impacts on the individuals and communities "classified out"
of insurance coverage, often for reasons beyond their control.

Chapter 5 examines the insurance industry's response to the urban crisis
of the late 1960s and attempts by civil rights activists and government officials
to combat insurance redlining—the practice of denying or limiting insurance
services and investments to specific neighborhoods, typically because their
residents are poor and/or people of color. Insurers justified redlining on the
grounds that some neighborhoods—particularly those populated primarily
by nonwhite residents—were statistically "more risky" than others. In debates
with activists, insurance companies denied charges of racial bias, claiming
that their impartial use of objective data allowed them to discriminate fairly.

Chapter 6 follows similar debates between the insurance industry and feminist activists, who identified the use of sex as a category in insurance underwriting as "discrimination in its most blatant form."[26] These activists hoped to
mandate what was called in the 1970s and 1980s "unisex" insurance, or the equal
setting of rates and coverage for women and men. Insurance leaders portrayed
their risk classification structures in both cases as apolitical applications of a
calculative science. Categories like sex and geographical location, they insisted,
were not only objective, but were also cost-effective and essential for ensuring
"actuarial fairness"—the principle that "good risks" should not be made to subsidize "bad risks." The widespread acceptance of this rhetoric by the American
public in the early 1980s hampered efforts to combat insurance discrimination

and signaled the triumph of market-based understandings of fairness over social commitments to equality.

Insurance and Neoliberal Governance

Insurance Era offers new insights into why attempts to reform the American
insurance system and expand collective forms of risk sharing have made slow
progress over the past half century. By selling the idea of "self-made" security, insurance leaders associated insurance with individual, rather than collective, responsibility. By investing heavily in the nation's economy and built
environment, the industry made a convincing case for private enterprise as
a state-like actor that could provide security, create jobs, and build housing
and infrastructure. By redefining discrimination as an acceptable actuarial
practice, insurers elevated fairness over equality as a central goal of American
social institutions and collective life. Each of these developments grew out of
the ability of insurance to govern, both beyond the state and in partnership
with it.

The insurance industry helped privatize security, shrink the state's commitment to ensuring social welfare, and transform the meanings of risk in the
twentieth-century United States. But private insurance shaped American life
in another, crucially important, way as well: by serving as an incubator for
new forms of social governance that were eventually adopted by other institutions. As recent work on the sociology of medicine, education, and criminology has shown, approaches to risk and governance devised and developed by
the insurance industry have permeated these institutions and are remaking
them in its image. Robert Aronowitz's study of the rise of "risky medicine,"
for example, argues that the experience of being at risk for disease has con-
verged since the 1980s with the experience of disease itself, transforming the
way medical professionals interact with patients and replacing the treatment
of illness with the treatment of risk.[27] Michael Peters has shown how actuarial
governance has helped privatize education and make "responsibilization of
the self" and entrepreneurial training centerpieces of primary and secondary schooling.[28] Bernard Harcourt has illustrated the disastrous impacts of
actuarial policing and paroling on communities of color, as well as how risk
became a proxy for race in the management of crime in the United States
over the past three decades.[29] Each of these authors identifies insurance as a
primary site of origin for governmental logics that have transformed, and are
transforming, the institutions they study.

Such claims will come as no surprise to social theorists of risk, who have
long identified private insurance as "the quintessential form of neoliberal

governmentality."[30] The insurance industry provided crucially fertile ground for early articulations of what scholars now call "neoliberal governance" in the United States.[31] More than any other institution during the postwar years, insurance bridged economic and social life. It wed questions of morality to economic calculation, linking insurance consumption to responsible action and citizenship. It promoted market values by expanding the language of investment to the family, to the future, to the self. Finally, private insurance served as a monetizing force, attaching cash value to noneconomic entities formerly considered outside the market—even, and perhaps especially, life itself.

Immediately after the birth of the American welfare state, insurance companies began selling an alternative vision of social governance that repudiated the Keynesian ideals and public institutions of the New Deal order. Combining the privatization of security with an anti-state message, postwar insurers offered a competing social and economic vision for the nation. This vision elevated private institutions and entrepreneurial action above representative democratic institutions and collective life. Before the word *neoliberalism* had entered the American lexicon, insurance companies were promoting its values, offering a vision of autonomous individuals and family units that could invest as entrepreneurs in their own lives and security while eschewing responsibility for the risks faced by others.

The efforts of private insurers to sell this vision were not always successful. They encountered resistance—in the form of consumer rights, civil rights, and feminist activism. The industry's ability to contain and combat this resistance deserves our attention. *Insurance Era* reveals the many ways leaders of private industry advanced governmental rationalities designed to limit and dismantle egalitarian and collective responses to life's uncertainties. In the process, it argues that insurance is much more than a business. As the sociologist Deborah Stone has claimed, insurance is "a social institution that helps define norms and values in political culture, and ultimately shapes how citizens think about issues of membership, community, responsibility, and moral obligation."[32] Examining the history of private insurance in the United States can help us better understand many of the social divisions and inequalities that have come to characterize American life over the past century. By arming ourselves with a deeper knowledge of the institutions that have participated in creating and perpetuating these divisions, we can begin devising new means of achieving security—means capable of extending the promise of our insurance era to those it has long excluded.

PART I

Selling "Self-Made" Security

Insurance Marketing in the Wake of the New Deal

Looking back in 1967 at a lifetime of service as the chief spokesperson for the American life insurance industry, Holgar Johnson declared, "We have come a long way over a very rough road."[1] Johnson had seen his share of trouble as president for nearly three decades of the Institute of Life Insurance, one of the first institutional public relations organizations formed in the United States. The institute launched in 1939, three years after the passage of the Social Security Act, with two primary goals in mind: (1) to boost esteem for the industry by convincing Americans of the central role insurance companies played in the nation's social and economic life, and (2) to protect the industry from nationalization and other incursions by government. As Johnson knew all too well, this last threat was very real during the New Deal era and the years the followed. "The life insurance business here could have readily been nationalized," Johnson recalled darkly in his history of the institute.[2] During his first decade as president, "socialism hovered in the air. Voices of discontent with capitalism were still loud in the land."[3] By the end of his career, however, Johnson could boast that the institute had helped secure a central place in American life for commercial insurance and the privatized vision of security it endorsed. The Institute of Life Insurance had also done much to stave off nationalization—not only at home, but also abroad. Johnson proudly reported upon his retirement in the mid-1960s that, by sharing lessons and expertise from America, his institute had helped counteract movements to nationalize life insurance in countries around the world.[4] The secret to preventing government expansion and intrusion into the insurance business in the United States, Johnson explained to his colleagues at home and overseas, lay in convincing individual companies to set aside competition, "speak with one voice," and "sell ideas instead of products."[5]

The ideas Johnson and other leaders of the insurance industry sought to sell Americans are the subject of this chapter. The birth of the American welfare state via the introduction of Social Security, unemployment insurance, and a host of other government programs presented the greatest threat ever encountered by the insurance business in the United States. If left unchecked, the newly empowered state threatened to dismantle the industry—directly through nationalization, or indirectly by feeding public demand for universal forms of coverage. Insurance leaders like Wallace Stevens and Holgar Johnson immediately recognized the ideological components of the coming fight. In the new insurance era, Americans would be faced with a choice: risk could be spread and security achieved through either public or private means. Public insurance promised universal security based in solidarity, collective affiliation, and trust in the state to provide for its citizens. Private insurance offered individual protection based on faith in the market and on the willingness of Americans to secure themselves by investing voluntarily in their own fates. The future of the insurance era, and the nation's system of social security provision, hung in the balance.

By the mid-1930s, the government held a distinct advantage in the battle to define the insurance era. The Great Depression marked a turning point in the relationships between security, insurance, and the American state. The economic disaster left millions of Americans without jobs, and even those lucky enough to maintain income faced rising prices and falling wages. The federal government responded to the crisis with an ambitious reworking of the role of the state in American social and economic life. The architects of the New Deal designed its diverse package of social programs to jumpstart the economy and provide for the welfare of the population, but they also sought to transform the way Americans understood the meanings and sources of security. Security, perhaps more than any other concept, became the central component of New Deal ideology. In his 1935 State of the Union address, President Franklin Roosevelt underscored this notion, with a promise that providing for the "security of the men, women and children of the nation" would be his "first and continuing task."[6] Increasingly framed as a basic right, economic security came to be seen as an entitlement of citizenship during the New Deal years. This vision of a providential state found an eager audience in a nation devastated by the Great Depression, a crisis many attributed to the excesses and failures of private enterprise.

Turning the tide of public sentiment away from universal insurance programs and toward private security would be a massive challenge. Private insurers met that challenge with determination and a willingness to draw on the industry's substantial resources in its bid to compete with government. Attempts to understand the stunted development of the American welfare state—its limited provisions in comparison to those of peer nations in the liberal West—have tended to emphasize "cultural" factors: a frontier ethos rooted in self-reliance, an exceptional American allegiance to individualism.[7] Little attention has been paid to the efforts made by private insurers to limit the growth of the American state and contain its commitment to collective risk spreading.[8] Those efforts, however, were significant. The pages that follow examine the strategies pursued by the midcentury insurance industry as it confronted the state and worked to produce social, political, and economic conditions that favored the privatization of security. Moving first to share risk in the face of adversity, leaders of one of the nation's most powerful industries banded together to resist government encroachment and to craft an ideological response to the New Deal's promise of universal security. That response imagined, and attempted to call into being, a new kind of American citizen and insurance consumer—one who took responsibility for their own security, rather than depending on the state to provide it for them. To sell this vision, insurance leaders turned to public relations and marketing.

"Speaking with One Voice": Institutional Marketing and the Power of Public Relations

Before the twentieth century, few insurers advertised. A handful of the largest companies dipped their feet into advertising during the final decades of the nineteenth century, publishing calendars and postcards for limited distribution and printing statistics in public forums that alerted consumers to the strength of company assets. In comparison to other major industries, however, insurance came late to the advertising game.[9] A long-standing reliance on the agent as a selling tool explains this delay. Insurers cited the personal nature of the insurance purchase, as well as its complexity, as the primary reason agents had been used to sell policies throughout the industry's long history. Agents were thought to give a human face to the business, and their interaction with consumers was deemed essential to sales. As the insurance advertising expert A. H. Thiemann explained, "The very nature of insurance demands a personal approach. When the agent is face-to-face with the prospect he can answer objections immediately and he can try again and again to close until the sale is finally made."[10] The impersonal nature of advertising and the ease with which consumers could simply "turn the page or dial" led many insurers to see it as antithetical to the agent system. These concerns lingered well into the twentieth century. As one skeptical executive reasoned in the 1950s, "Advertising may sell soap but it can't sell life insurance: agents sell life insurance."[11]

Despite this enduring commitment to agents and a widespread skepticism concerning the virtues of marketing, most large life insurance companies had embraced advertising of some form by 1910s. The reasons for this shift were largely political. The much-publicized 1905 Armstrong investigation and hearings, which took place in New York and found the nation's three leading life insurers guilty of extensive corruption and fraud, damaged the entire industry's reputation as a faithful guardian of the nation's savings. In a quest to regain the trust of the public, Equitable Life and Mutual Life, two of the companies targeted directly by the investigation, hired leading marketing firms to help craft and publicize their responses to the hearings. These responses, published as letters in leading newspapers, sought to assure Americans that "the extravagance has been stopped" and that new management had been installed at the firms.[12] The historian of advertising Roland Marchand argues that Equitable and Mutual were the first American corporations to use the medium of advertising in this way, making the insurance industry a leader in the use of marketing to construct and maintain a desirable "corporate image."[13] Other life insurers—even those not involved in the investigation—also suffered from the suspicion and distrust generated by the Armstrong hearings. These firms followed the lead of Equitable and Mutual, turning to advertising in hopes of recapturing the goodwill of the public.

Life insurance advertisements from the first decades of the twentieth century reflected this goal by emphasizing the social value of insurance and the work insurance companies performed in the service of the public. Metropolitan's decades-long public health campaign, discussed in chapter 2, offers one example of this kind of advertising. Prudential's disturbing "loss after lapsation" series, launched in the 1920s, offers another. The Prudential campaign, which focused on the plight of widows and orphans, is representative of much life insurance advertising from the era. One example from the series, titled "Two Widows: The Husband of One Let His Life Insurance Lapse," depicts a happy mother surrounded by her children in her home, and her maid, who wears a sorrowful expression. Unsupported by a breadwinner's life insurance policy, the maid (presumably a social equal to her employer before her husband's untimely death) has been forced to work for a wage outside her home.[14] Another Prudential ad from the same series, titled "They Said Father Didn't Keep His Life Insurance Paid Up!," pictures a young boy speaking with a concerned woman, framed by the gates of an orphan asylum (see fig. 1.1). This advertising approach, which sold life insurance as a necessity for

FIGURE 1.1. Prudential "loss after lapsation" advertisement from the mid-1920s. Companies like Prudential portrayed life insurance as a social good that preserved status and decreased demand for public aid and charity programs. (Prudential Insurance Company of America, "They Said Father Didn't Keep His Life Insurance Paid Up!," *Saturday Evening Post*, c. 1925, private possession of author.)

breadwinners charged with the care of dependents, remained popular among insurance advertisers well into the 1930s. These ads trafficked in fear, but they also depicted life insurance as a valuable social good capable of preserving status and the class system while also reducing demand for public aid and charity.

By the end of the 1920s, advertising campaigns depicting insurance companies as beneficent public servants had done much to mitigate the damage wrought by the Armstrong hearings. One industry analyst even claimed that, by 1930, the industry had successfully demonstrated its "moral superiority," striking deep "at the problem of protecting the virtues of the home."[15] Still, skepticism toward advertising continued to linger among insurance industry leaders. Most large insurers advertised, though not to the extent of other major industries; medium and small insurers tended to avoid advertising altogether.[16] Cost was one barrier for smaller companies, but there were others as well. More than anything, insurance was notoriously difficult to sell. A. H. Thiemann called life insurance "one of the most difficult sales imaginable, one that entails persuading people to forgo the pleasure of spending their money today in exchange for a promise which will be made good under circumstances almost impossible to imagine: one's own death."[17]

This, again, was one of the reasons the industry had relied so long on agents. Their physical presence was seen as a necessary obstacle to consumers for whom "the rules of common courtesy prevent from peremptorily terminating an interview" and who might otherwise refuse to think of a potentially disastrous future.[18] Insurance was also expensive, even when payments were spread out over time through annual or semiannual premiums. As the advertising expert Colin Simkin argued, life insurance cost more than most consumer goods, including cars, and "even the accumulated equity in a home."[19] Still, the high cost might not be such a problem if insurance weren't also so abstract. "In spite of the number of dollars involved" in an insurance contract, Simkin reasoned, "it is for a long period, and intangible. There is nothing to display in one's home. Unlike other products, it is not visible daily on shelves or in showrooms. It is even something from which the purchaser may never secure direct benefits."[20]

Life insurers were particularly prolific producers of literature on the difficulty of selling their products, but the same problems faced companies specializing in other insurance lines, all of which could be associated with danger and disaster—or worse, the notion that insurers profited off of fear and misfortune.[21] For this reason, and because many of the strict divisions between insurance fields had begun to crumble by midcentury with the advent of "multiline" firms selling numerous forms of coverage, industry leaders began moving toward "institutional marketing" in the 1940s. Institutional marketing differed from traditional advertising in the sense that it entailed selling the industry itself and the "idea" of private insurance, rather than specific companies or policies.[22] "The *concept* of insurance protection must be sold," explained one institutional marketing advocate. "Every advertisement placed by an individual company benefits the industry as a whole by improving consumer acceptance of the basic idea."[23] Institutional marketing encouraged individual companies to set aside competition and imagine their industry as a singular entity with shared goals. Under this system, insurers of all stripes could work together to sell their business, and, more than anything, the *idea* of private insurance.

No organization made greater strides in the field of institutional advertising—or in unifying the insurance business—than the Institute of Life Insurance (ILI). Referred to as an "instrumentality" by industry insiders, the ILI was a fully staffed organization that managed public relations for the entire industry. In 1939, when the institute was founded, its directors established a set of defining goals: to educate Americans about life insurance, to conduct research on "social concerns" affecting the industry, and to "translate public viewpoints to companies in such a way that would smooth relations with broad publics."[24] The ILI ultimately did much more. It gathered in one place, for the first time, industry-wide statistics; it managed interactions with the press and helped shape media coverage of the life insurance business; it directed all lobbying efforts for the industry out of its Washington office; and it oversaw the publication of millions of textbooks, filmstrips, pamphlets, and advertisements. As one of the first institutional public relations agencies in the nation, the ILI also exerted significant influence in the business world. The institute quickly became the voice of the entire insurance industry, but it also advocated for American business in general. Holgar Johnson, the institute's first president, often bragged that the ILI was a first-of-its-kind organization that "revolutionized" the field of public relations and "pushed forward new frontiers in communication between American business and the American people."[25]

It was no coincidence that an organization tasked with "speaking with one voice" for a unified insurance industry came into being in the late 1930s. Competition from the New Deal state and the specter of nationalization struck fear into the hearts of every insurance executive, leading to calls for unity and action like those issued by Wallace Stevens in "Insurance and Social Change." But the industry faced other challenges during this period as well. Millions of Americans defaulted on their mortgages during the Depression.

As a one of the nation's largest holders of farm mortgages, the life insurance industry became a reluctant owner of millions of acres of dispossessed farmland, almost overnight. Many Americans viewed insurance companies as heartless for foreclosing on struggling farmers. The industry's reputation also suffered as hundreds of thousands of policyholders, who could no longer afford payments, lost coverage when their insurance policies lapsed. The industry abandoned these consumers, even though they had paid premiums for years, if not decades, leading to further criticism. To make matters worse, insurance companies raised the price of premiums as interest rates dropped during the Great Depression. Companies also lowered the dividends paid out on policies to make up for lost income.[26] These moves angered struggling Americans. The public trust the industry had worked so hard to recover after the Armstrong revelations tanked once again.

In response to widespread concern surrounding the power wielded by the nation's financial institutions, President Roosevelt appointed a Temporary National Economic Committee (TNEC) in 1938. Launched by a joint resolution of Congress, the TNEC set out to study the financial sector's contributions in causing the Great Depression and its control over production and distribution of the nation's goods and services. Much to the chagrin of life insurance executives, Congress singled out their industry for special consideration. The TNEC's investigations—which one commenter called "more a federal investigation of insurance than a study of the concentration of economic power in the modern community"—lasted two years and resulted in charges that closely resembled those made by the Armstrong hearings only a few decades earlier.[27]

The TNEC accused the industry of engaging in predatory selling practices that led to high lapse rates, skimping on benefits, and concentrating power in the hands of executives and managers, who were not held accountable to policyholders and showed little regard for their interests.[28] On the lookout for monopolistic behaviors, the committee also called into question the large size of insurance companies and their "inclination to cooperate with one another" by fixing prices and "thus further concentrating their power."[29] Finally, the TNEC noted with suspicion that the insurance industry, which had foreclosed on untold numbers of farmers and done nothing to prevent the policies of millions of Americans from lapsing, was sitting on over $29 billion in assets—more than any of the largest companies in the nation, including the American Telephone and Telegraph company, General Motors, Standard Oil, and all the railroads combined.[30]

Industry leaders immediately realized the danger of the TNEC investigation, which was more far reaching and potentially disastrous than the

1905 Armstrong investigation. Unlike Armstrong, which had criticized the managerial policies of fifteen life insurance companies and suggested alterations to existing regulations, the TNEC targeted the entire industry, calling for additional investigations into "all forms of fire, casualty, and marine insurance," and a completely new regulatory structure overseen by the federal government.[31] Though the committee stopped just short of recommending complete nationalization of private insurance, frequent comparisons between the insurance business and public utilities during the hearings were enough to send industry leaders into paroxysms of dread.[32] If the investigation went unchallenged, one industry analyst stated bluntly, "the technique of insuring would be changed radically, perhaps to such an extent that private insuring would no longer continue."[33]

Executives of leading life insurance companies responded to the hearings by accusing the TNEC of bias, calling its investigation "a springboard for bringing life insurance under the control of the bureaucratic system in Washington," based on "half-truths, incorrect data, and the omission of facts."[34] These leaders struggled, however, to produce industry-wide statistics that could account for the use of industry assets. They also lacked a mechanism through which to respond to the hearings as a unified force. A group of concerned executives, led by Connecticut General's president, Frazar Wilde, swiftly formed a committee to devise an appropriate response to the investigation and determine the extent to which it reflected public sentiment.

The committee's first step was to hire the newly formed Elmo Roper polling organization to interview five thousand Americans, from a variety of walks of life, about the life insurance business.[35] Results from the Roper survey revealed what the executives feared most: large numbers of Americans believed that the presidents of insurance companies were paid too much, that the fine print in insurance policies had been designed to confuse consumers, and that industry sales agents were dishonest peddlers interested only in profit and personal gain. This last charge struck a particularly powerful blow, as industry leaders regarded agents as the heart of the business. Wilde circulated the results of the Roper study to the presidents of the largest insurance firms in the nation and organized a meeting in New York to discuss a response. These executives formed the Institute of Life Insurance, an organization representing seventy-six of the nation's largest firms (a number that grew to more than three hundred by the 1960s). Each company agreed to contribute toward the institute's operating budget.

Wilde and his colleagues agreed that the ILI should serve as a public relations organization, not a professional organization. Directed by the presidents and "top management" of the industry's largest firms, it was designed from the start to function from the top down. The ILI's first president, Holger Johnson, admitted that this kind of structure conflicted with the values of "a democratically oriented society," but justified the move by stressing that, in business, "few innovations come from the lower echelons."[36] Johnson and other members of the ILI jumped into work almost immediately, launching their first public outreach campaign late in 1939, while the TNEC hearings were still ongoing. The campaign emphasized the strength of the state insurance supervisory system and the valuable public service performed by the industry in a weekly "newspaper column" written by Johnson. These columns, printed in hundreds of newspapers across the nation, depicted the leaders of the TNEC as "woefully unsophisticated about the economics of American business" and suggested that the committee had misunderstood the industry and treated it unfairly.[37] The ILI also began collecting statistics on the insurance business that could be used to refute charges of corruption and improper use of policyholder premiums. The ILI eventually compiled this data and published it annually in what became a staple of industry research, the *Life Insurance Factbook.*

When the final TNEC report was released in March 1941, insurance leaders were relieved to find that many of the accusations leveled at the industry had been softened, creating what one life insurance executive called "a very different impression" than the hearings themselves.[38] Though the report recommended federal regulation of the industry, it kept open the possibility of a strengthened state supervisory system and encouraged companies to *voluntarily* improve policy provisions, cost factors, and selling practices. Many industry insiders suspected that the ILI had played a key role in tempering the TNEC's recommendations and applauded the organization for securing an important strategic win in what Provident Mutual president Albert Linton called "the mortal conflict between two opposing philosophies of government and human liberty."[39]

The danger had hardly passed, however. Though the industry's conflict with government was put hold by the nation's entry into World War II shortly after the release of the TNEC's final report, the state still loomed as a potential threat. Negative sentiment and distrust from the public had also not been remedied. To foster unity, the ILI hosted annual meetings throughout the war, where the nation's top insurance executives gathered together to discuss business strategy. Typical discussions at these meetings involved how best to communicate to the public the valuable contributions life insurers were making to the war effort. Meetings also regularly addressed politics and whether public sentiment was moving to the right or the left, or as industry leaders put it, "to the right or the wrong."[40] During the war years, the institute launched a research division and an education division and continued to work with polling organizations, like Roper, to determine changes in public attitudes toward private insurance. Significantly, the ILI also hired the J. Walter Thompson Company (JWT), one of the oldest and most respected marketing firms in the nation, to oversee its public relations efforts. Together with the ILI, the marketing experts at JWT set about creating a far-reaching "program of public education" designed to win back the trust of the public and to combat what Johnson called "the increasing amount of public sentiment in favor of collective security."[41]

Selling "Self-Made" Security

Having staved off federal intervention, at least for a time, the ILI returned to its primary objective during the postwar years: convincing a nation that had largely come to associate security with collective affiliation and public provision to embrace instead a new vision of security rooted in individual responsibility and private consumption. The ideological pressures exerted by the nation's entry into the Cold War assisted the insurance industry in this task. During the early years of the Cold War, national security became the driving force of American foreign and domestic policy. This focus also expanded beyond the realm of political culture. As the United States clamored to protect its interests in the deepening Cold War, popular culture and major media outlets framed American citizens as the primary warriors in a battle depicted as a face-off between two inherently contradictory ways of life. Cold War ideology in the United States called for the active participation of citizens in defending "distinctly American" values from the threat of communism. This demand reshaped the political, cultural, and social landscape of postwar America.[42] It also aided the insurance industry in its efforts to privatize security and elevate individual responsibility over collective risk sharing. The New Deal had framed security as a right of citizenship. Postwar insurers drew on Cold War ideology to help them transform security into a private responsibility, a vital form of civic duty demanded of all citizens.

The quest for national security became a central topic of insurance advertisements during the late 1940s and early 1950s. Insurance advertisers regularly portrayed the nation's future success as contingent on the ability of American citizens to "secure themselves." To do so, insurers introduced a new and unprecedented focus on individuals to their marketing materials. Prewar ads had primarily emphasized insurance as a means of providing for dependents. Postwar ads shifted this focus, underscoring connections between insurance consumption and individual freedom, responsibility, and autonomy. Widows and orphans—omnipresent figures in life insurance advertising from the pre-war era—faded from view as insurance advertisers opted increasingly to emphasize robust individuals: entrepreneurial subjects who faced the future with confidence.

The ILI, as the voice of the industry, led this charge. In 1949, the institute launched its influential "Do-It-Yourself American" campaign, which ran nationally in hundreds of magazines and newspapers (see fig. 1.2). The goal of the campaign was to present life insurance as "one of the best examples of the free enterprise system in action," while also depicting the individual as "his own best source of security."[43] The ILI created the campaign in conversation with a team at JWT to reflect "the native Yankee ability to use their own hands and wits," and to encourage American men to assume full responsibility for their families, "as opposed to relying on the government."[44] Touted by the institute as "an antidote to the trend toward statism," the campaign featured biographies of hard-working American "men who, since the War, found opportunities to get ahead and made the most of them." Instructing readers that "America is what it is because it sees more in the 'do-it-yourself' spirit than in spoon-fed security," the campaign combined a celebration of free enterprise and entrepreneurial action with a thinly veiled critique of public provision.[45]

The ILI opted to revise and update this campaign in 1950, giving it a new look and a new focus on "self-made" security. In ads with titles like "The Only Real Security Is Self-Made!," "Creating His Own Security!," and "Why These Americans Believe in Self-Made Security," the ILI celebrated Americans who had successfully embraced private insurance as a route to autonomy and self-sufficiency (see fig. 1.3).[46] While the reality of family life is present in ads from the series—a recurring catchphrase is "Life insurance: helping American families to help themselves!"—the campaign overwhelmingly featured representations of individuals. One early ad from the campaign, typical of the series as a whole, offered the following copy:

> By their own thrift and initiative, and by their own free will, 80 million men and women are using life insurance as a means of making their *own* security for the future. . . . And since it helps people do so much for *themselves*, life insurance is used by more and more people every year. Individual life insurance companies compete actively in the forward-looking American way to fill America's growing needs for *self-made* security. As a result, the next year will see life insurance helping even more people to make their own security . . . *on their own.*[47]

Avoiding discussion of care for dependents, much less the collective sharing of risk, the newly updated "self-made" security campaign offered a vision of a thoroughly privatized insurance era in the making.

FIGURE 1.2. Institute of Life Insurance "Do-It-Yourself" advertisement celebrating entrepreneurial action and private insurance consumption as a source of autonomy. (ILI, "Meet Glenn Graber: Another Do-It-Yourself American!," 1950, J. Walter Thompson Company, Domestic Advertisements Collection, David M. Rubenstein Rare Book & Manuscript Library, Duke University.)

FIGURE 1.3. Institute of Life Insurance "Self-Made Security" advertisement depicting private insurance as a superior alternative to public insurance programs offered by government. (ILI, "The Only Real Security Is Self-Made!," 1950, J. Walter Thompson Company, Domestic Advertisements Collection, David M. Rubenstein Rare Book & Manuscript Library, Duke University.)

The new campaign continued in the spirt of the "Do-It-Yourself" ads but offered a bolder articulation of the differences between security offered by government and insurance sold by private industry. Citing again "the continuing drift toward statism," the ILI expanded its critique of public provision in the 1950 campaign's copy. "Security provided by the government must be paid for out of the earnings of all the people," the ads read. "Government itself earns no money. The only REAL security comes out of what is earned—it is self-made."[48] In the years to come, the institute would continue this kind of messaging, amending it to keep up with changing conditions and changing times. Both the "Do-It-Yourself" and "Self-Made Security" campaigns represent early attempts on the part of the industry to articulate and emphasize the "Americanness" of personal security achieved through private means.

As the ILI focused on selling the distinctly personal virtues of privatized security, individual life insurance companies pursued similar messaging, often turning to representations of entrepreneurs to sell ideas instead of products. The John Hancock Mutual Insurance Company's distinctive "American Heroes" campaign, for example, ran nationally in magazines throughout the nation from 1948 through the late 1950s. The series featured colorful portraits alongside biographical sketches of "great men" in American history, emphasizing the contributions to the nation of businessmen and entrepreneurs. Each individual featured in the ads received a catchphrase: Frank Woolworth "sold happiness for nickels and dimes," Henry Ford "earned his success," the Revolutionary War financier Robert Morris "made money talk for freedom," and Horatio Alger "inspired the nation's boys to succeed." Occasionally, the Hancock series celebrated composite figures. The Great American Salesman, for example, "sold progress door to door." I. Jones, Prop., a fictional representative of the American small businessman, was "big in self-respect" and "bigger in influence on a national way of life that lets any man be his own master." At the end of each biography, Hancock linked these "great men" to the life insurance consumer, who, the copy read, "makes up his own mind, stands on his own feet, and provides security for his own future through savings and life insurance."[49] Like other insurance advertisements of the era, Hancock's "American Heroes" campaign depicted insurance as a responsibilizing tool— one that helped build an investor mentality and encouraged a general ethos of self-improvement, self-sufficiency, and autonomy.

Other companies offered up their own employees as exemplary models of entrepreneurial action and self-made security. In a July 1950 ad titled "Free Enterprise at Work," the Philadelphia-based North America Insurance Company announced its commitment to supporting independent agents, "who, in the service they provide, make vital contributions to free enterprise in action." A 1779 portrait of Joseph Marshall, "owner of a successful iron works that sold munitions to George Washington's Continental army" and member of the original board of directors for the company, occupied the top third of the advertisement. A celebration of entrepreneurs past and present, the ad impelled readers to purchase North America insurance by underscoring the company's dedication to "a dynamic system that anticipates and responds to the changing needs of the public." By emphasizing entrepreneurialism as a company tradition, North America Insurance sought to align its agents and company with a distinctly American capitalist past. This particular advertisement took an extra step by enlisting the insurance consumer as an ally in securing "for the public interest" such American staples as the entrepreneurial spirit and the free enterprise system.[50]

This emphasis on the enterprising character of agents was not limited to the North America Insurance Company, or even life insurance firms. Insurance companies in a variety of segments of the industry stressed similar values in marketing campaigns throughout the era. A National Board of Fire Underwriters advertisement from 1953, for example, underscored the importance of fire insurance as a means of "enabling men to invest in the future with confidence." The full-page spread emphasized the necessity of financial protections against loss of property to smoke and flame, while also setting out to demonstrate the entrepreneurial commitment of the National Board of Underwriters. Praising board agents for "offering security to millions of families," the ad copy promised that these "hard-working entrepreneurs" were "in business for *themselves*, showing that private enterprise—which has given America the highest standard of living in the world—provides the best way to meet your insurance needs."[51] Here, insurance was portrayed not only as a means of achieving personal security, but also as an industry whose representatives themselves embodied the spirit of free enterprise.

The unmistakable message of these and other insurance marketing campaigns from the era was that Americans should take responsibility for their own safety, security, and well-being by becoming entrepreneurial investors in their own lives. Industry advertisers depicted insurance as a tool through which individuals could achieve this self-securing state, rather than a crutch on which to lean and depend (the way insurers coded public programs). Industry advertisers depicted the personal security of individuals as the primary and most desirable outcome of the insurance purchase, but they also cited additional benefits offered by private insurance consumption to the nation as a whole. These companies stressed the need to defend free enterprise, individualism, and the American entrepreneurial ethos in an unstable political world. Linking responsible citizenship to the private procurement of personal security, insurance industry marketing impelled Americans to sustain their nation by securing themselves, their property, and their futures.

By portraying private insurance consumption as an exercise that preserved free enterprise, industry advertisers offered consumers an opportunity to participate actively in the defense of the nation and an American way of life, while at the same time selling a new understanding of the relationship between citizenship, security, and the state. This connection between good citizenship and the achievement of personal security through private means was made explicit by the businessman and Connecticut senator William Purtell in a 1953 address commemorating the one hundredth anniversary of the Aetna Life Insurance Company. In his address, Purtell articulated a vision of security identical to that of insurance ads from the era. "We can have no security as a nation unless we have security as individuals," he announced. "The success of [Aetna] over the last 100 years offers further proof of the desire of the average American to be responsible for his own security."[52] While the insurance industry's critique of a providential state may not have reached all Americans, this ringing endorsement of "self-made" security from a United States senator suggests that it found traction among business-friendly leaders of government.

Anti-inflation Messaging and the Politics of Issue Advertising

The evolution of insurance marketing during the postwar era reflected a change in the industry's understanding of its role in American life. Selling the idea of private security—a focus of institutional advertising analysts— remained a priority for insurance advertisers; but as selling the "basic idea" became less vital, industry leaders increasingly worked to change the conditions under which their business operated. By the mid-1950s, insurers had thoroughly embraced advertising as a powerful tool for shaping the political, legal, and economic frameworks that governed the industry. Many of these efforts directly confronted the state, railing against government spending, corporate taxation, and industry regulation, while at the same time positioning private insurance as a superior alternative to government provision.

Insurers first began experimenting during World War II with what advertising analysts from the period termed "issue" advertising. These campaigns were not designed to increase sales. Instead, their goal was to influence public opinion concerning abstract political, legal, and economic processes. Institutional marketing advocates encouraged individual companies and organizations like the ILI to adopt issue advertising, citing its value as a powerful political device, "a communications medium that influences the public attitude."[53] This type of advertising, experts argued, enhanced the industry's prestige, developed "a more favorable climate for all of its operations," and could "influence public attitudes in such areas as health insurance," a field many in the industry feared would be nationalized first.[54] Issue marketing avoided direct discussion of insurance consumption and instead addressed topics like inflation, price control, taxation, government spending, and insurance industry regulation.

The earliest of these issue campaigns discussed the problem of rising prices and sought to educate and alert the public to the causes and dangers of inflation. The ILI once again served as a leader, producing thousands of anti-inflation advertisements and industry-penned news stories over the course of the 1940s and 1950s. The institute's first issue campaign, the "Anti-inflation Bulletin," launched in December 1943. The ILI distributed the bulletin to seven thousand newspapers and nine hundred radio stations across the country. It also cultivated relationships with editors at large newspapers to ensure that the bulletins were presented as news, not advertisements.[55] The ILI supplemented the bulletin with extensive advertising. The institute's first dedicated anti-inflation ad campaign, launched in 1944, stressed the importance of saving as a means to combat wartime inflation and impelled Americans take individual responsibility in waging the battle. An ad from the campaign, titled "Why Your Life Insurance Companies Urge You to Keep Up the Fight against Rising Prices," for example, insisted that "the financial health of America as a whole depends on the financial health of every individual."[56]

In ads like this one, the ILI depicted individual economic behaviors—and particularly, planned consumption and saving for the future—as essential ingredients of responsible citizenship. Other ads emphasized duty and responsibility as well, featuring titles like "Who's to *Blame* If the Cost of Living Gets Out of Hand" and "Keeping America Strong Is Everybody's Job!"[57] Every American, the ILI argued, was responsible for defending the nation by maintaining economic prosperity. "By saving instead of spending," the ads promised, "you will guarantee the safer, happier future you have always wanted. You will help hold down your present cost of living. And—you will be doing your patriotic duty towards helping win the war."[58]

When inflation slowed with the end of World War II, the ILI discontinued its anti-inflation campaign and returned to its regular programming. Entrance into a new war in 1950, this time with Korea, brought the return of inflation, and with it, ILI messaging updated to reflect changing political currents. "The enemy's sixth column is inflation!" one 1950 ILI ad proclaimed, insinuating that communists were seeking to create inflation in the United States as a means of forcing America to "spend itself into destruction."[59] Over the course of the next decade, the institute closely followed inflation rates, launching anti-inflation public outreach campaigns when rates reached troubling levels. The ILI's education division even joined the fight, producing an animated filmstrip, titled *Trouble in Paradise*, that emphasized the dangers of inflation and argued for the superiority of life insurance investments in the economy over government spending on social services.[60] The film argued that individual Americans could play an active role in defending their nation by embracing austerity, prudence, and thrift—and encouraging government to do likewise.

The ILI and insurance leaders argued that anti-inflation issue campaigns were presented as a service to the nation in the interest of consumers and the general public. One institutional advertising guide described these campaigns, for example, as devoted to "preserving the power of the dollars guaranteed to policy owners and beneficiaries."[61] Of course, anti-inflation advertising also served the industry itself. Most obviously, these ads encouraged the purchase of private insurance by identifying saving and investment as patriotic behaviors linked to engaged and active citizenship. Anti-inflation messaging served the industry in less obvious ways as well. Inflation often leads to profit losses for industries like insurance that engage primarily in long-term investments. It can also make markets unpredictable, creating difficulties for long-term institutional budgeting and planning (essential to insurance operations). Finally, inflation produces widespread uncertainty concerning the future purchasing power of money, which tends to inhibit consumer willingness to save through mechanisms like insurance. Anti-inflation advertising presented the ILI and other insurance advertisers with a means to bolster the industry's image as a public servant while at the same time protecting its investments and profit margins.[62]

Notably, this form of issue advertising also allowed insurers to position their industry as a custodian of the national economy on par with the state, and to call into question government spending on social services. "One of the greatest dangers to the purchasing power of the dollar lies in expecting the government—whether federal, state or local—to play Santa Claus and bring us new services year after year," cautioned one ILI ad from 1959. "We simply can't expect to have all the services we would like, however desirable they may be."[63] Wedding an anti-inflation message with a call for restricted government, the nation's largest organization of life insurers urged Americans to actively oppose state spending by contacting their elected representatives. "Let your senators and congressmen know your point of view about cutting government spending," one ad urged readers, noting that Congress "may hear mainly from pressure groups who demand more services and projects"—a situation that might make it hard for public servants to "hold the line against inflation."[64]

Even during times when inflation did not pose a danger to the industry, the ILI continued to produce issue ads encouraging Americans to contact their elected representatives and request fewer social services. An ad titled "Why Should <u>You</u> Help Your Representatives Keep Down Government Spending?," for example, featured an image of a well-dressed couple placing a stamped letter in a mailbox. Beneath this image, the copy encouraged readers to denounce government spending: "You must tell your government representatives that you support their efforts to spend carefully and not wastefully. . . . *Insist* that the federal, state, and local governments cut out *all* unnecessary spending. Tell them you do not expect more government services now." A clear attempt to check desire for public insurance programs, this ad and others like it reminded Americans that "government dollars are *your* dollars," and warned against expecting the state to "do for us what we can do *for ourselves*" (see fig. 1.4).

The ILI's anti-inflation campaigns won several prizes from advertising and public relations organizations, and were widely lauded as a valuable service to the public. One insurance advertising analyst even claimed in 1964 that insurers had "thoroughly educated" the American people about inflation.[65] This success encouraged industry leaders to continue pursuing political-issue advertising throughout the 1950s and 1960s. In a 1958 meeting with JWT, which had handled the institute's marketing for nearly two decades, the leaders of the ILI laid out a ten-year advertising plan devoted almost entirely to a continuation of its already extensive issue campaigns. In this meeting, the ILI leadership presented JWT with the following questions:

1. Can advertising play any role in helping to prevent the insurance business from being taxed?
2. Can advertising dealing with the manner in which the business is operated assist in softening the effects of a congressional investigation of the insurance business?
3. Public relations—how can advertising create a more favorable attitude toward life insurance?[66]

The directness with which insurers revealed these hardly philanthropic intentions can no doubt be explained by the private nature of such meetings, the proceedings of which were not intended for public consumption. Archived review board minutes documenting conversations between insurers and marketing firms like JWT, however, provide undeniable evidence of the political

FIGURE 1.4. Institute of Life Insurance issue advertisement encouraging Americans to resist expansion of government programs and social services. Insurance organizations like the ILI used advertisements like this one to shape public opinion and pursue political goals. (ILI, "Why Should You Help Your Representatives Keep Down Government Spending?," 1952, J. Walter Thompson Company, Domestic Advertisements Collection, David M. Rubenstein Rare Book & Manuscript Library, Duke University.)

goals of insurance marketing and call into question the public-minded nature
of issue advertising.

JWT was the oldest, largest, and most respected marketing organization
in the United States. As members of the nation's premier marketing firm, its
representatives were certainly no strangers to shrewd and calculating corporate clients. Yet in meeting minutes throughout the 1950s and 1960s, JWT
workers regularly came into conflict with ILI leaders over their demands for
political-issue campaigns. After being asked by the ILI to produce a series of
antitaxation ads, for example, JWT representatives continuously expressed
confusion concerning the purpose of such efforts. "Now they want anti-tax
ads to go along with their anti-inflation ads?" one JWT analyst asked doubt-
fully. "I just don't see how much good these actually do for the client."[67] When
instructed to create a campaign discouraging federal and state regulators
from investigating insurance companies by suggesting that the industry was
"clean as a hound's tooth," JWT workers again expressed doubts. "Let's focus
down," one representative reasoned. "If there's going to be an investigation by
a congressional committee, what can we do? It's too late now if that's our sole
motive."[68] The discomfort expressed in these meetings by the seasoned advertising professionals at JWT suggests that the ILI was rare, or even unique,
among advertisers of the era in demanding that its ads be directed toward
overtly political ends having little to do with sales.

Indeed, it was the "educational" nature of political campaigns requested
by the ILI that elicited the most criticism from JWT workers. "The institute
insists on education campaigns," a JWT copywriter complained, "but also
that ads be written in a vein where we appear to be talking *with* the reader,
not *to* him."[69] Pointing to ILI requests that emphasis in ads be placed on complex legal procedures and tax policy, another JWT representative confessed,
"I just don't feel any enthusiasm for these educational campaigns. I just don't
see what's to be gained."[70] On the question of antitaxation advertising, still
another noted, "The question of how the life insurance business is taxed is
not only too complex for public discussion, but also one in which not even
a limited segment of the public would be interested."[71] JWT representatives
expressed unease, as well, at the ILI's disregard for sales (the traditional focus of advertising) and its insistence that new marketing campaigns instead
shape the political, legal, and economic conditions of business operations.
In most meetings, JWT workers channeled this hesitance toward convincing ILI leadership to "tone down" the overtly political rhetoric of their ads—
but occasionally it dissolved into contempt. In one review board meeting,
a JWT representative complained bluntly, "This 'educational copy' scares
me. It sounds like a Martian colossus and I find myself thinking, 'gee, if

they've got 20,000,000 for a shopping center, I guess my premiums may be too high.'"[72]

Despite these conflicts, JWT produced thousands of political-issue ads for the institute over the course of the 1950s and 1960s. Many of these ads addressed the question of industry regulation—a topic close to the hearts of insurance leaders. On this front, JWT and the ILI adopted a strategy that avoided direct discussion of proposed legislation or investigations into insurer conduct and instead focused on the ways in which the industry was *already* regulated, and how it administered itself "in the best interests of its policy holders."[73] An ad titled "How Do Life Insurance Companies Figure Premiums?," for example, explained the internal mechanisms companies employed to determine policy pricing, emphasizing their efficiency and objectivity.[74] Another, "What Standards Govern the Life Insurance Companies in Investing your Money?," took a similar approach to the question of regulation, describing the industry's already existing commitment to safety, diversification, and returns for policyholders. Assuring readers that companies "endeavor to place life insurance money where it does the most good for the country and the people," the ad celebrated the industry's commitment to public service and suggested that investigation into, or increased regulation of, insurance investment practices would be costly and unnecessary.[75]

Along with discouraging industry regulation, ILI issue ads also sought to paint private industry as a superior alternative to the state and state-based services. These ads continued to emphasize the responsibilizing force of insurance consumption on individuals and its ability to offer "self-made" security, while also noting the contributions of "insurance dollars" to the nation as a whole. An ad entitled "How Does the Money People Put into Life Insurance Benefit All of Us?," for example, stressed the role played by private insurance investments in securing economic prosperity and the "quality of life" of all Americans:

> Look around you! The houses we live in, the cars we drive, the telephones we use, the electricity that lights our homes, the food we eat, the clothing we wear, all of the things that really affect our lives every day are probably financed by life insurance funds in some way. Invested in every part of the country, this money touches potentially every phase of American life. It helps provide the capital necessary to build America. It helps finance business, both large and small. All of this adds up to more jobs and more goods for more and more people. So, you see, your life insurance dollars benefit you and your family, your community, and the country as a whole.[76]

The providential nature of private enterprise, so clearly articulated here, was extolled in other insurance issue ads as well. "Is America a Better

Place Because <u>You</u> Own Life Insurance?," another ILI ad from the same investments-focused series, assured Americans that "life insurance money is carefully put to work—and with purpose." Linking insurance dollars to the building of factories, the creation of jobs, and the construction of new housing, the ad promised that "insurance money makes America better." In the ad's closing statement, the ILI infused this celebration of private enterprise with another critique of public provision. "Through life insurance," the copy vowed, "you're building security for yourself and your family—on your *own*. You're not depending on somebody else to do it for you."[77]

While seemingly innocuous in their focus on the mundane technicalities of insurance operations, midcentury insurance advertisements were, in fact, political documents. These materials called for a retreat from democratic, public institutions and elevated private enterprise as a site of individual protection, economic stewardship, and nation building. The clearly political goals of these ads expose the fallacy of insurer claims that issue advertising and other marketing materials were offered in the service of the public. They also reveal the extent to which the insurance industry feared the state and sought to combat its expansion. The ILI provides an early example of the private insurance industry's organized attempts to shape public sentiment by channeling corporate resources toward antigovernment goals. Corporately funded think tanks and research institutes that sprung up later in the twentieth century owed much to the strategies and ideological tools developed by the ILI. The institute's success in selling ideas—chief among them the superiority of individual enterprise over public provision and collective risk sharing—would prove influential in later corporate interventions into American social and political life.[78]

These ideas also helped transform the shape and direction of the insurance era in the United States. Though historical reception of advertising and marketing messages is notoriously difficult to measure, there can be little doubt that the activities of the ILI and other leaders of the insurance industry helped shift the balance of the American security system away from a collective national body and toward autonomous individuals tasked with the management of their own security. By directing substantial resources toward securing political and economic conditions favorable to a privatized insurance era, the ILI and the insurance executives who oversaw its interventions encouraged small government, the deregulation of industry, and the privatization of social services. Perhaps most important, these industry leaders also developed a compelling ideological response to the New Deal state, one that channeled the patriotic desire of Americans to serve their nation by encouraging them to take charge of their own risks. This response positioned private insurance institutions in competition with the state both in the market for security as well as in the provision of a wide range of social services, including public health, education, maintenance of economic growth and stability, job creation, and infrastructure building. This commitment to social governance, discernable in the advertising messages disseminated by the ILI, was deepened and expanded in public service campaigns launched by life insurance companies and other segments of the industry during the same era. Chapter 2 examines these campaigns as evidence of the industry's dedicated efforts to privatize not only security, but risk itself.

2

"Facing the Future's Risks": Governing through Education and Public Service

During a weekend in the spring of 1952, more than three hundred of the top property and casualty insurance professionals in the United States gathered in New York City to celebrate the two hundredth anniversary of the founding of mutual insurance in America. Organized by the presidents of the largest insurance firms in the nation, the three-day conference featured an impressive lineup of speakers—from industry luminaries and business leaders to academics in fields as diverse as chemistry, sociology, economics, political science, and criminology. The proceedings of the conference were published a year later as *Facing the Future's Risks: Studies toward Predicting the Unforeseen*, a unique collection that offers a rare glimpse into the soul of the mid-century American insurance industry and the concerns that shaped its social and political visions for the future.

Topics under consideration at the conference included such industry standbys as probability, statistics, economics, and finance, as well as less obviously insurance-related inquiries into chemistry, crime, information technology, psychology, the motion picture industry, and the sociological status of American women. The speakers, invited to address "risks facing the nation," reflected the diversity of fields deemed crucial by insurers in their struggle to envision a predictable future, and also, ultimately, to help shape it. Looking forward with optimism concerning such a project, Lyman Bryson, one of the chief organizers of the conference, declared approvingly, "We are showing newer and stronger signs of being interested, not only as individuals, as has always been the case, but as members of a professional group, in *the whole context of our civilization*."[1]

The efforts of the 200th Anniversary Committee to position their industry at the center of the nation's political and economic life should come as no surprise to business historians of the era, who have noted an uptick in "business activism" during the postwar years, as well as an expansion of political influence exerted during this period by leaders of private industry.[2] Yet the remarkable scope of the *social* vision on display at this conference also points to something more than a drive for political power. The insurance industry's quest to shape "the whole context" of American civilization, as Bryson put it, reveals a commitment to a larger and more abstract project—one best understood as a program of social governance. The insurance industry's engagement in public service and educational initiatives supported and deepened this program.

The Uses of Public Service

Chapter 1 illustrated how insurers used marketing tools like advertising to achieve several institutional goals. First, insurers used advertising to sell the basic idea of private coverage. Second, advertisements produced by organizations like the ILI encouraged "self-made" security and sought to tie insurance consumption to individual autonomy and entrepreneurial action. Third, advertising provided a powerful political tool that insurers used to influence public opinion on issues important to the industry, including inflation, corporate regulation, and taxation. Finally, insurance companies and public relations organizations turned to advertising as a means of discouraging public support for government spending and the expansion of public insurance programs. Advertising was not the only tool insurers used to reach the public. More than any other industry, and long before the advent of "corporate social responsibility," insurance companies and their professional organizations actively embraced public service programming as a primary form of public relations.

Historians of insurance have typically viewed the public service commitments of private insurers as a means of increasing esteem for the industry by associating it with good works.[3] Metropolitan Life Insurance Company president Louis Dublin, who oversaw one of the first public health programs in the nation, helped define this vision, calling insurance public service work "an example, characteristic of the American way of life, of private enterprise promoting public welfare."[4] The esteem generated by public service activities attracted goodwill, but it also had political value. Even in the business-friendly climate of the booming postwar years, insurance leaders maintained a fear of government. Clarence J. Myers, president of the New York Life Insurance Company, admitted as much in a 1959 address to the Rotary Club of New York. "Let us face it," he cautioned, "the industrial strife and trust

busting early in this century, and the antipathy to business during the Depression have left their mark."[5] Myers called on his fellow businessmen to
respond to these threats by investing in public service—to attract goodwill,
but more important, to stave off government encroachment. One year later,
Eugene Thore, president of the Life Insurance Association of America, offered a similar message. "Unfortunately, many students of our social security
system think of it as something more than a floor of protection," he warned.
"One of the major challenges facing the insurance business is this view that
government should do the entire job."[6] Noting a "desperate need" for a "broad
educational program to combat this thesis," Thore, like Myers, called on insurance providers to participate in service initiatives and publicize those efforts widely.[7]

For an industry seeking to privatize security, public service offered a valuable tool that could shield it from government intervention while also portraying private enterprise as a contributor to social welfare on a par with the
state. Safety education, health programs, and other initiatives launched by insurance providers "in the service of the public" also functioned as important
components of a system of claims reduction. Safer, healthier people were, put
simply, less costly to insure. Public service and educational programs helped
insurance companies reduce claims by teaching individuals to actively manage and take charge of their own risks. This form of "self-made" security
encouraged individuals to become their own private risk managers, to take
responsibility for their own health, safety, and welfare. Educational materials
produced by insurers pursued these goals by emphasizing calculation, planning, and self-monitoring as central components of a happy and healthy life.
By influencing the daily habits and behaviors of individuals as well as their
understandings of risk, insurance companies and their professional organizations hoped ultimately to transform the population—to make it safer, more
secure, and more reflexive in matters of health, family, and finance. This form
of insurance governance sought to individualize risk, making it the domain
of individual responsibility and management.

Public service and educational campaigns had other uses too. Many public service and educational initiatives included a component of surveillance,
generating data that insurance companies used to refine the risk-rating and
classification structures used to price and determine availability of insurance
coverage. Some of these surveillance efforts collected data without consent.
Others asked Americans to voluntarily surrender private details about their
lives, or to surveil themselves by participating in programs that encouraged
self-monitoring and self-regulation. Though we often think of corporate attempts to control private data as a recent phenomenon, insurance companies

began pursuing this project during the early years of the twentieth century. Insurers gathered mountains of data, often through programs purporting to serve the public, and eventually used it to build a system in which private companies served as gatekeepers charged with regulating access to basic features of social life. By the end of the postwar era, data collected by insurance companies played a significant role in determining who could drive a car, buy a home, or start a business—not simply who had access to insurance or how much they paid for it.

Public service offered commercial insurance providers opportunities for surveillance and data gathering, an effective means of encouraging self-governance and individual responsibility for risk, a tool for reducing claims, and a shield against government competition and intervention. This chapter explores each of these uses of public service through a study of twentieth-century insurance industry health, safety, advice, and educational programs. It begins with a discussion of industry-sponsored public health campaigns, which launched during the early decades of the twentieth century and continued into the postwar era. It then moves to a study of industry-penned educational and advice literature. The chapter concludes by examining the efforts of automobile insurers to take charge of the nation's roadways and position their industry at the center of driver education and governance in the United States.

"The Greatest Single Institution Dedicated to Public Welfare in America": Life Insurance and Public Health

In the first decades of the twentieth century, insurance industry leaders identified the public service campaign as a powerful tool that could shape not only public perception of the industry, but also the behaviors and habits of Americans. The Metropolitan Life Insurance Company's public health program was one of the earliest—and by far the most influential—of such projects. The company's efforts to improve the health of Americans began in the early years of the twentieth century and continued into its final decades. The most widely recognized public health campaign in the history of the United States, Metropolitan's multifaceted health program comprised data collection and medical research, the establishment of visiting nurse programs in cities across the country, and the publication of vast quantities of public health materials. These materials included health notices, which ran in national and local newspapers and magazines; textbooks, filmstrips, and other educational materials designed for use in schools; and health-related pamphlets and brochures, distributed to individuals and families across the country. The scope of the program was massive: by 1959, Metropolitan had distributed well over a million health and safety messages in the United States and Canada.[8]

Metropolitan launched its forays into public health after the company restructured its medical department in the early years of twentieth century. As the historian Dan Bouk argues, insurance companies first introduced medical departments in the mid-nineteenth century with the goal of identifying and rooting out sick or suspect applicants, classified as bad insurance risks.[9] It did not take long, however, for insurers to realize that these same departments could be reengineered to keep existing policyholders, and potential ones, well. Fire and employer liability insurers had already turned risk prevention into standard practice by the end of the nineteenth century. Hartford Fire Insurance Company, for example, employed an army of "loss-prevention" engineers who consulted builders of proposed structures, performed inspections, and taught owners of properties how to reduce fire hazard.[10] Two important developments in the early years of the twentieth century convinced life insurers like Metropolitan to follow along a similar path, transforming their medical departments into prevention laboratories geared toward improving public health.

Scandal was one of the primary factors motivating Metropolitan and other insurance companies to pursue public service initiatives during the early twentieth century. For much of the nineteenth century, strong connections between insurance and gambling, as well as the taint of "dealing in death," had led many Americans to distrust insurers and consider their work immoral.[11] Attempts to shake this reputation—mostly through insurers' efforts to associate their industry with statistical expertise and objective authority— had achieved success by the turn of the century. The highly publicized 1905 Armstrong Committee investigation and hearings hampered these efforts. Bad press generated by the hearings harmed the entire industry—even those companies, like Metropolitan, that had not been involved in the investigation. After the hearings concluded, life insurers stepped up efforts to win back the trust of Americans. The formation of public relations organizations like the ILI offered one way to do so. Portraying the industry as a reformed and beneficent public servant offered another.[12]

The rapid growth of "industrial insurance" around the turn of the century provided an additional impetus for life insurers to enter the field of public health. Industrial insurance offered minimal coverage to workers, who paid low premiums to visiting agents on a weekly basis. Unlike traditional life policies, industrial plans typically covered little more than burial expenses and did not require thorough medical examinations. Though first introduced in the nineteenth century, industrial insurance expanded rapidly during the early years of the twentieth century as mass immigration swelled the ranks of the nation's working classes. Eager for the premium dollars of workers but concerned about the potential for excessive claims, leading industrial insurers like Metropolitan turned to public health as a promising tool for improving the morbidity and mortality rates of their poorest policyholders.

Once committed to the project of public health, Metropolitan poured millions of dollars into the effort. Along with devoting significant resources to research (it founded a research-based "Life Extension Institute" in 1913), the company also enlisted its marketing and publishing wings in the program.[13] From the 1910s through the late 1950s, the company produced millions of informational health notices and pamphlets, and distributed them widely in cities across the nation. Typical subjects of Metropolitan health materials included contagious diseases like syphilis, diphtheria, measles, typhoid fever, tuberculosis, pneumonia, and influenza. Health notices and pamphlets also offered information on simple health practices like first aid, home safety, and healthy food preparation. Many of these materials included interventions that targeted and sought to eradicate traditional forms of medicine and "folk healing" practiced by immigrant groups. They also emphasized the need to consult insurance representatives and other medical experts, rather than friends and family, for health advice. One 1927 Metropolitan pamphlet on syphilis, for example, featured a drawing of a devil-like creature speaking with a young man, and warned readers that twelve million Americans suffered from syphilis, "many not knowing it and still more being hoodwinked by quacks and charlatans."[14] Another 1940 notice cautioned against entertaining "curbstone medical advice" and advised readers to beware "the danger of diagnosis by uninformed, unqualified advisors."[15]

Metropolitan first addressed this need for "qualified advisors" in 1909, launching what would become one of the signature features of the company's public health program. The Metropolitan Visiting Nurse Service, which sent trained nurses to the homes of policyholders free of charge, began on a provisional basis in New York, then quickly expanded to cities across the nation.[16] In its early years, the company worked closely with already existing nursing organizations, beginning with the Henry Street Settlement nurses of New York, an organization led by Lillian Wald. Over the next decade, the company formed alliances with more than six hundred visiting nurse associations across North America. Responding to the popularity of the program as well as the shortage of nurses in some locations, Metropolitan created its own nursing service in 1911. The company launched the service in Saint Paul, Minnesota, and later expanded it to cities across the country.[17] Nurses employed by the company received extensive training, including, in some cases, postgraduate study. Their primary tasks, as stated by Metropolitan, were "accurate reporting, home instruction, and treatment" of policyholders, especially those covered by industrial policies.[18]

The nursing service was a massive success. Metropolitan reported that the nurses helped lower morbidity and mortality rates in the cities where they operated—a finding the company used to justify the cost of the program.[19] The high quality of care offered by nurses also earned the gratitude of existing policyholders and attracted new ones. The visiting nurse service garnered widespread praise for Metropolitan, and, as the historian of medicine William Rothstein has argued, portrayed life insurance public service work as an "alternative to socialized medicine."[20] Nurses rounded out Metropolitan's extensive health programming, adding in-home care to the growing suite of health services performed by the company—including medical research, public education, and data collection and analysis. Proudly boasting, "We are teaching the State its duty," Metropolitan president Haley Fiske opted repeatedly to expand the program.[21] By the 1940s, Metropolitan nurses operated in 7,728 communities across the United States and Canada.[22] By 1953, they had made 107 million visits to more than twenty million policyholders.[23]

Outward success, however, masked internal discord. As the nursing historian Diane Hamilton has illustrated, the nurses employed by Metropolitan regularly came into conflict with company leadership.[24] Battles over pay and structure of management were common, as were disputes over how best to treat and care for patients. Metropolitan insisted, for example, that nurses focus on infectious diseases and limit their visits to patients suffering from chronic conditions. This, according to the company, ensured that the program yielded "the largest practical returns."[25] Nurses objected to this directive and other attempts by Metropolitan leadership to promote efficiency over proper care—but they lacked the power to win such battles.[26] Notably, the company also enlisted nurses as collectors of data, instructing them to keep detailed records of all patient visits for use by the company's vast statistical department.[27] Fiske identified this function of the program as one of its greatest virtues. "Our nurses are most invaluable," he declared in 1921, "for collecting numberless statistics for various medical research purposes."[28] The nurses resisted but eventually performed this surveillance grudgingly, gathering, for decades, data about the health and living conditions of the working-class populations that made up the bulk of the company's consumer base.

Metropolitan discontinued the visiting nurse service in 1953. A decline in the volume of home visits as medical care moved increasingly to hospitals, along with rising employment opportunities and wages for nurses, drove the cost of the program higher than Metropolitan was willing to pay. The company continued to pursue health campaigns well into the postwar era, however, adjusting its messaging for changing times. The foci of Metropolitan's health materials shifted during this period to reflect the primacy of individual responsibility and self-management that infused insurance marketing and other aspects of industry practice during the era. Metropolitan had emphasized individual agency in managing health since the 1910s. One of the more successful health books sponsored by the company, for example, was titled bluntly *How to Live*. Published in 1915, the book remained popular well into the 1920s.[29] Postwar health materials produced by the company continued this tradition, while at the same time shifting attention away from environment as a central field of intervention and doubling down on the individual management of risk. As the twentieth century wore on, Metropolitan's health work focused less on communicable, "social," diseases (a preoccupation of the company's prewar campaigns) and more on noncommunicable conditions related to individual behavior.[30]

Many of the topics covered by the company's postwar public health materials cited changes in medical knowledge concerning what were, at the time, relatively new sources of illness: stress and depression. One health notice from this period, for example, instructed readers to "remember to relax!" and avoid worrying too much or getting "upset emotionally."[31] Another, titled "Most Likely to Succeed . . . in Getting Over a Stomach Ulcer," emphasized the need to develop "mental or emotional discipline" in order to maintain a healthy relationship to stress.[32] These new medical concerns reflected a shift in the meaning of health in relation to individual conduct. From the perspective of the medical establishment—of which the insurance industry had become a crucial arm—"disease control" could no longer be achieved simply by changing the social behaviors of Americans. Public health now also depended on encouraging new forms of self-monitoring, reflexivity, and vigilance. Insurance health notices promoting relaxation, having fun, and controlling emotions thus replaced materials encouraging the covering of coughs or the importance of immunization.

Weight became another regular topic of health messaging for Metropolitan and other insurance companies during the postwar period. Attempts to integrate height-weight ratios in risk rating began in the mid-nineteenth century but were haphazard, and typically used as a means of selecting out underweight applicants, thought to be prone to disease. By the 1910s, medical research conducted by insurance medical departments had identified overweight as an equally troubling classification. Over the next few decades, life insurance companies drew on actuarial data to construct standardized height and weight tables. By the 1940s these tables had shifted away from a record of national averages and instead began listing "ideal" weights in relation to gen-der, age, height, and build.[33] Postwar health materials distributed to the pub-lic by companies like Metropolitan popularized and publicized these tables, while at the same time encouraging individuals to *find themselves* in the data and take active steps to fit into appropriate categories and ideals (see fig 2.1).

The philosopher Ian Hacking argues that this form of communication represents an attempt to "make up people," to wield statistics in such a way that they not only describe but also create new categories and groups. "You can't just print numbers," Hacking writes. "You must print numbers of objects falling under some category or other."[34] For Hacking, statistics, particularly those communicated to the public, are productive—it is "beneath their vari-ous categories" that different kinds of people come into being. Identifying, or as Hacking argues, *creating*, "types" of people had been a central goal for the statistical and actuarial departments of life insurance companies since their establishment in the nineteenth century. Postwar insurance advertise-ments that publicized ideal weight distributions in the form of charts and graphs offered a promising new approach to "making up people" by enlist-ing individual Americans as active participants in the process. Health notices asking Americans questions like, "Checked your weight lately?" also helped individualize risk by emphasizing the necessity of calculated and vigilant self-monitoring, and by underscoring the importance of taking individual responsibility for one's own health.

Metropolitan scaled back several features of its public health program-ming in the late 1950s, but the connections the company forged between health, individual conduct, and responsible self-management remain em-bedded in American culture and medical practice to this day. Notably, the company's pathbreaking health work also cemented connections between insurance and public service. The historian of advertising Roland Marchand credits Metropolitan with "a reputation as the most philanthropic advertiser of the era."[35] Observers at the time of the campaign's heyday, including Her-bert Hoover (then US secretary of commerce), concurred. Hoover applauded Metropolitan in a 1923 speech as "the greatest single institution dedicated to public welfare in America."[36] The massive popularity of its health campaigns helped Metropolitan become the largest insurance company in the nation and gained the firm a reputation as America's leading authority in the sphere of public health.

Noting Metropolitan's success, insurance marketing experts and organi-zations like the ILI encouraged industry-wide adoption of similar campaigns. The institute even launched its own public health effort, the Life Insurance Medical Research Fund, in the early 1950s. Designed to distribute funds from

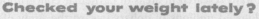

Checked your weight lately?

MEN*
Fully clothed,
1 inch heels

HEIGHT	5'3"	5'4"	5'5"	5'6"	5'7"	5'8"	5'9"	5'10"	5'11"	6'	6'1"	6'2"	6'3"
Small Frame	119-128	122-132	126-136	129-139	133-143	136-147	140-151	144-155	148-159	152-164	157-169	163-175	168-180
Medium Frame	127-136	130-140	134-144	137-147	141-151	145-156	149-160	153-164	157-168	161-173	166-178	171-184	176-189
Large Frame	133-144	137-149	141-153	145-157	149-162	153-166	157-170	161-175	165-180	169-185	174-190	179-196	184-202

WOMEN*
Fully clothed,
2 inch heels

HEIGHT	4'11"	5'	5'1"	5'2"	5'3"	5'4"	5'5"	5'6"	5'7"	5'8"	5'9"	5'10"	5'11"
Small Frame	104-111	105-113	107-115	110-118	113-121	116-125	119-128	123-132	126-136	129-139	133-143	136-147	139-150
Medium Frame	110-118	112-120	114-122	117-125	120-128	124-132	127-135	130-140	134-144	137-147	141-151	145-155	148-158
Large Frame	117-127	119-129	121-131	124-135	127-138	131-142	133-145	138-150	142-154	145-158	149-162	152-166	155-169

If you are one of the many millions of Americans who've gained unneeded pounds, consider these facts:

1. At ages 20 and over, men and women who are considerably overweight have a mortality rate about 50 percent higher than their "trim" contemporaries.

2. High blood pressure occurs more than twice as often in overweight people as in thinner people.

3. Studies show that 85 percent of adult diabetics were overweight at the onset of their disease.

So, it's evident that excessive poundage burdens more than your two feet. In fact, overweight can impair the function of many vital organs and hence is associated with many life-shortening conditions.

On the other hand, if you reduce . . . *and keep your weight down* . . . you should increase your chances for long life and good health. You will certainly look and feel better . . . and have greater stamina, too.

Yet, some quick-reducing diets may be almost as bad for your health as the constant stress of overweight. All diets, therefore, should be avoided, unless prescribed by your doctor.

So, when you plan to reduce, start with a visit to your doctor. He will determine your desirable weight . . . and, most important, he will give you a sound, balanced, varied diet that everyone needs whether reducing or not.

If you are overweight and want to reduce surely and safely, these "do's and don't's" may help you:

Do say "no" to all high-calorie foods . . . rich desserts, gravies, sauces and social-hour tidbits.

Do exercise moderately to keep in trim and help burn up unneeded calories.

Don't use "reducing drugs" except on your doctor's recommendation.

Don't give a second thought to second helpings . . . no matter how tempting they may be.

Don't expect immediate good news from the scales. One or two pounds a week is a safe, sensible rate of weight loss.

Metropolitan's booklet *Overweight and Underweight* gives a number of helpful low-calorie menus, lists calorie values of 200 foods and offers other suggestions which may help you shorten your beltline and lengthen your lifeline. Mail the coupon below for your free copy.

* *Desirable weights for men and women of ages 25 and over based on numerous Medico-Actuarial studies of hundreds of thousands of men and women.*

**Metropolitan Life
Insurance Company**
(A MUTUAL COMPANY)
1 MADISON AVENUE, NEW YORK 10, N. Y.

Metropolitan Life Insurance Co.
1 Madison Ave., New York 10, N. Y.
Please send me a copy of your booklet *Overweight and Underweight.* 556-F.

Name_____
Street_____
City_____State_____

FIGURE 2.1. Metropolitan public health advertisement encouraging Americans to fit into ideal weight categories. Insurance companies like Metropolitan engaged in public health campaigns as a means of attracting goodwill for the industry and to reduce costs by limiting claims made by policyholders. (Metropolitan Life Insurance Company, "Checked Your Weight Lately?," *Forbes* (May 1, 1956), 29, Roy Lightner Collection of Antique Advertisements, David M. Rubenstein Rare Book & Manuscript Library, Duke University.)

the industry toward research in areas of particular concern for life insurers, the program donated millions of dollars toward the study of heart disease and sponsored research fellowships at medical schools around the country. To make the most of this virtuous giving, the ILI's press bureau sent "specifically written news stories to each city where the grants and fellowships were made."[37] As part of this publicity effort, the institute also produced a film in 1954, *A Matter of Time*, which detailed and celebrated the insurance industry's work in improving the health of Americans. Television stations across the nation broadcast the program more than six hundred times.[38] Dedicated publicity efforts of this sort, combined with the work of individual firms like Metropolitan, helped cement associations between insurance and public service. By the 1950s, public service and educational programs had become synonymous with insurance providers.

"Education for Living": Industry-Penned Curricula and Interventions into Daily Life

Recognizing the many uses of public service and seeking opportunities to expand the industry's influence beyond the sphere of health, life insurers launched "educational departments" in the 1950s with the goal of introducing industry-friendly curricula to public schools. These materials encouraged private insurance consumption while at the same time associating the industry with an altruistic commitment to the public good. Distribution of educational materials also offered a means of encouraging Americans, from an early age, to apply calculation, planning, and future-oriented thinking in their daily lives. Curricular materials designed by the industry depicted the purchase of life and other forms of insurance as a mark of responsible citizenship, as well as a means through which students could learn valuable concepts like thrift, prudence, and the individual management of risk.

The ILI embraced the notion that insurance could train safer, more responsible individuals proudly in its Education for Living series, an extensive curricular library produced by the institute's education division. The series included textbooks, workbooks, filmstrips, and teaching guides—all distributed by the institute to public schools and libraries free of charge (see fig. 2.2). Some of these materials focused on insurance specifically. A comic book directed at elementary-age children, titled *The Man Who Ran Interference*, for example, followed the adventures of an insurance agent who helped a family "protect itself from potential financial trouble."[39] The textbook *Arithmetic in Action*, designed for integration into elementary mathematics courses, promised to "add zest" to the classroom by teaching students about life insurance.[40]

The advertisement reads:

*Young people **do** want to know the facts of life insurance*

Our schools are not only teaching them how to make a living ... but equally important, *how to live!*

For more than 80% of our children, graduation from high school marks the end of formal education. Today's high schools are putting an increasing emphasis on training that will prepare young graduates for productive jobs and careers.

And in more recent years, there has been a definite trend to "education for living" and the addition of such courses as home and family living, family relations and money management.

As a central source of information about life insurance, the Institute of Life Insurance is continually answering requests of teachers and students for in-

formation and educational material on life insurance.

As part of its educational program, the Institute prepares teaching aids for classroom use, consisting of booklets, charts, motion pictures, and other items for which teachers may indicate a need.

In addition, the Institute sponsors a nationwide scholarship program to improve the teaching of money management and financial security. This is done through summer workshops at eight major universities which give intensive training in teaching techniques and subject matter to educators who, in turn, pass on their knowledge to their students and to other teachers.

Through these services, the Institute of Life Insurance is helping to broaden the understanding of a subject that is a major source of financial security for the American family.

What Life Insurance Means...

TO OUR FAMILIES
TO OUR ECONOMY

moderns make money behave

The booklets shown above are just two of the many aids prepared by the Institute of Life Insurance. They are useful to radio editors, writers and commentators, as well as educators. Copies are available on request.

Institute of Life Insurance

Central Source of Information about Life Insurance
488 Madison Avenue, New York 22, N. Y.

5457-B

This advertisement appears in
Broadcasting-Telecasting—March 9, 1953

FIGURE 2.2. Institute of Life Insurance advertisement selling textbooks for use in public schools. Industry-penned curricula encouraged young people to take responsibility for their own risks and view private insurance as an essential part of economic life. (ILI, "Young People Do Want to Know the Facts of Life Insurance," 1953, J. Walter Thompson Company, Domestic Advertisements Collection, David M. Rubenstein Rare Book & Manuscript Library, Duke University.)

The Mathematics of Life Insurance, another ILI textbook, claimed to make high school math courses "more fun" by generating "stimulating classroom discussions" about insurance products.[41]

Other curricular materials produced by the ILI's education division focused more generally on instilling economic habits and behaviors amenable to insurance consumption. Textbooks like *Blueprint for Tomorrow* and *Moderns Make Money Behave* introduced high school students to virtues of "the free enterprise system" while underscoring the importance of responsible investment, saving, and financial planning for the future.[42] The ILI also introduced materials to its Education for Living curriculum library geared specifically toward female students. A filmstrip titled *Directing Your Dollars*, for example, offered home economics students lessons in "how to live" by "making money management a personal virtue."[43] These materials proved exceedingly popular among educators, despite their seemingly dull subject matter. The institute proudly reported that schools requested over two million copies of the comic book *The Man Who Ran Interference*, and regularly noted the popularity of its other curricular offerings in reports to its members.[44]

The ILI presented its curricular materials as educational documents provided to schools out of a commitment to public service. Their value to the insurance industry, however, expanded beyond the goodwill that service work was known to generate. One textbook on insurance, written for a high school audience, instructed students, "This is your workbook—when you are through with it, take it home. Your parents will be interested in the information presented and to see the work you've done"—a fairly transparent attempt to get more mileage out of the text, persuading parents as well as students of the value of life insurance. The same textbook included a pitch to students to seek future employment in the insurance industry, promising in its early pages, "You will learn something of the vocational opportunities which exist in insurance, opportunities which you may want to investigate for yourself when you graduate from school."[45] This move—significant during a period of concern surrounding a future shortage of clerical workers—suggests yet another way that insurers made use of their educational materials.

Public relations experts at the ILI skillfully introduced industry-penned curricula into public schools across the nation. "We moved cautiously at first because we did not want to be subject to a charge of trying to put propaganda into the schools," ILI president Holgar Johnson explained, noting that "other segments of American Business had been accused of this."[46] Despite this danger, the institute forged ahead in hopes of nurturing what its leaders called "a closer relationship between the business world and the educational world."[47] Curricula designed by the institute helped young people develop a "long range interest" in private insurance, and was thus seen as a crucial tool in the quest to manage future risks to the industry.[48] To smooth the adoption of these materials—and avoid accusations of peddling propaganda—the ILI took extra care to stress the educational value of its curricula and hired credentialed educators and nationally renowned experts to help develop content.

Establishing relationships with experts outside the field of insurance became a central task for the directors of the ILI and other industry leaders during the postwar years. As the industry moved beyond health and school curricula in its efforts to shape the behaviors and habits of Americans, insurers relied heavily on experts to determine which habits required intervention. The ILI worked closely, for example, with polling organizations like those run by George Gallup and Elmo Roper to predict the direction of public habits and values that might need changing.[49] The research conducted by mid-century pollsters—which involved creating "microcosms" of the population by sorting individuals into groups by geography, age, gender, occupation, and income—appealed to an industry that employed similar techniques to sort and classify populations.[50] The ILI hired polling organizations to track changes in the "consumption habits, bodily habits, and emotional habits" of Americans.[51] Insurers also paid special attention to the nation's changing attitudes toward government, and particularly whether the public was moving closer to an acceptance of "statism or socialism."[52] As Arnold Brown, vice president of the American Council of Life Insurers explained, looking back on the postwar years, "the concept of a moving line of demarcation between government and the insurance business attracted much attention, and a number of the industry's leaders wanted to find ways to determine how and why that line moved."[53]

The ILI also used pollsters to track changes in family structure, especially the evolving social roles of American women. After learning from polling data in the early 1950s that wives made more economic decisions (including decisions about insurance) than husbands, ILI leaders altered their marketing and educational massages in order to attract the attention of what they called "the newly articulate feminine half of the population."[54] Polling data provided the impetus for the ILI's decision to launch a "women's division" in the early 1950s. This wing of the institute conducted research on changing gender roles and developed public service and educational materials for female consumers. The women's division oversaw publication of a weekly newsletter, titled the *Family Economist*, which was printed in the women's pages of newspapers and magazines around the country.[55] It also formed relationships with women's organizations, including the General Federation of Women's Clubs, the National Federation of Business and Professional Women's Clubs, the Girl

Scouts, and a variety of women's church groups. By the mid-1950s the institute had developed a reputation as a leader in the field of "women's issues"
and received requests for educational materials from a variety of organizations, including the US Department of Agriculture's "home management"
division.[56]

To help analyze data produced by polling organizations and to prepare for
an uncertain social and political future, the ILI also enlisted the services of
academics in the mid-1950s. The institute worked closely, for example, with
the Harvard sociologist Talcott Parsons, who helped shape the ILI's research
on the changing structure of the American family and other changes to social
life—including increased social and geographic mobility, changing gender
roles, and the continued waning of the extended family structure.[57] Enthusiastic about the prospect of predicting future changes to the population and
"the nature of society," ILI leaders regularly invited sociologists like Parsons
to speak at the institute's annual meetings. These scholars introduced cutting-
edge sociological research to the nation's top insurance executives. "We were
essentially asking our business leaders to go back to college and major in
sociology," Johnson joked in his history of the institute.[58]

Sociologists proved useful in the insurance industry's quest to "predict
the unforeseen" and face the future's risks. Psychologists offered a different
but equally valuable skill set, one called on by insurance leaders to help direct their interventions into social life. The ILI's Johnson, like many business
executives during the postwar years, was an avid reader of psychological literature.[59] Johnson often quoted his favorite psychologist, Henry Allen Over-
street, author of the popular 1925 book *Influencing Human Behavior*, in his
writings and speeches, and directed the ILI to draw on psychological research
to help dictate the course of its public service messaging and educational
activities.[60] From sociologists, Johnson and other leaders of the industry
learned the value of making "intelligent diagnoses" about the public "as a
unified aggregate of habit-systems."[61] Psychologists offered tools for shaping
those systems, providing lessons on how to speak to various segments of the
population and appeal to their "drives," hopes, and desires. "The problem of
social and political advance becomes fundamentally a problem of discover-
ing the crucial habit-systems of a people," Johnson explained, "then devising
means for changing them."[62]

Pollsters, sociologists, psychologists, and other experts offered valuable
knowledge and strategies that insurers drew on in their efforts to govern
the conduct of Americans—or as the ILI put it, to teach Americans "how
to live."[63] Insurers used this knowledge to transform their approach to marketing by infusing their advertising materials with "educational" content,

self-help messaging, and advice. The ILI, for example, supplemented its post-war "self-security" and issue marketing with hundreds of advertisements and informational pamphlets advising the public in diverse aspects of economic, social, and private life. Public relations organizations like the ILI became leading producers of these kinds of materials, but individual companies contributed to this trend as well, filling national newspapers and magazines with "educational" copy on a vast array of topics, including how to stretch the family food budget; how to plan future education and careers for children; how to prevent juvenile delinquency, manage debt, and secure marital happiness. Few of these materials mentioned insurance. Though they tended to encourage saving and thrift, for example, most lacked a sales pitch and avoided referring to insurance consumption directly. The absence of an overt shill no doubt contributed to the idea that insurers and their affiliated experts offered advice as a public service.

The family and family life were by far the most common topics of postwar insurance "educational" advice literature. Many ads, for example, addressed marriage as an occasion to plan for the future, and stressed the necessity of preparation for healthy marriages and family life. One ILI advice ad from the early 1950s featured an image of a mother advising a daughter dressed in a wedding gown. "Remember, dear," the mother announces in the title, "happiness doesn't just *happen!*"[64] Another advice ad from the same series asked readers, in a large headline floating over an image of a happy couple in a boat, "Why is marriage like a canoe? because to manage either takes proper balance and teamwork."[65] Other advice ads stressed more specific marriage-related questions, such as the proper age to marry and whether or not wives should work outside the home. "How Young Should People Marry?," for example, introduced readers to the Joslins, a couple who had married at the (relatively young) age of twenty, but had nonetheless managed through "hard work and creative financial planning" to "make their own security." The Joslins, the copy concluded, "were right to marry as young as they did" and "prove to all of us that we can solve our own problems by our own efforts."[66]

Many insurance advice advertisements included essays penned by nationally recognized experts—a move designed to cater to the expertise-obsessed culture of the era.[67] An ILI advice ad featuring an image of a woman dressed in work clothes, juggling a grocery bag while leaning over an oven, for example, asked readers, "Does the extra paycheck always pay?" The subtitle, "When wives work, more money often means more problems, too!," is followed by copy featuring "an authoritative discussion of this very modern question by Frank J. Hertel, General Director, Family Service Association of America."[68] A year later, in another ILI advice ad, Hertel addressed readers again, declaring, "In many cases wives can work *and* run happy homes . . . but it takes careful management."[69] Experts stepped in to advise on other topics, including debt management, budgeting for food, and saving for college and professional training for children. In "The Birthday Tommy tried to FORGET!," a child dreams of a new bicycle but does not receive a birthday present because his parents toil under "the great burden of debt that has made many American homes unhappy." In the copy, a "renowned family planning expert" advises parents how to avoid such unhappy situations by creating a budget and planning for the future by saving.[70]

"The *Real* Culprit Was Never Tried!," an ILI ad that portrayed a young boy in court, took a similar tack. Here, David Armstrong, executive director of the Boys Clubs of America, instructed parents to integrate activities for children into their family budgets, "just as you would save money for your children's food." Rising juvenile delinquency and national burglary rates, Armstrong explained, could be prevented through the enterprising work of parents who sought security for their families through financial planning.[71] Metropolitan offered a similar argument in "The Restless Years: 9–12," which advised parents to monitor the reading materials of their preteen children as a means of preventing juvenile delinquency. The copy urged parents to teach children "the value of money" and "how to budget allowance," warning that "the school can't be expected to solve all your child's difficulties."[72] Significantly, this last warning implied that government programs like the justice system and the public schools offered inadequate solutions to national problems like delinquency.

Insurers never lost track of the real purpose of their advice advertisements and educational materials. "We were building, through indirection, a foundation for the use of insurance," Johnson admitted in his history of the ILI.[73] In the face of rapid and unpredictable social change, building that foundation required a dedicated program of social governance. The amazing breadth of seemingly non-insurance-related topics covered by postwar industry advice campaigns underscores their governing character. Even faith was portrayed as a pursuit that required calculated planning and a willingness to manage the future's risks. "I Pray the Lord My Soul to Keep," an ILI ad that ran nationally throughout the early 1950s, for example, urged readers to seek out faith as "a bedrock of family unity" and instructed readers that "to keep alive the family's faith calls for a positive plan—just as you plan for your family's material welfare."[74] This message, like so many others insurers produced during this period, argued that the management of private life, and even spirituality, must be strategic and subject to calculation.

Taking the Wheel: Auto Insurance as Governance
and the Corporate Roots of Driver Education

Life insurers were not the only insurance companies that pursued educational
programming with a governing bent "in the service of the public." Property
and casualty insurers also participated in such projects, contributing actively
to the midcentury "safety movement" alongside government agencies and
other industries, like manufacturing.[75] Fire insurance companies launched
fire safety campaigns; home insurance providers published pamphlets and
produced curricula on safety within the home; and group insurance providers worked tirelessly to train companies and their employees to prevent
workplace accidents. No field within the property and casualty fold, however,
made deeper inroads into safety education than the auto insurance industry.

When cars first became widely available in the 1920s, they posed a serious
threat to public safety. Few regulations existed to govern their use, accident
rates were high, and the carnage they introduced to America's roadways was
as horrifying as it was new. Americans at this time were no strangers to the
damage machines could inflict on human bodies, but until the 1920s, accidents had been largely confined to the industrial sector. The new accessibility
and popularity of automobiles brought the industrial accident into the public
sphere and put new and ever larger segments of the population in danger.
The rising toll of automobile accidents and the question of how to best govern driving elicited a number of responses during the early years of expanding car ownership. Governments set speed limits, imposed traffic laws, and
put in place licensing and registration requirements. The question of liability
for accidents fell mostly to the tort system, which struggled throughout the
1920s to resolve a number of problems—chief among them the fact that many
American drivers had few assets and were unable to pay settlements. Auto
insurance, a relatively new invention at this time, was a luxury available only
to the privileged few. But as cars became more prevalent and accidents piled
up, more and more commenters began to wonder if insurance might play a
role in solving the problems of traffic safety and governance.

The market for auto insurance grew rapidly throughout the 1920s and remained steady even during the Depression years of the 1930s. It was during
this era that insurance first emerged as a potential solution to the troubles
afflicting the nation's roadways. Legal scholars became particularly enthusiastic proponents of insurance during this period, celebrating its potential to answer crucial questions like who should be allowed to drive, how
to assess liability, and how to secure compensation for victims of accidents.

Legal thinkers considered a number of approaches to structuring the auto insurance system, the most comprehensive of which was the Columbia plan, widely recognized as the first "no-fault" auto insurance scheme. A team of law professors at Yale and Columbia developed the plan, modeled after workers' compensation, in 1932. It mandated that all drivers be required to carry third-party insurance coverage—to protect victims injured by their vehicles—and promised compensation for those victims without regard to fault. Noting that auto accidents shared much in common with industrial accidents, the Columbia plan's authors argued that driving had become a *social* risk that demanded a collective solution.

With this in mind, the plan's architects argued that comprehensive social insurance offered a better and more efficient structure for compensating victims than the courts and the tort liability system. As Jonathan Simon has argued, this new approach to liability and compensation represented a turning point in the history of auto insurance, and also driver governance.[76] The plan emerged at the dawn of the insurance era, when Americans were first beginning to identify the need to spread risk across collectives as an essential feature of modern life (Congress passed the Social Security Act only three years later, in a similar spirit). Fierce opposition to the Columbia plan from auto insurance companies, who predictably feared that it might lead to a government takeover of the industry via nationalization, helped prevent it from being adopted in the United States.[77] The fact that the plan was widely discussed in legal circles and the media, however, signaled a change in thinking about collective risk and liability, as well as a new willingness to turn to insurance as a viable system of social governance.[78]

Americans rejected no-fault and other forms of mandatory liability coverage in the 1930s; the private auto insurance industry continued to grow. Following World War II, car ownership rates in the nation skyrocketed once again, helping insurance gain ground as an important tool for mitigating the social and economic impacts of accidents. Massive growth offered the industry clear opportunities for profit, but it also presented challenges. With so many new cars and drivers on the roads, how would companies set prices and control claims? Eager to compete for the consumer dollar, individual firms began seeking new ways to lower premiums and attract what the industry referred to as "good risks"—safe drivers with a low probability of filing claims. The primary way companies did this was by refining the risk classifications they used in setting rates and determining availability of coverage. Age, sex, and marital status became standard underwriting categories during the 1950s, as did geographical location (the subject of later debates over redlining, the focus of chapter 5).

In order to create these refined rating categories, insurers stepped up their surveillance efforts, assembling massive quantities of statistical data on car ownership, accidents, and driving behaviors. Some companies approached the need for data creatively, experimenting with cutting-edge methods of risk rating. The Kemper Companies, a national conglomerate of twelve auto insurance providers, for example, pioneered the use of psychological testing, focusing on male drivers under the age of twenty-five. Kemper launched the program in California in 1961 and mass-tested it in New England over the next two years. The companies' "psychological staff" designed the Kemper Young Driver Education Test to "reveal the feelings, drives, attitudes and other facets of the basic personality which have a direct bearing on his performance behind the wheel of a car." Though Kemper admitted the test was not an "infallible underwriting tool," the organization insisted on its predictive value and offered young drivers who achieved a satisfactory score a 10 percent discount on their premiums. By 1969 the Kemper Companies had administered more than ten thousand psychological tests throughout the country.[79]

As underwriters scrambled to refine their rating mechanisms, the scourge of automobile accidents continued to plague the nation—and the claims departments of insurance companies. In an effort to boost esteem for the industry and stem the rising tide of claims, auto insurers dove headlong into public service work, just as life insurers had done decades earlier.[80] The statistics departments of insurance companies had long known that the accident rates of young drivers were higher than those of older ones, making education an obvious site of intervention. The industry also clung to a belief—expressed repeatedly in internal literature and conferences—that individual drivers, not enforcement of traffic laws or the design of vehicles or roadways—were the root cause of accidents. As Stanley Withe, secretary of Aetna Casualty and Surety Company, succinctly claimed, "It is the man behind the wheel that causes most accidents."[81] With this in mind, insurance companies and their professional organizations focused on educational efforts that could reach drivers while they were young and instill in them a "safety mindset."

Early educational efforts focused on the production of curricular materials. Auto insurance companies published thousands of textbooks and pamphlets offering lessons in traffic safety to young American drivers. These materials presented driving as an activity that involved calculation, prudence, and the individual management of risk. Insurance companies also produced educational filmstrips and distributed them, free of charge, to schools. Films like the National Association of Mutual Insurance Companies' *Caution at the Crossroads*, Liberty Mutual's *Teenage Road-E-O*, and Aetna's *Live and Let*

Live emphasized automobile use as an individual responsibility and broke the driving process down into quantifiable, repetitive movements.[82]

Government leaders, school officials, and the press applauded auto insurers for their good work in the field of traffic safety, and this praise encouraged the industry to continue its efforts to educate American drivers. In 1953, Aetna unveiled "a new driver education concept" to supplement the company's already extensive traffic safety programming: the Drivotrainer system, a course devised to teach students driving basics from the safety of the classroom (see fig. 2.3). The centerpiece of the course was an exciting new machine: a driving simulator called the Aetna Drivotrainer. Designed to replicate the driving experience, the machine looked and felt like an actual car—complete with a functional steering wheel and column, braking and acceleration pedals, turn-signal indicator, shifting mechanism, and headlights. The machine represented the culmination of decades of experimentation with simulators on the part of the company, combining features and functions of earlier devices the insurance giant had designed in hopes of quantifying the driving process and producing safer, more responsible drivers; these included the Steerometer and the Reactometer, both developed by Aetna in the 1930s.[83] Unlike these earlier devices, which primarily served as entertaining curiosities at world fairs and other similar venues, Aetna developed the Drivotrainer to be a part of a comprehensive driver education program.

Aetna set up its own in-house "moving picture bureau" to shoot and distribute films designed specifically for use with the simulator.[84] These films, projected on a screen in the front of the classroom, offered realistic depictions of roadways from the first-person perspective of a driver behind the wheel. The first Drivotrainer course offered a fifteen-film pilot. The course was extended in the early 1960s to include twenty-one films, all shot using a technique the company called "tri-angle vision," which allowed students to see side and rear mirrors in all first-person scenes. Aetna claimed that this technique offered students "a total view of the traffic situation."[85] As students operated controls in reaction to developments that unfolded on screen, their actions (including braking, shifting, and steering) were processed and delivered electronically to a device at the back of the room. This "master control unit" automatically recorded and scored each student's performance.[86] Specially trained instructors oversaw the master unit, watching carefully to spot student errors as they occurred. Aetna argued that close interaction with these instructors, who could intervene as they spotted mistakes, helped students learn faster while also developing "proper attitudes and good judgement on city and suburban highways."[87] At the end of each course unit, data gathered by the master control unit was printed out on paper rolls. At the end

FIGURE 2.3. Students at the Brooklyn School of Automotive Trades learning to drive using the Aetna Drivotrainer simulator. Driver education programs like the Drivotrainer system attracted goodwill for the auto insurance industry, helped reduce claims, and produced proprietary data used by companies to set rates. (*Driving Stationary Aetnacars*, 1953, *Brooklyn Daily Eagle* photographs, Brooklyn Collection, Brooklyn Public Library.)

of the course, instructors combined rolls for each student, producing a final scoresheet.

The Drivotrainer system represented a unique opportunity for Aetna. Instructors encouraged students of Drivotrainer courses to purchase coverage from the company, and those who completed the program with high marks received discounted insurance rates. Student scoresheets also provided Aetna with valuable new data on the driving performance of young male and female drivers. Expansion of the program promised the company a treasure trove of proprietary data on this problematic category of potential consumers—a category that had previously proven difficult to classify and measure. Association with cutting-edge technology and with the laudable goal of training safer drivers also stood to earn the company goodwill from the public. The multiple dividends offered by the program convinced Aetna to pour additional resources into expansion. After successful early trials at the Brooklyn High School of Automotive Trades, Hollywood High School in Los Angeles, and State College of Iowa at Cedar Falls, the company set out to make the Drivotrainer system a national program.

Paul Cullen, the superintendent of Aetna's new Public Education Department, oversaw the expansion and sold the Drivotrainer system to schools around the nation. Cullen penned articles describing the virtues of the program and traveled the country speaking to educators, safety experts, and school boards. Citing divorce and accident statistics, he argued in one pitch, "There are two licenses in this country which we get with inadequate preparation: a marriage license and a driver's license."[88] Though the industry had been classifying young drivers as bad risks for years, Cullen argued that, if educated properly, these youngsters represented "the brightest hope for future traffic safety."[89] Cullen sold the Drivotrainer as an economical alternative to behind-the-wheel training, the high cost of which had prevented many schools from offering driver education courses. The typical Drivotrainer classroom included ten simulators, though the system could handle up to twenty-four. This volume, Cullen argued, allowed a single instructor to teach a large number of students at the same time, leading to "a 30% reduction in cost-per-pupil."[90] Moving beyond the question of cost, Cullen also promoted the program's ability to provide "realism without risk" by conducting "drills without danger" that gave students experience responding to emergencies, which could not be done safely on the road.[91]

Cullen succeeded in attracting attention to the Drivotrainer system and advancing its acceptance among educators. At a conference on driver education in 1955, the National Commission on Safety Education, a department of the National Education Association, adopted a policy allowing simulator training to serve as a substitute for one-half of the training the commission typically recommended for on-the-road instruction. The National Safety Council supported the policy.[92] Enthusiastic about the prospect of installing Drivotrainers in schools across the nation, Aetna sponsored a conference at its headquarters in Hartford, Connecticut, early in 1957, hoping to convince educators, traffic safety experts, and other auto insurers to join the company in encouraging government to subsidize driver education programs, including those that employed simulators, in the nation's public schools.[93] Six months later, Aetna's secretary, Stanley Withe, joined Cullen in Washington, where they testified in front of Congress in support of a bill "to promote safety in transportation by motor vehicles in interstate commerce by assisting the states to establish programs for driver education."[94] This willingness to lobby the state and support its expansion reflected a new strategy on the part of the industry. Property and casualty insurers, like life companies, had spent most of the century criticizing government and arguing that private enterprise offered the best and most efficient solutions to social problems. When government could be used to further the goals of the industry, however, tactics of this sort were set aside. The substantial control auto insurers already wielded over the nation's driver education system no doubt contributed to the industry's willingness to enlist government as a partner.

When called to testify, Withe and Cullen offered House representatives a number of arguments in favor of a federal subsidy for driver education. "In this day of modern motor travel, the California driver in a crash on an Indiana highway may be the victim of a Maryland driver," Withe reasoned. "As the key to future highway safety, therefore, driver education should be the universal concern of us all."[95] Arguing that a patchwork of state and local programs could not sufficiently ensure national safety, Withe insisted that "only when education encompasses all drivers can it achieve maximum effectiveness."[96] Cullen focused his testimony on the "revolutionary" Drivotrainer, and even brought one along to exhibit at the hearings. Both men encouraged the assembled representatives to revise the current bill, which offered only limited funding to schools for "equipment purchases" and thus might deter the adoption of simulators. The insurance men also repeatedly returned to the question of cost, offering detailed statistics that depicted the Drivotrainer system as an efficient and economical means of training the nation's drivers.

The assembled representatives responded enthusiastically, agreeing to amend the bill to allow funding for Drivotrainers. Representative Kenneth Roberts of Alabama, who led the hearings, however, was unmoved by the insurance men's statistics and discussion of cost. He asked if the Drivotrainer course would "build up proper social attitudes on the part of students" or respond adequately to what he considered the *real* problem with young drivers. "We have too much, I would say, juvenile delinquency today," he mused, and asked if "perhaps, delinquency is reflected somewhat in bad driving in the teen-age groups?" Cullen responded that Aetna's Drivotrainer system did, indeed, encourage "good attitudes and good judgment," and could even be used as an efficient tool to identify "personal deficiencies" early on in young drivers. He added, "If you can catch the youngsters in their formative years and inculcate an attitude of safety, you can go a long way toward licking the traffic-safety problem." Satisfied, Roberts urged the remaining witnesses to move quickly through the rest of the hearing.[97]

Though Aetna deemed the presentation a success—Roberts and several other representatives expressed gratitude to Withe and Cullen and lauded the company's efforts to train safer drivers—the 1957 bill failed to pass, due to budgetary concerns. The hearings attracted national attention to driver education, however, and strengthened the reputation of Aetna and the auto insurance industry in general as leaders in the field of driver safety. Proponents of driver education disappointed by the failure of the 1957 bill were rewarded for their efforts several years later with the passage of the Highway Safety Act of 1966, which imposed a 10 percent reduction in federal aid to states that failed to implement comprehensive driver education. By that point, Aetna had already installed the Drivotrainer system in high schools and colleges across the country. The 1966 act only boosted its popularity, allowing states a cost-effective way to expand driver education programs and avoid a cut in federal aid. By 1967, 1.5 million students had enrolled in Drivotrainer courses, with thirty thousand trained annually at more than five hundred high schools in thirty-seven states.[98] The simulators found their way to the plains of South Dakota, where Aetna boasted that "teenage Sioux Indians" had enrolled in the program, and eventually to the UK, Thailand, Switzerland, Sweden, and a number of other countries around the world.[99]

Aetna continued to update and improve the system. In 1967 the company released the Mark V, a computerized Drivotrainer manufactured by the Raytheon company.[100] Touted as "the ultimate in realism," the new computerized model was "smartly styled with a compact fiberglass body and bucket seats."[101] As with earlier versions, the dashboard included an ignition switch, speedometer, gas gauge, headlight switch, dimmer switch, and horn—all of which were operative. On the new model, when the gas gauge reached empty, the motor stalled.[102] Other improvements to the system included new films, updated for added realism. Produced now in color for widescreen viewing, the films gave students a "panoramic view" designed to "closely approach" normal windshield vision.[103] Brake lights depicted in the new films flashed realistically. Sound effects included "the swish of passing cars, the beep of horns, the squeal of tires in emergency situations."[104]

The new Mark V Drivotrainer offered other advantages, including a less active role for the classroom instructor. This meant less time and money spent training teachers. In a loving description of the updated system, Aetna's administrator of Driver Education Services, Dean Cook, described the up-dated classroom: "As the students drive to the filmed highway on the screen, a computer monitors their actions. When a driving error is committed, the computer signals the student, telling him how to correct it. This information appears on the student display panel just above the dashboard."[105] Computer-ized displays that automatically reported progress to students did more than cut down the cost and time required for instructor training; Aetna claimed they also aided in the learning process by allowing students to set their own pace and "take charge" of their own education.[106] The *Journal of Secondary Education* praised the Drivotrainer as a scientifically advanced "teaching ma-chine" that promoted "self-instruction" by providing students with "an op-portunity to participate and deliberate upon the complete philosophy of safe driving under the programmed conditions of the films."[107] Aetna had sold the system to legislators in the 1950s by emphasizing student interaction with instructors who were specifically trained to promote "proper social attitudes." By the end of the 1960s, this interaction had been replaced by a computerized "teaching machine" designed to train self-governance.

Numerous attempts to gauge the effectiveness of driving simulator train-ing were made during the 1950s and 1960s. Studies sponsored by Aetna and Allstate (who released their own simulator, the "Good Driver," in 1961) found that students with simulator training received fewer traffic violations and ex-perienced fewer accidents than students who had participated in standard behind-the-wheel educational programs.[108] Later studies conducted by educa-tors and traffic safety researchers in the 1970s, however, found that simulators like the Drivotrainer failed to affect performance skills in a meaningful way. These studies concluded that no discernable difference existed between sim-ulator and behind-the-wheel training.[109] With their effectiveness called into question—and as increasingly underfunded public schools opted to discon-tinue driver education programs in the 1970s—the simulators gradually fell out of use. Aetna sold the Drivotrainer to educational electronics manufac-turer Doron Precision Systems in the late 1970s (and the property and casualty wing of their business to Travelers Insurance not long after). The few Drivo-trainers that survive today are mostly housed in museums—relics of what one educator called "Space Age Education," but what might just as easily be described as the heyday of private industry's incursion into public schools.[110]

The auto insurance industry's efforts to take the wheel of the nation's driver education system during the postwar years helped reduce claims and increase sales while supporting the notion that insurance companies offered an appropri-ate and desirable solution to the problem of driver governance. But these efforts carried additional benefits as well. In congressional hearings—which occurred frequently in the 1970s in response to public outrage over unpredictable and sometimes exorbitant premiums charged by auto insurers—representatives of the industry regularly pointed to their record in the field of traffic safety in order to stave off regulation and paint the industry in a flattering light. Developing a reputation as an industry that served the public also helped deflect potential criticism of the industry's often-contradictory practice of pooling risks while simultaneously individualizing them. Refined risk-rating structures, devised in the 1950s, that drew on age or gender worked on a "class" basis, for example, while surveillance technologies like psychological testing or Drivotrainer scoring measured individual behaviors and characteristics, then set rates accordingly. Though these contradictions would attract criticism in the 1970s and 1980s, during the 1950s and 1960s the public largely overlooked them.

The governing efforts of auto insurers did not go completely unchallenged, however, during the postwar years. In his 1962 book, *The Highway Jungle: The Story of the Public Safety Movement and of the Failure of Driver Education in Public Schools*, Edward Tenney, a driver training educator critical of private industry's intrusion into the field, delivered a scathing critique of corporate involvement in public education. Tenney accused insurers and other corporate interests of using driver education to "prime" young people for entry into the market. "Highway safety is, indeed, everybody's business," he scoffed, "but some people make more money at it than others."[111] Reserving special ire for insurance companies, Tenney devoted dozens of pages in his book to a critique of the industry. "It would be an exaggeration to say that commerce both owns and operates driver education," he noted wryly. "It would be less an exaggeration to say that commerce owns it and that the life adjusters run it."[112] Tenney was especially disdainful of insurance industry attempts to speed passage of compulsory driver education laws, and accused insurance companies of using their influence over driver education to boost business. "It is obvious that insurance companies stand to make a direct profit from those states that enact driver-education laws," he argued.[113] Tenney closed his book with an appeal to Americans to resist the intrusion of private enterprise into public education, of exactly the sort perpetuated by insurance companies and their professional organizations throughout the postwar era: "Every citizen should be aware of the basic conflict between education for adjustment to the marketplace and education for enrichment of the life of mind and spirit. It really comes down to the large question of who is to control our schools. Shall the schools be opened up to reflect the competitive struggle for markets?"[114]

Though Tenney's critique focused on the insurance industry's entry into the field of driver education, the questions he raised spoke more generally to the changing role of private enterprise as a shaper of individual behavior and social governance in the United States during the postwar years. Insurance companies and their professional organizations led this transformation as they attempted to predict and manage the future's risks. Though insurers' commitments to public health and driver education waned over time, the industry did not abandon its efforts to shape social life, or the "whole context of our civilization." By the late 1960s industry insiders had identified a new field of intervention: what the ILI called "the poverty, frustration, decay, and ugliness" of America's cities.[115] As insurers turned their gaze toward the nation's troubled urban centers, launching ambitious new public service programs, they made sure to publicize their efforts widely.

The industry did not enter this new field of intervention with clean hands, however. In fact, insurance companies played a central role in creating the very problems they set out to solve in America's cities during the late 1960s and early 1970s. Chapters 3, 4, and 5 examine the origins and complicated legacies of the industry's investments in the postwar built environment—in housing developments, shopping centers, office buildings, and infrastructure projects. In each of these sites, insurance companies developed new strategies of governance and new partnerships with the state to help enact them.

PART II

Investing in Privatization

3

"Public Enterprises in Private Hands":
Investing in Urban Renewal

In *Eleven Stories High: Growing Up in Stuyvesant Town, 1948–1968*, Corinne Demas offers a memoir of her childhood in Stuyvesant Town, a massive private housing development built during the 1940s in Lower Manhattan by the Metropolitan Life Insurance Company. Demas recalls a regulated, manicured environment, where "order always prevailed" and security was a staple of daily life.[1] In Demas's memoir, the handpicked residents of Stuyvesant Town lived sensible lives characterized by thrift. Longtime residents "socked away" savings, choosing modesty over extravagance, some dying with estates "totaling up to half a million."[2] The homogeneous residents, all white and middle class, were predominantly families of World War II veterans. Stuyvesant Town's fireproof walls were not thin, but "conductive."[3] Every night at the same time, "as if on schedule," a symphony of "tooth brushing, wiping, flushing, and washing" echoed through the columns of the development's imposing towers.[4] Individual apartments featured intimate views into parallel others, a product of the density and "bewildering" symmetry of the carefully planned space.[5] Fathers returned home from work as dentists and doctors, occasionally mistaking their own buildings for indistinguishable ones across the way. They rode identical elevators to identical floors, entered identical doorways, and were greeted by screams of wives who were not their own.[6] In her memoir, Demas muses about the impact of so much sameness on Stuyvesant's residents:

> A friend of mine who grew up in Stuyvesant Town believes the sameness made people crazy—the fact that everything appeared identical, but on closer inspection, really wasn't. I disagree. For children especially, I think the sameness was comforting. The layout of buildings, playgrounds, walks, and drives, was all predictable, once you mastered the design.[7]

In contrast to much of what has been written about urban housing developments built by insurance companies during the years surrounding World
War II, Demas's image of Stuyvesant Town is sympathetic. Most commentators have been less kind, focusing on the negative aspects of these sanitized,
segregated spaces—their participation in destructive urban renewal projects
that displaced thousands of low-income families, their discriminatory racial
politics, their aesthetic ugliness. Demas offers a more positive, though conflicted, vision. In *Eleven Stories High*, density begets conflict, but the sameness of residents also leads to a sense of community. Although rigorous policing and regulation produce feelings of anxiety and suspicion, the general
"orderliness" and predictability of the environment also, according to Demas,
provides comfort for residents, and a sense of security.

Demas's memories of Stuyvesant Town offer a personal account of what
it was like to live in the enclosed, dense, private housing developments designed, constructed, and managed by insurance companies during the late
1940s and early 1950s. Developments like Stuyvesant Town—just one of dozens of housing projects built by life insurers in cities across the country—have
attracted the attention of a number of architecture and urban studies scholars
in recent years. Drawing on early work by Arthur Simon, Arnold Hirsch, and
Roberta Moudry, which highlighted insurance housing developments as important participants in midcentury urban renewal programs, these scholars
have produced detailed studies of the impacts of the industry's housing investments on specific communities.[8] Individual communities matter immensely,
but the "life insurance housing boom," as the urban planning scholar Adam
Tanaka has recently called it, was a national trend.[9] To understand this trend,
we need to examine the goals and motivations of the industry that shaped it.
This chapter positions the midcentury life insurance urban housing boom
within the larger context of the industry's changing role in American life,
focusing on the power of insurance as (1) an institution of social governance,
(2) a promoter of racial and class-based discrimination, and (3) an agent of
privatization.

Construction and management of large housing developments in urban
centers expanded the industry's governing reach, allowing insurers to actively
shape spaces of residence and consumption as well as the laws that dictated
the circulation of capital throughout the nation. As some of the first large-
scale construction projects financed, built, and managed by life insurers,
they also serve as key sites through which to examine the industry's ability
to export techniques of risk management to new spheres beyond insurance
practice. Insurers took their control of these developments seriously, applying
the logic of risk at every stage. Nearly every aspect of the building process,

FIGURE 3.1. Aerial view of Stuyvesant Town and Peter Cooper Village, built by the Metropolitan Life Insurance Company in Manhattan in 1947. Metropolitan designed private, racially segregated housing developments like Stuyvesant Town to be self-contained "urban utopias" structured around the management of risk and governance of tenants. (*Aerial View of the Stuyvesant Town–Peter Cooper Village in New York City*, © New York On Air/Offset.com.)

from selection of construction materials (most were fireproof) to selection of tenants (segregated by race and class), turned on a calculus of risk. The physical layouts of housing developments were no exception. Figure 3.1, an aerial photograph of Stuyvesant Town, one of several urban housing developments built by Metropolitan, reveals the overwhelming uniformity and symmetry of these spaces. The architects of these developments intentionally limited entrances and exits, restricting access to outsiders and channeling inhabitants through an open, central area as they came and went. The result was a tightly controlled space in which the movements of residents were strictly monitored—not only by patrolling guards hired by insurance company management, but also by neighbors (a phenomenon Demas discusses at length in her memoir). The ability to wield this kind of control over space was a primary motivating factor for insurers entering the housing field. As Metropolitan president Frederick Ecker argued in 1952, building and managing housing developments offered his company unprecedented authority in overseeing its investments, allowing "direct control" over operations "to a much larger extent than would be possible if [the company] merely held the mortgage on a project."[10]

Insurance housing developments worked both socially and spatially as tools of governance. As the architecture historian Roberta Moudry argues, "carefully wrought formal designs" in insurance housing "were matched by education and social guidance: financial, physical and social stability within company housing were secured by a combination of physical and social planning."[11] Insurance company leaders regularly cited the "social implications" of their urban housing developments as an important reason for pursuing such projects. Discussions of social factors not directly related to insurance were not new to this period—insurance companies, as we have seen, had been involved in social engineering projects that extended beyond their policy-holding contingents for decades. Metropolitan's public health campaign, for example, served as an important element of the company's public relations efforts, but was also designed to influence the conduct and behaviors of the general population. Connections between the industry's public health work and its midcentury housing investments were made often by the press. In an article about New York Life's late-1940s Lake Meadows development, for example, *Architectural Forum* praised the city of Chicago for "attracting the medicinal money of the insurance company to its sick South Side."[12] Insurers encouraged these connections. Metropolitan's Ecker argued, for example, that "clean and desirable housing accommodations" of the sort his company created were laudable for "their tendency to reduce disease, the volume of crime, and in general produce a more wholesome environment."[13]

Just as Ecker hoped, insurance housing developments reshaped the cities around them. As significant contributors to a national pattern of urban renewal, the companies that built these developments participated in slum clearance and redevelopment projects that redrew the class and racial lines that had characterized urban spaces before World War II. Though these patterns were prevalent in most urban renewal projects of the era, insurance companies—members of an industry that specialized in discrimination through its underwriting function—brought a special zeal for exclusion to their building projects and were instrumental in perpetuating and deepening racial and class-based discrimination in housing. In his study of Stuyvesant Town, the historian Samuel Zipp argues that insurance companies like Metropolitan "planned to rescue a portion of the 'rundown city' for white, middle-class family life."[14] Their success in doing so hinged on their ability to privatize formerly public space, or as the civil rights and housing activist Charles Abrams put it in 1947, to transfer "public enterprises" to "private hands."[15] Shrewdly evading discussion of land grants and tax breaks provided by state and city governments as enticements to build, insurers emphasized the positive contributions of their housing developments to the public good.

The housing they created, however, was privately owned and managed. Insurance companies eagerly advertised their contributions to urban renewal, seeking to elevate their industry as an institution on a par with the state that was capable of creating both new housing and new civic forms. In the process, they made a powerful case for both racial segregation and privatization as the future of America's cities.

Entering the Field of Urban Housing

How did life insurance companies come to invest in urban housing in the first place? During the first decades of the twentieth century, laws in most states allowed life insurers to invest in mortgages but prohibited companies from purchasing or managing real estate. Barred from owning or operating property "related to any business other than insurance," the real estate holdings of most insurers included their home office buildings and little else.[16] Most of these laws originated around the turn of the century, when widespread distrust of corporations, aggravated by the Armstrong Committee findings of 1905, spurred public demand for regulation of the industry.[17] During this era, states across the country passed legislation restricting the investment practices of insurers, which had previously been unregulated and often involved speculative deals that adversely affected policyholders. Real estate, because of its perceived lack of liquidity at this time, was considered speculative and therefore ill suited for insurance investment.[18]

State regulation also prohibited insurers from investing in stocks, once again because of their association with speculation. Thanks to these regulations and a conservative approach to investing that emerged out of the Armstrong debacle, the stock market crash that devastated the nation's financial system and helped launch the Great Depression in 1929 left the life insurance industry relatively unharmed.[19] Only twenty of the life insurance companies registered in the United States failed during the Great Depression; this compares to the more than four thousand state and national banks that failed at the height of the crisis in 1933. Nearly every insurance company that did fail turned to solvent reinsurers to honor claims. Bank failures, by contrast, resulted in losses to depositors of about $1.3 billion from 1929 to 1933.[20] Though the industry was not left entirely unscathed by the Great Depression—lapsed policies and rising mortality and disability rates drained cash flows—life insurers offered a substantial amount of liquidity at a time when such sources were limited.[21] By the mid-1930s, the industry was sitting on millions of dollars and looking for places to put them. Laws limiting insurers' options for investment posed a serious problem not only for companies seeking to diversify their holdings and receive good returns for their policyholders, but also for capital-poor cities and states.

An early attempt to revise investment law in order to free up insurance dollars was made by New York in 1922. In response to housing shortages in the state following World War I, regulators temporarily amended New York's insurance statutes to allow life insurance companies to invest in housing. State and city leaders turned immediately to Metropolitan, the largest insurer based in New York, and offered the company a ten-year period of tax exemption on a property located in Long Island City. Metropolitan agreed to spend $7.5 million on a housing development that would contain 2,125 units composed of fifty-four five-story walk-up apartment buildings. This development, called the Metropolitan Apartments, opened in 1924 and remained fully occupied well into the 1930s. Though deemed a success by all parties, the housing amendment passed by New York in 1922 expired after four years. The state didn't amend its insurance investment codes again until the late 1930s, when decreased building during the Great Depression caused another housing shortage.[22] Unlike the earlier shortage following World War I, the housing crisis launched by the Depression lasted for more than a decade and devastated cities and states across the nation.

Partnerships between state and city governments, desperate for new sources of capital for building, and the life insurance industry, flush with investment dollars and actively seeking to diversify its holdings, offered an attractive solution to the unfolding housing emergency. Drawing on its experiences in the 1920s, New York State opted to again amended its insurance code in 1938, passing a new law that allowed life insurance companies to invest up to 10 percent of their assets in moderate-income rental housing in cities with populations of three hundred thousand or more.[23] Metropolitan, having been consulted in advance on the terms of the legislation, announced it would invest $100 million in housing and immediately began plans to build Parkchester, a Bronx development discussed in the pages that follow.[24] The nation's entry into World War II in 1941 only deepened the housing crisis, leading New York to continue revising and updating its investment laws.[25] As home to both the largest city and the largest insurance companies in the nation, the state became a leader of a national trend. New York's Urban Development Corporation Act of 1941, which offered incentives to private investors willing to finance housing, and the Redevelopment Companies Law of 1942, which allowed cities to condemn land using the power of eminent domain and turn it over private corporations, were replicated in states across the nation. The 1942 law, designed specifically to entice insurance investors, offered a twenty-five-year tax abatement on housing redevelopment properties and became an

TABLE 3.1. Number and cost of housing projects constructed or purchased by life insurance companies, 1941–1952

Company	Number of projects	Year of acquisition	Cost to company as of December 1952
Bankers National Life Insurance Company	3	1947	$1,424,769.72
	1	1948	66,184.90
Colonial Life Insurance Company of America	1	1946	349,643.91
Connecticut Mutual Life Insurance Company	2	1946	159,954.64
	1	1948	880,415.72
Equitable Life Assurance Society of America	1	1941–1942	10,030,051.64
	1	1946–1950	17,393,422.51
Guardian Life Insurance Company of America	1	1947	360,101.40
	1	1948	240,562.40
	1	1949	345,426.50
Home Life Insurance Company	1	1946	1,056,584.37
John Hancock Mutual Life Insurance Company	1	1946	11,715,919.26
Metropolitan Life Insurance Company	3	1941	129,190,139.71
	1	1943	108,843,755.91
	1	1944	12,003,843.75
	1	1945	38,673,522.41
Mutual Benefit Life Insurance Company	3	1947	1,125,048.95
New England Mutual Life Insurance Company	1	1948	3,816,770.53
	1	1949	4,479,617.65
	1	1950	4,036,564.30
New York Life Insurance Company	1	1946	1,864,456.64
	1	1946–1949	62,148,139.29
	1	1947–1949	20,809,770.37
	1	1952	1,598,678.40
Phoenix Mutual Life Insurance Company	1	1947	1,160,162.21
Prudential Insurance Company of America	1	1945	2,287,668.51
	2	1946	2,158,341.49
	2	1947	2,826,221.88
	1	1947	636,658.91
Security Mutual Life Insurance Company	1	1947	703,583.36
Western and Southern Life Insurance Company	1	1946	527,171.86

Source: Robert Schultz, *Life Insurance Housing Projects* (Philadelphia: S. S. Huebner Foundation for Insurance Education, 1956), 35–36.

important driver of slum-clearance efforts in New York and other states that adopted similar legislation, including Illinois and New Jersey.[26]

By the mid-1940s, laws prohibiting investment in residential real estate by life insurance companies had been amended or repealed in all but seven states.[27] Eager to diversify investments, improve "social conditions" in cities, and showcase the industry's aptitude as a nation builder, life insurance companies dove enthusiastically into urban housing. Table 3.1, a chart developed by Robert Schultz for his 1956 study of insurance-financed housing, illustrates the profusion of such projects between 1941 and 1952. It also reveals the widespread interest in urban housing among life insurance companies of all sizes, and the massive amounts of capital insurers invested in these projects during this period. Metropolitan was one of the more prolific builders, but other large insurers, such as New York Life, New England Mutual, and Prudential, also participated extensively in this trend. By 1952, the combined housing developments built and managed by life insurance companies in the United Sates provided residences for approximately two hundred thousand people— roughly the population, at that time, of Salt Lake City, Tulsa, or Hartford. Metropolitan's Parkchester, the largest of such projects, housed a population equal to a city the size of Reno, Nevada, or Newport, Rhode Island.[28]

The industry's new role as the nation's largest landlord was celebrated early and often by insurance trade publications, architectural journals, and the mainstream press. In an approving 1949 article that chronicled the industry's investments in housing, the *Eastern Underwriter* claimed that insurance developments did much to "improve the appearance of cities" while "furnishing attractive examples of urban living," and concluded that "life insurance rental housing has always represented an improvement over the type of housing it has replaced."[29] Other trade publications stressed the developments' role in creating jobs. The *Weekly Underwriter*, for example, pointed out that construction of insurance housing offered full-time employment for thousands of servicemen returning from World War II.[30] A lengthy 1946 *Fortune* article on Metropolitan's housing developments marveled at the company's ability to build efficiently at scale while still providing "protection without regimentation," and noted that no company had "a vaster stake in public welfare and the national economy."[31] *Architectural Forum* wrote several glowing reviews of developments built by insurers, praising the industry in 1950 for its role in urban renewal projects that "bandaged" the nation's "sores."[32] Even the influential architecture critic and *New Yorker* essayist Lewis Mumford, who savaged Stuyvesant Town as a disastrous example of "prefabricated blight," found it in his heart to applaud other insurance developments, and particularly New York Life's Queens project, Fresh Meadows.[33] Mumford called that development a "a slice of the City of Tomorrow" and deemed it "skillfully put together" in 1949.[34]

Despite this praise and the visibility that massive building projects offered individual firms, the industry's move into urban housing ultimately produced mixed results. Investment returns from housing developments did not meet the expectations of most companies, and construction and management costs in many cases were higher than anticipated. The contributions these developments made toward ameliorating the nation's midcentury housing shortage also failed to attract the same degree of goodwill and public support as health, safety education, and other service programs pursued by insurers during the same era. The industry's insistence on a policy of racial segregation in its housing projects—a move considered a moral misstep by a growing number of Americans—proved crucial in this failure. The pages that follow offer examinations of midcentury life insurance housing developments built in two influential sites: New York and Chicago. In both, the industry's attempts to manage risk by privatizing both urban space and social governance collided with rapidly changing national politics surrounding race and housing.

New York: The Quest for Control and the Privatization of Public Space

PARKCHESTER

Following the amendment to New York State's insurance code in 1938, Metropolitan immediately set about planning a housing project of epic proportions. Though located only eight miles from Times Square, the 129 acres the company selected in the Bronx for the project were largely uninhabited.[35] The New York Catholic Protectory, owners of the site since 1865, had operated an orphanage and reform school on the land, and sold the property to Metropolitan for $4 million, or 71 cents per square foot.[36] From the earliest days of planning, the company sought direct control over the development, resisting interference from outside entities. Though the city was initially charged with building roads and infrastructure, for example, Metropolitan opted to take over construction in order to avoid delays—and to illustrate that privately financed housing could be built quickly and efficiently without assistance from government.[37]

This was no small task. The development that would become Parkchester was the largest housing project ever conceived in the late 1930s. Nothing like it had been attempted by either the private or public sector. The scale was massive. Upon completion, Parkchester's fifty-eight buildings, ranging from two to thirteen stories high, would offer 12,272 units and house forty-two thousand people.[38] It would contain a shopping center with more than two hundred stores and a two-thousand-seat theater; five large parking garages with a capacity of 4,500 cars; and twenty-two recreational areas containing basketball, handball, badminton, and shuffleboard courts, gyms, slides, swings, and wading areas.[39] As construction commenced, a number of commenters noted that the insurance company was in the process of building "a city within itself."[40] These claims proved true. When the development opened—on a piecemeal basis in 1940 and 1941, and in completed form in 1942—it became an almost entirely self-contained community. Though Metropolitan turned over the streets it had constructed to the city for upkeep, the company controlled nearly every other aspect of the development. Parkchester had its own police system and childcare facilities, as well as a large maintenance staff, equipped with snow-removal trucks, power lawn mowers, a machine shop, an electrical shop for repairing cars and refrigerators, and a carpentry shop for providing other repairs.[41]

Metropolitan relished the notion of self-containment as an important aspect of its control over Parkchester. When interviewed in 1946 about Parkchester and other developments built by his company, Frederick Ecker argued that isolation was necessary to insulate these projects from surrounding neighborhoods, "which may be relatively unattractive to begin with or may deteriorate."[42] Creating self-contained developments that functioned as cities-within-themselves helped Metropolitan protect its investments, but it also allowed the company manage risk by checking the influence of outsiders. Metropolitan intentionally limited access to nonresidents. The development's layout, for example, featured just two through streets and only a handful of entrances and exits. The company also chose not to include schools or churches in Parkchester's plan. As Moudry argues, this move grew out of Metropolitan's awareness that it could not control the policies or constituencies of such institutions, the presence of which may have led to a steady flow of "unregulated" persons into the development on a daily basis.[43]

The company also pursued direct control during the tenant selection process. Metropolitan's zeal in carefully screening applicants to its self-contained "model community" became legendary, a central element of what residents referred to decades later as "Parkchester lore."[44] The intensive vetting process began with an examination of applicants' financial status, including a review of their bank accounts. All Parkchester tenants were expected to have an annual income of $1,800 to $4,500 (85 percent of those selected in the first round of screenings earned over $2,000 annually—placing them solidly in the middle class).[45] Income checks were followed by a visit to the current homes of applicants by specially trained tenant selection officers. During these visits, Metropolitan representatives examined the living habits of prospective tenants and conducted interviews designed to determine both "general character" and "financial responsibility."[46] According to one tenant, these "white-gloved" officials asked "intimate and penetrating" questions: Was the applicant "neat and self-respecting?" or "careless and uncouth" and "likely to be loud and cantankerous neighbors?"[47] Once Metropolitan completed the in-home interview, the company surveyed the applicants' neighbors and acquaintances. Despite this grueling process, demand for housing in Parkchester was enormous. Roughly forty-eight thousand families applied for tenancy upon the development's initial opening in 1940.[48]

Once selected, the individuals and families that settled in Parkchester found that Metropolitan's quest for control was not limited to the application process. Leases were labyrinthine, containing regulations typical to such documents (dogs were not welcome), as well as prohibitions against leaving personal items outside apartments, hanging laundry to dry outdoors, sitting on beach chairs on lawns, allowing children to roam unsupervised, and performing "unbearable annoyance to other tenants."[49] Violation of any lease item could lead to eviction. This included infractions committed by children. A 1944 *Herald Tribune* article, for example, published the "dossier" of Robert Simmons Jr., a seven-year-old Parkchester resident whose unsupervised activities attracted the attention of the "Parkchester police"—uniformed company guards that patrolled the development's quiet streets. The young boy received numerous citations over a two-year period, amassing the following record: "November 1, 1942—Robert caught on a lawn; February 1, 1943—Robert apprehended throwing a snowball; June 24, 1943—Robert trampled shrubbery retrieving his ball; October 10, 1943—Robert picked a flower in one of the development's gardens."[50] To aid residents in keeping order, fifteen full-time employees joined the "Parkchester police" in supervising recreational areas for both children and adults. An additional eighty-five employees performed clerical duties in an on-site rental office, and four hundred others performed maintenance and oversaw the grounds.[51] As Moudry has argued, Metropolitan had a "constant and visible presence" at Parkchester and considered residents "part of the maintenance system that preserved property values."[52] Tenants may have chafed at the insurance company's efforts to govern their conduct, but controlled supervision was likely seen as a low price to pay for a clean and affordable place to live in the midst of a housing crisis. As one resident put it in 1944, "For the lower-middle-class—I guess that's our class—it's fine."[53]

Aside from a handful of good-natured exposés mocking the company's iron-fisted control of tenants, media coverage of the development during its first few years was overwhelmingly positive. In a move that no doubt pleased industry leaders eager to compete with the state, journalists regularly emphasized the fact that Parkchester had been privately financed. *American Magazine* announced in 1939, during construction, that the project was "showing Uncle Sam the way."[54] The *Christian Science Monitor* noted that the development featured "larger rooms, better landscaping, and more accommodations than any U.S. Housing Authority project," adding: "and nobody has been taxed to pay for it."[55] This last claim was not entirely true. Metropolitan's refusal to include a school in the plans for Parkchester meant that the city was forced to build one next to the property to accommodate the community's thousands of children.[56] The influx of traffic caused by Parkchester also inundated the Pelham Bay Park subway line, making it necessary to build new tracks at the taxpayers' expense.[57] These details were easily overlooked, however. Praise for the community buoyed Metropolitan's leaders, who found that their total investment of $63 million had bought the company public goodwill and a chance to expand its social governance efforts.[58] What's more, the development performed well financially during its first five years, comparing favorably with the average earnings of other industry investments.[59]

Positive press coverage of the development continued unabated well into the final decades of the twentieth century. The Pulitzer Prize–winning architectural critic Paul Goldberger, for example, called Parkchester "utopian," and a product of "developers who truly believed that better housing could create a better society" in his 1981 study of urban housing in the New York Times.[60] "The whole place stands as a crucial reminder," he glowed, "that it is possible to build housing on a mass scale and not lose touch with what we like to call the human values."[61] Goldberger, like many commenters before him, neglected to mention that the "better society" imagined by Metropolitan when it built Parkchester included racial segregation as one of its "human values." The insurance company's homogenous "utopian" community at Parkchester didn't only exclude tenants by class, selecting out low-income applicants; it also excluded tenants by race. The company's "whites only" housing policy eventually attracted criticism—at Stuyvesant Town, the company's first major slum-clearance project, and at Parkchester in 1953, when Metropolitan forcibly evicted a Black family who had sublet an apartment in the development from a friend.[62] For the first several years of Parkchester's existence, however, its significant contribution to racial segregation in American housing was largely ignored.

STUYVESANT TOWN

Urban and architectural historians have credited Parkchester's success as the reason Metropolitan dove further into the urban housing field, and also why several other large insurance companies followed the company's lead.[63] In 1943, only a year after Parkchester opened in its completed form, Metropolitan announced it would build a new project in Lower Manhattan. Unlike Parkchester, this development was planned under New York's new

Redevelopment Companies Law. In exchange for the insurance company's estimated commitment of $50 million, the city of New York agreed to use its power of eminent domain to condemn the eighteen-block site selected for the project—deemed a "blighted" slum by city authorities—and hand it over to Metropolitan for redevelopment. Advocates of urban renewal in New York, including parks commissioner Robert Moses, were confident that an agreement with Metropolitan would attract other private money to the city. To sweeten the deal, they offered the company a twenty-five-year tax abatement on the property, as permitted by the Redevelopment Companies Law. The agreement reached between Metropolitan and the city led to Stuyvesant Town, the first privately financed slum-clearance effort in New York.

Riding high on the success of Parkchester, Metropolitan's leaders anticipated a positive public response to its efforts to aid the city in creating Manhattan housing. This, to their chagrin, was not to be. From the earliest stages of planning, the development attracted controversy. The problems began with the considerable challenge of clearing the area slated for redevelopment, a process that launched in 1945. Manhattan's "Gashouse District," the site that would become Stuyvesant Town, was home to roughly 3,400 working-class families, or an estimated ten thousand people.[64] A 1945 study conducted by the Community Service Society, a local social work organization, found that nearly half of those residents had lived in the area for more than twenty years, and that many had strong ties to the area's ethnic communities and churches.[65] Although New York's elites in government and business supported the project unequivocally, housing reformers and members of the press expressed concern that the insurance development would dislocate the poor and leave them nowhere to go.[66] The projected rents for Stuyvesant Town were listed at $14 a unit—a price even the strongest backers of the project knew only 3 percent of the low-income residents of the Gashouse District could afford.[67] In a process that would be repeated in other slum-clearance projects across the country, many of the people dislocated by Stuyvesant Town were forced into nearby neighborhoods that were also considered substandard, contributing to further overcrowding and leading to calls for the clearance and redevelopment of additional regions.

Despite concerns expressed by the press, social organizations, and housing activists, Metropolitan forged ahead. By 1946, the residents of the area had been cleared, demolition in preparation for Stuyvesant Town was progressing at the rate of a million cubic feet a week, and the company was accepting applications from prospective tenants.[68] When the development was completed in 1947, it was capable of housing twenty-four thousand people in its 8,755 apartments, distributed among thirty-five buildings that stood twelve to thirteen stories high. The company also included six underground parking garages with room for 1,500 cars, plus off-street parking for an additional 400.[69] The entire cost of the project upon completion reached $90 million—significantly higher than the $50 million Metropolitan expected to invest.[70] This was just one of the many problems faced by the company at Stuyvesant. Though applications for tenancy in the development far exceeded the number of available units, criticism of the project continued to plague Metropolitan.

Just as it had at Parkchester, the insurance company managed risks to its investment by carefully screening prospective tenants and strictly regulating the behaviors and conduct of residents. Stuyvesant Town was located in an area more densely populated and more ethnically and racially diverse than Parkchester. Fearful of outside influences, Metropolitan doubled down on its commitment to self-containment as a technique of risk management in its new development. While two through streets were included in the plans for Parkchester, no outside traffic was allowed to penetrate Stuyvesant Town. The "Metropolitan Oval," a large park located at the center of Parkchester, was replicated in the new development, but it was lined with towers that blocked views to the park from the outside. The entire development, including all its pedestrian paths, were marked with signs that read "Private property," and uniformed company security guards patrolled the area.[71] Metropolitan also stepped up its efforts to govern Stuyvesant residents. The company distributed numerous pamphlets and booklets to every tenant. These texts offered useful information about amenities provided by the development, but they also encouraged residents to conduct themselves "properly" and assume "wholesome" behaviors.[72]

While Metropolitan's quest for control at Parkchester attracted only light-hearted criticism, it became the basis of sustained and scathing condemnation at Stuyvesant. Few commenters judged the insurance company's efforts to govern spatially though design more harshly than Lewis Mumford. The acclaimed writer, known for his studies of the influence of architecture on urban life, attacked Stuyvesant Town in a series of articles published in the *New Yorker* during the late 1940s. In "Prefabricated Blight," a particularly harsh 1948 takedown of the development, Mumford lambasted the fortress-like nature of Stuyvesant and compared Metropolitan's architectural vision to that of a "police state."[73] In a passage that might have easily described Parkchester, Mumford accused Metropolitan of "employing all of the vices of regimentation associated with state control at its unimaginative worst."[74] He added that the development appeared to have been created for residents "with no identity but the serial numbers of their Social Security cards."[75] This last charge—unfortunate for its conflation of public and private insurance systems—drew a direct connection between the power exercised by the state and that exercised by private industry. Though the life insurance industry had encouraged these kinds of connections for decades, it is doubtful that its leaders welcomed this particular jab.[76]

Mumford focused his critique of Stuyvesant on architecture, design, and aesthetics. Other critics found more profound reasons to loathe the development. Metropolitan's "whites only" policy of racial segregation at Stuyvesant Town, largely overlooked at Parkchester, became a lightning rod for criticism from the earliest stages of planning.[77] When the company met with the New York Citizens Housing and Planning Council to discuss the project in 1943, the group demanded to know why no schools were included in Stuyvesant's plans. Metropolitan's president, Frederick Ecker, responded that a school would draw children from outside the project, including local Black children.[78] He also noted blithely that Black tenants would not be admitted to the development, because their inclusion would "depress all the surrounding property."[79] When pressed to explain this stance in an interview with the New York Post following the meeting, Ecker defended his company's "whites only" policy, insisting, "Negroes and whites don't mix. Perhaps they will in one hundred years, but they don't now."[80]

The oft-quoted interview drew a firestorm of criticism over the next several months, especially from civil rights activists. The efforts of these activists to desegregate housing and other institutions in the United States received a powerful boost from the wartime "Double-V" campaign, which sought victory against tyranny and racism, both at home and abroad. The campaign received strong support and promotion from the Black press, which flourished during the era.[81] The New York Amsterdam News, the oldest and largest Black newspaper operating in the city, demanded a response from Metropolitan on its "Jim Crow policy." Accustomed to questions about his company's policy after months of criticism, Ecker pleaded with the paper: "The colored people should try to understand our problems. We are trustees for the funds of hundreds of thousands of people, and we can't risk their money in investments that may not prove profitable."[82] Ecker's plea did not attract sympathy from the Black press or Black New Yorkers. Civil rights activists, joined by a growing number of labor organizers, housing reformers, and liberal critics, stepped up pressure on the company to desegregate Stuyvesant Town.

In response to these efforts, the city adopted a measure in 1944 that prohibited racial discrimination in all private housing projects that received public subsidies. The law did not apply to Stuyvesant Town, however, because the project's contract had already been approved. The protests and condemnation of Metropolitan continued, but the company refused to change its policy.

The conflict finally reached the courts in 1947. A group of Black veterans, recently returned from combat in World War II, filed suit against Metropolitan after applying and being rejected for housing in Stuyvesant Town. Backed by the NAACP and the ACLU, the three veterans—Joseph Dorsey, Monroe Dowling, and Calvin Harper—based their case against Metropolitan on the claim that the company had violated the equal protection clause of the Fourteenth Amendment. Stuyvesant Town should be considered public housing, the veterans argued, because it was built on public land given to the company by the city, and because tax concessions had been granted by the state for its purchase and construction. Upholding the private ownership of the development, the New York State Court of Appeals held in favor of Metropolitan. The court majority claimed that the Redevelopment Companies Law, under which Stuyvesant was built, "deliberately and intentionally refrained from imposing restrictions upon a redevelopment company in the choice of tenants," and reiterated that the intent of the act was "to leave private enterprise free to select tenants of its own choice."[83] The majority added that access to housing accommodation in private developments "is not a civil right."[84]

Metropolitan's leaders insisted throughout the proceedings that their policy of racial segregation did not, in fact, constitute discrimination, and was instead a necessary aspect of pooling and managing risk—they were, according to the company, simply "protecting the soundness of their investment."[85] Parks commissioner Moses, a passionate backer of urban renewal, supported the insurance giant, denouncing "those who insist on making projects of this kind a battleground for the vindication of social objectives . . . and who persist in claiming that a private project is in fact a public project."[86] Others disputed this claim, including the attorney and civil rights advocate Charles Abrams, who represented Dorsey, Dowling, and Harper in their suit against Metropolitan. Furious that the case had not been decided in favor of his clients and concerned about its implications for the future, Abrams called the decision in *Dorsey v. Stuyvesant Town Corporation* "a precedent that may have the most ominous consequences for our whole American democratic pattern of government."[87]

Why did Abrams believe the ruling endangered democracy? The answer to this question can be found in the new role the insurance industry had carved out for itself as a partner to government, and the legal immunity the *Dorsey v. Stuyvesant Town* case guaranteed the company and other private investors. In his critique of the ruling, Abrams emphasized the public nature of the project, again pointing to the fact that Metropolitan had received a grant of tax exemption by the city totaling $55 million—more than three times the cost of the land. He also reminded New Yorkers that the city had condemned and turned over to the company public streets amounting to a fifth of the area occupied by the development, displacing in the process "some ten thousand low-income tenants from their homes, as well as a host of storekeepers, churches, schools—and even another publicly regulated housing project." Metropolitan closed these streets to the public following acquisition of the land and barred the construction of public playgrounds or schools inside the development, effectively privatizing what was once public space. Abrams emphasized this notion in a series of articles he wrote following the decision. "Public enterprises in private hands are now held free to segregate, discriminate, and stand above the law," he argued in *Commentary Magazine*. Worried that the decision would lead to consequences that expanded beyond the question of segregation in housing, Abrams insisted that the case "reached down to the very roots of American freedom." He concluded his article with a warning: "Private corporations may now be lawfully handed the powers and funds of government, and use them unhindered by constitutional restraint."[88]

Though Metropolitan won the case, critiques like Abrams's and the unfavorable publicity generated by the lawsuit forced Ecker and other company leaders into a corner. Unwilling to embrace racial integration but eager to appease critics, Metropolitan announced during the appeals process that a new project, designed to provide "model housing for colored folks," was in the works.[89] At the urging of Robert Moses, the company selected a twelve-acre site next to the Harlem River, between 135th and 138th Streets, for the Riverton Houses—the first private housing development in New York built specifically to house Black Americans.[90] Continued pressure to desegregate Stuyvesant finally forced the company to budge in 1950. No doubt aware of pending legislation that would force integration, Metropolitan announced in August of that year that it would officially accept Black tenants at Stuyvesant. Company representatives insisted, however, that the move was voluntary. "No change in basic policy is involved," Metropolitan told reporters. "The company has successfully established its right to select tenants of its own choice, and management will continue to exercise its best judgement."[91] Though hardly an endorsement of racial equality, the announcement appeased some of the company's critics. Actual integration, beyond token inclusion of a handful of nonwhite tenants, came slowly to Stuyvesant Town and other developments built by the company. Most remained 99 percent white well into the 1970s.

RIVERTON

While controversy swirled around Stuyvesant Town, Metropolitan set about building the development it had promised in Harlem. Though technically open to "mixed-race tenancy" (because the contract was signed following passage of the 1944 measure barring discrimination in private housing), Riverton was, from the start, a Black development. Built under the same Redevelopment Companies Law as Stuyvesant, the project involved substantial slum clearance. Metropolitan received land condemned by the city as well as the standard tax abatement on the site, described by Robert Moses as a "blighted" area and by others as "little more than a drab assortment of junk shops, coal pockets, and a few tenements."[92] Despite these descriptions, the area that would become Riverton Houses was, in fact, home to a dense population. Though details about the families and individuals who lived on the site before construction of Riverton are unavailable, the population was likely similar to that of surrounding areas, which were also cleared and redeveloped during the same period. In 1949, Moses announced his Harlem Slum Clearance Plan—an agenda made possible by Riverton—that targeted a three-block area just southwest of the insurance development for privately financed redevelopment. That plan documented 7,419 persons residing in the fifteen-acre area slated for clearance. Riverton's twelve acres, cleared and redeveloped only three years earlier, were likely home to a similar number of people.[93] Having gained experience at Stuyvesant, Metropolitan succeeded in removing these families and individuals in less than a year.[94]

Slated for an area desperate for new housing, Riverton promised to accommodate roughly 1,200 families in clean, modern accommodations. The response was immediate. Metropolitan received more than twenty thousand applications in advance of the development's launch in 1947. Like the company's other housing projects, returning veterans were given priority in the application process. Concerned that the "unique nature" of the Riverton development, as well as its location, might attract "undesirable" tenants, Metropolitan took extra care in selecting "higher bracket colored residents" during its rigorous screening process of prospective tenants.[95] Constance Wright, one of the first tenants to move in on opening day, for example, was visited by representatives of the insurance company during the months-long wait to see if she would be granted housing in Riverton. Wright recalls company agents picking through her apartment, taking notes, and looking, as she put it, to "see how you kept house."[96] Dr. Billy Taylor, another Riverton resident, recalled, "They were really screening people very closely—because they wanted a very special kind of grouping of people who had certain aspects of education, certain aspects of other things that were good for the community."[97] Though the screening process for tenancy at Riverton was rigorous, few applicants complained. Some even celebrated the company's efforts. Clifford Alexander, the first resident-manager of the development, credited the project's initial success to the intense screening of prospective tenants.[98]

After opening to much fanfare—both the mainstream and Black press covered the project's launch—Riverton quickly became a model development in Harlem. The first residents included Wallace Bertram, a World War II veteran and linotype operator for a publishing house downtown, his wife, Lula Mae, and their twelve-year-old son, Frank; the Fords—a psychiatric social worker, his wife, Dora, and their daughter, Dianne (a student at the University of Wisconsin); and Emmett O. Smith, a mail clerk for the *New Republic* (also a vet), and his wife.[99] These families moved in during the summer of 1947, right as the New York Supreme Court upheld Metropolitan's decision to bar Black tenants from Stuyvesant Town. Despite controversy surrounding the company's policy of racial segregation, many Riverton residents—like the Demas family and others who found homes in Stuyvesant, Parkchester, and insurance housing developments across the country—relished the opportunity to live in clean, modern apartments, among people of common experience, common age, common ambitions."[100] This was particularly the case for Black middle-class professionals unable to find good housing elsewhere in the city. As one Riverton resident fondly recalled, "We were truly like an oasis in central Harlem."[101]

Just as Robert Moses and other redevelopment backers hoped, Riverton set a precedent that attracted other private investors to the area. This included backers of a second private development, the high-income Lenox Terrace apartments—the product of Moses's 1949 slum-clearance plan. Lenox Terrace opened adjacent to Riverton in 1958 amid controversy over forced displacement of residents and "inadequate efforts" to assist in their relocation.[102] No doubt pleased that high-income housing had come to the area, Metropolitan still took extra steps to manage risk and protect its investment, employing a policy of class segregation at Riverton that paralleled its policy of racial segregation in other developments. The company closed the playground at Riverton to nonresidents, for example, and company guards strictly supervised the area. Metropolitan justified this move by explaining that Black children "from lesser classes" might infiltrate the space. "We had a big problem with that [policy]," one resident who grew up Riverton recalled, "because we as kids didn't feel that there was any difference between us and them—but some of the other folks made it a point that there was a difference."[103]

The compromise that led to the development of Riverton mirrored the lives of many tenants. James and Denise Foster, who moved into Riverton with their two children in 1960, offer one example. James, a margin clerk at

Bear Stearns, made the commute from Harlem's Riverton to Wall Street six days a week. A veteran of World War II, Foster hoped to use his experience on Wall Street to someday build his own investment firm. Denise Foster's two passions included shopping at Bloomingdale's and giving her children a sense of their family's history, which included a proud display of her grandmother's high school diploma in their home. Though James Foster believed in supporting "black institutions," he donned the conservative suits of Wall Street and his family shopped downtown. The Fosters subscribed to *Ebony* but also to *Good Housekeeping* and *Glamour*. Before moving to Riverton, the family lived in a low-income development near upper Park Avenue, but they were drawn to Harlem—for both the feeling of "black brotherhood" and the presence of good, middle-income housing. The Fosters didn't "participate much" in Harlem's political life. Denise Foster worked part time as a social worker in the neighborhood but avoided local politics. James Foster, for his part, was consumed by "job demands." Despite being willing, as he put it, "to express opinions about politics," he kept a low profile.[104]

Though many residents of Riverton, like the Fosters, were willing to look past the development's role in the racial and class politics of the city, outside observers were not. In "Fifth Avenue, Uptown," a 1960 essay penned for *Esquire*, James Baldwin blasted Riverton as a potent symbol of Jim Crow, an inadequate and degrading answer to criticism of the company's commitment to racial segregation. "Harlem watched Riverton go up," wrote Baldwin, "in the most violent bitterness of spirit, and hated it long before the builders arrived. They began hating it at about the time people began moving out of their condemned houses to make room for this additional proof of how thoroughly the white world despised them."[105] Baldwin emphasized the fact that Riverton and other urban renewal projects in Harlem were controlled by whites:

> Even if the administration of [Harlem's housing] projects were not so insanely humiliating (for example: one must report raises in salary to the management, which will then eat up the profit by raising one's rent; the management has the right to know who is staying in your apartment; the management can ask you to leave, at their discretion), the projects would still be hated because they are an insult to the meanest intelligence.[106]

Comparing insurance company management at Riverton to the white police who arrogantly patrolled Harlem's streets, Baldwin claimed that both represented "the force of the white world," a world intent on keeping "the black man corralled up here, in his place."[107]

Baldwin pointed out that the middle-class residents of Riverton faced the same demeaning racism as their poorer neighbors: "They get up in the morning and go downtown to meet 'the man.' They work in the white man's world all day and come home in the evening to this fetid block. They struggle to instill in their children some private sense of honor or dignity which will help the child to survive."[108] He insisted that even private developments constructed in Harlem were destined to become slums due to neglect from the outside world. Perhaps referring to a series of much-publicized crime waves that swept the development in the mid- to late 1950s, Baldwin noted that middle-income Riverton was no different from other housing projects constructed in the area.[109] In a move that would attract fierce criticism, and may have been intended as a sarcastic jab at Metropolitan's strict supervision of tenants, he wrote of the development's residents: "They had scarcely moved in, naturally, before they began smashing windows, defacing walls, urinating in the elevators, and fornicating in the playgrounds."[110] Adding fuel to the fire, Baldwin accused middle-class Riverton residents of thinking themselves better than their surroundings and reminded readers that the majority of Harlemites knew they lived there "because white people [did] not think they [were] good enough to live anywhere else."[111] He concluded his article with an indictment of efforts to attract private investors to redevelop Harlem and other Black urban communities: "Whatever money is now being earmarked to improve this, or any other ghetto, might as well be burnt. A ghetto can be improved in one way only: out of existence."[112]

By calling out Riverton specifically, Baldwin drew the ire of Metropolitan management, elite Harlemites, and the Black press, all of whom contested his demeaning description of life in Riverton. In an article critical of his *Esquire* essay, the *New Amsterdam News* came to the defense of the development, offering a list of prominent residents currently living in the community. Perhaps unaware of the fact that the writer had grown up in Harlem, the paper attacked Baldwin as a preening intellectual and "self-styled expert" on their community.[113] In response, Baldwin penned a scathing letter to the editor of the paper, accusing the residents of Riverton of "closing [their] eyes to the anguish and despair" around them.[114] Citing the Stuyvesant controversy that had forced the insurance company to build in Harlem in the first place, Baldwin reminded his critics: "Riverton was constructed in order to keep the Negroes of Harlem segregated."[115]

Critiques like Baldwin's challenged the notion that "separate but equal" Black insurance housing developments offered viable substitutes for racial integration. Few insurance investors, however, were willing to risk endorsement of integrated housing in the late 1940s and early 1950s. Other insurance companies looked on with concern as Metropolitan struggled to manage the growing chorus of criticism surrounding its race-based policies. Fearful of experiencing a publicity disaster of the sort that unfolded at Stuyvesant, for example, the John Hancock Mutual Life Insurance Company left the integration question open when planning a private housing development for Dearborn, Michigan, just outside Detroit, in 1948. The white residents of Dearborn, with the support of its segregationist mayor, Orville Hubbard, quickly organized and protested the project. Handbills that read "Keep Negroes out of Dearborn: Vote no on the John Hancock rental housing project" and "Wake up, Dearborn! Wake up! Open your eyes wide! John Hancock gives housing double talk" circulated widely.[116] Although Hancock never explicitly stated intentions to open the project to nonwhite tenants, the company's silence on the question enraged white Dearborn residents, who successfully killed the project in the early stages of planning. Other companies faced similar challenges in the years that followed as they attempted to navigate the politics of race and housing in cities beyond New York.

Chicago: "Negro Removal" and the Pursuit of Insurance Dollars

LAKE MEADOWS

As New Yorkers lined up for a chance to live in insurance housing, other cities looked on with a combination of interest and envy. The largest insurers had focused the bulk of their investment dollars on New York, but the housing shortage was a problem faced by urban centers across the country. Chicago's housing situation had turned especially bleak by the early 1940s. Construction had slowed virtually to a halt during the Great Depression, exacerbating long-standing problems related to overcrowding and overuse of the city's aging housing stock. As the historian Arnold Hirsch has illustrated, the housing shortage hit Chicago's Black residents hardest. A special 1934 census found that the average Black household in the city contained 6.8 persons, while the average white household contained 4.7.[117] Another study found that 375,000 Black residents lived in the central section of the city's South Side, an area equipped to house no more than 110,000.[118] The start of World War II and the jobs it created in defense manufacturing and other fields only made the problem worse. Hirsch reports that by 1941 the city's vacancy rate had dropped to 1.5 percent. It had plummeted even further, to 0.9 percent, by 1942.[119] Prevented from obtaining housing in the surrounding suburbs, Black Chicagoans were restricted to city's "Black Belt," a dense and rapidly expanding region with a population that was 98 percent nonwhite in 1940.[120] This expansion, feared by white city leaders and residents, was partly a product of population growth fueled by wartime migration. The process was also driven by landlords, who profited by converting standard apartments along the fringes of the Black Belt into cramped, windowless "kitchenette" units leased to Black tenants so desperate for housing that they were willing to pay exorbitant rents—up to ten times higher than those charged to whites.[121]

Anxious for a solution to the housing crisis and eager to stem expansion of Black Belt slums, state and city leaders launched a campaign in the early 1940s to attract private housing financing to Chicago. They began by creating a favorable legislative climate, passing the Illinois Neighborhood Redevelopment Corporation Act in 1941. This law, like the one passed in New York, empowered privately financed corporations to invest in urban housing. That same year, the Illinois Metropolitan Housing and Planning Council and the Chicago Housing Authority jointly crafted and published a plan, *An Opportunity for Private and Public Investment in Rebuilding Chicago*. The council designed the plan specifically to entice insurance companies to invest in the city's South Side—a long-established part of the Black Belt" deemed a "blighted" slum by the city's Planning Commission. South Side institutions, including the Illinois Institute of Technology and the Michael Reese Hospital, threw their weight behind the plan. Both institutions expressed fears that local conditions threatened their vitality and future expansion. As representatives from the Michael Reese Hospital put it, "Even a healthy island cannot exist long in a sea of blight."[122]

The city's efforts paid off. In 1945, the Equitable Life Assurance Society announced that it was considering at least one, and maybe two, $10 million housing developments for Chicago. These developments would contain two thousand to three thousand units and would rent at approximately $15 a month.[123] That same year, the New York Life Insurance Company also announced that it would consider building housing in Chicago. Leaders of the two companies met separately with Chicago's mayor, Edward Kelly, to discuss their terms. Both told Kelly that they preferred to build on land that had already been cleared, and insisted that the city take responsibility for slum clearance before any agreement could be made. Kelly and the city agreed to these terms, promising to acquire land considered "blighted" and in need of redevelopment before handing it over to the insurance investors. Despite this concession, both companies withdrew.[124] Equitable argued that while insurers did have "an obligation to provide decent housing," the company was not ready at that time to make a commitment to Chicago.[125] New York Life punted, agreeing to consider building at a later date. Frustrated, state and city leaders reached out to other insurance companies, asking their leaders directly to consider building in Chicago. Metropolitan responded that it had already invested in urban housing to an extent the company found satisfactory.

Northwestern Mutual of Milwaukee, one of the largest life insurance firms in the Midwest, also passed, adding that large developments of the sort that had been built in New York were "highly questionable investments."[126]

By 1947, the nation's Second City was feeling slighted. "New York Gets Big Housing Units; Midwest Pays," declared the *Daily Tribune*. Treating insurance premiums as though they were tax dollars, the paper complained that large, national insurance companies had ignored the city, "despite the fact that Chicago and the middle west, through their insurance payments, contributed a substantial part of the funds used to put up the imposing developments in New York."[127] The Illinois Manufacturers' Association urged a "comprehensive inquiry" on the part of state agencies to determine why insurers had snubbed Chicago. The association demanded to know why New York had "received $100 million in housing developments from insurance companies while Chicago received nothing." Noting that both land and labor were cheaper in Chicago than New York, the manufacturers blamed the city for failing to create sufficient tax concessions and inducements.[128] Other groups joined the association in criticizing the city. The Chicago Building Congress issued an appeal to municipal leaders to "sell large insurance companies on the idea of making direct investments in redevelopment projects."[129] Charles Nicol, president of the congress, suggested that "misinformation and poor civic selling" had deterred insurance companies.[130] Like the *Daily Tribune*, Nicol endorsed the notion that premium dollars should pay for more than insurance converge. "Life insurance companies take millions of dollars out of Chicago," he reasoned, "so we believe they would only be too glad to invest if a big redevelopment program were put into operation."[131] Nicol urged civic leaders to speed up condemnation proceedings and begin clearing large sites in order to bring insurance premium dollars *back* to the city.[132]

The life insurance industry often argued during this era that it functioned as a state-like entity, circulating capital in ways that served the public good. Insurance companies were not obligated to invest their dollars in particular sites or ventures, however. Contrary to the claims of Chicago leaders, insurers could put their money wherever they wanted—so long as it adhered to laws prohibiting "risky" investments and offered a solid return for policyholders. Urban developments had already proven lucrative in New York, and Illinois had passed laws allowing insurers to invest in urban housing. So why did the industry give Chicago the cold shoulder? When asked by reporters and city officials, the most common response from insurance executives was their desire to keep developments "under close surveillance."[133] Staying close to New York, where most large insurance investors were headquartered, meant an ability to "more closely watch" operations from the home office.[134] This argument, though consistent with statements from insurance leaders concerning their desire for "direct control" of investments, does not explain why New York–based companies were willing to build housing in Los Angeles and San Francisco, but not Chicago.[135] The second-most common response from insurance executives, when asked why they would not invest in Chicago housing, was "insufficient return on investment"—a vague and open-ended excuse that could easily mask concerns more political than fiscal. The housing Chicago sought was intended to stem expansion of the Black Belt, not to house the white middle-class. The city made it clear from the start that any South Side development would be a "Negro project," and ideally, an integrated one.[136] Racial politics—and a deep-seated belief that integrated housing was a risky investment—almost certainty kept insurance investors away. Some observers in the Chicago press assumed as much, speculating that the "unpleasantness" associated with racial disputes at Stuyvesant Town may have made insurance companies cautious about investing in their city.[137]

Despite these concerns, Chicago finally found a taker in the summer of 1948. Passage of the state's 1947 Blighted Areas Redevelopment Act—which allowed the city to acquire "blighted" areas, clear them, and then convey the property to private investors—convinced the New York Life Insurance Company, which had withdrawn from negotiations with the city three years earlier, to reconsider its position.[138] The company announced that it would spend roughly $20 million to build 1,400 apartments on one hundred acres of the city's South Side. Though not as prodigious a builder as Metropolitan, New York Life had already entered the housing field a couple of years earlier and was in the process of completing both the Stanworth Houses, a garden-style development designed to house faculty and graduate students at Princeton University, and the much-lauded Fresh Meadows development, another garden-style project located on a former golf course in Flushing, Queens. These developments barely qualified as urban, and neither involved massive slum clearance of the sort required in the South Side. To make room for the insurance development, more than eight hundred existing structures would need to be cleared, and roughly 3,400 families, the overwhelming majority of which were Black, would need to be relocated.[139] Concerned about the cost of such an undertaking, New York Life agreed to build only with the aid of newly designated state and municipal slum-clearance funds, totaling over $3 million, and with a promise from the city that it would acquire and clear the area before construction began. Finally, the company also negotiated the price of the land, to be sold by the city at 50 cents per square foot. In his 1956 study of insurance-financed urban housing, the finance professor Robert Shultz applauded New York Life for securing such a good deal. Adding up the projected price of acquisition, clearance, and preparation of the land for redevelopment, Shultz found that the cost to the city was "undoubtedly considerably in excess of the purchase price to the developer."[140]

Once a deal was struck, New York Life announced that construction would begin in two years. It ended up taking four, as numerous conflicts delayed the project. The insurance company and the city fought endlessly over how to zone the area and adjacent regions, how to secure construction of a nearby school (deemed necessary by New York Life to attract white tenants), and how to efficiently remove the thousands of residents already residing in the area.[141] One of the biggest conflicts arose when New York Life demanded expansion of the territory originally marked for clearance and construction, "so as to afford the development better views of the lake."[142] The company argued that lake views would allow units to be sold as "luxury apartments," and were thus necessary to ensure a solid return on the investment.[143] Even the city's staunchest proponents of redevelopment balked at the new plan, which involved demolition of "a well-kept Negro area where the bulk of property is resident owned, its taxes paid, and its maintenance above par."[144] Controversy erupted as residents of the area protested, arguing that New York Life had wrongfully ousted them from land in which they had invested "thousands of dollars in upkeep and improvements."[145] These protests—and charges from the community that the project was not slum clearance but "Negro clearance"—delayed demolition, but ultimately did not prevent it.[146] The area was cleared by 1952, and construction of Lake Meadows began.

Widely recognized as one of the most destructive redevelopment projects in the nation's history, Lake Meadows has been studied primarily as an example of the damage wrought by slum clearance and the problems associated with the private-financing model for urban renewal.[147] The project succeeded in producing housing for Black middle-class tenants in Chicago's South Side, but its apartments replaced only a small percentage of the units that were demolished, exacerbating the city's housing shortage. What's more, rentals in the new development cost 300 percent to 600 percent more than the 1940 average for the same area.[148] The residents who eventually found homes in Lake Meadows were not the same individuals and families who had been cleared from the area. In a glowing review of the development, *Architectural Forum* echoed the sentiment of many elites in Chicago and other cities around the nation, arguing that eviction of the poor was unfortunate but necessary. "This is no gentle therapy," the magazine declared. "It is drastic surgery."[149] Lacking other options, the low-income Chicagoans removed to make way for the insurance development were eventually forced into the city's public housing projects (where the population was found to be 99 percent Black in 1969).[150]

As the city scrambled to build public projects, former residents of the area moved to surrounding neighborhoods, and particularly Hyde Park and Kenwood. The flood of new residents led to calls for additional slum-clearance and renewal projects in those areas. Hyde Park's redevelopment, backed by the University of Chicago and financed in part by the federal government, displaced more than four thousand families. It was singled out by the urbanist Jane Jacobs in 1961 as a prime example of city planning gone wrong.[151]

Chicago's long process of slum clearance and redevelopment, launched by Lake Meadows, ultimately led to the dislocation of fifty thousand families (with an average of 3.3 members) and eighteen thousand individuals between 1948 and 1963.[152] Though urban renewal in the city would have certainly proceeded without the aid of insurance dollars, there can be little doubt that the demands made by New York Life to manage risk and secure their investment played a major role in shaping both Lake Meadows and the city's approach to redevelopment. Arnold Hirsch argues that in dealing with the insurance company, Chicago's leaders were searching for a "formula" that would launch a chain reaction, attracting additional private investors to the city.[153] If the plans with New York Life failed, city leaders and observers in the press feared that private capital would continue to snub the city, perhaps indefinitely. The insurance company thus held a distinct advantage in negotiations, eventually receiving from the city "everything it wanted in virtually every dispute."[154] Milton Mumford, Chicago's city housing coordinator, celebrated the 1948 deal with New York Life, for example, by declaring that other insurance companies "waiting for someone to take the lead" would almost certainly invest as well.[155] That never happened. The life insurance urban housing boom ended in the early 1950s, only a few years after it began, as insurers began moving their money to more lucrative sites in the suburbs. Lake Meadows remains the only large insurance-financed housing project in Chicago—a reminder of the destructive force of urban renewal, and a testament to the lengths city and state governments were willing to go in pursuit of insurance dollars.

Getting Out of Urban Housing

By the early 1950s, insurance companies began turning away from urban housing as an investment outlet. Bad publicity generated by protests over racial segregation policies caused the biggest headaches, but there were other problems as well. Although some companies hired outside contractors to build their developments, most opted to control entire projects from start to finish, essentially setting up "separate businesses within the insurance company," responsible for managing negotiations with municipal governments, slum clearance, planning and design, construction, and tenant relations.[156] While direct control of housing investments remained attractive to insurers, the logistics of managing rental facilities—many of which housed thousands of residents—were often overwhelming. Despite the industry's success in gaining greater influence over urban "social conditions" through investments in housing, construction of new projects slowed nearly to a halt by 1953.[157]

Many companies continued to hold on to their existing properties, however, enjoying tax abatements granted by state and city governments for decades. Their experience was soured by increasingly organized tenants, who protested racial segregation, rent hikes, evictions, and the controlling policies of their insurer landlords. When company guards seeking to evict a Black subletter arrived at the door of a Parkchester apartment in 1953, for example, they were greeted by a crowd of at least seventy residents and area activists. This "wall of determined people, arms intertwined," had been brought together by the Committee to End Discrimination in Parkchester, an organization formed by tenants and consisting of a mixed-race group of local activists described by the journalist Elihu Hicks as "Bronxites who know that democracy is meaningless unless it includes all people . . . Negro and white, Catholic and Protestant women and Jewish housewives, some with their children, some tenants in Parkchester and others from the area nearby."[158] Stuyvesant residents formed their own Committee to End Discrimination; its membership of more than 1,800 remained active well into the 1960s. Riverton's tenants, accused of lacking political mettle by James Baldwin, marched on city hall when Metropolitan proposed rent hikes at the development in 1951 and 1954.[159] They also formed a mixed-class neighborhood association with residents of a nearby public development, the Abraham Lincoln Houses, and successfully advocated for improvements to the area.[160] Companies struggled to contain tenant activism, employing red-baiting tactics and evicting residents who attempted to organize neighbors.[161] Their efforts achieved only limited success.

Outside New York, residents of housing developments also battled their insurer landlords. Metropolitan's San Francisco development, Parkmerced, housed 8,200 people and was built in two stages, just before and after World War II. The community became a hotbed of activism, with residents fighting the company from almost day one. In 1951, shortly after the development opened, women living in Parkmerced launched a protest against Metropolitan's ban on hanging laundry to dry on outdoor clotheslines. They claimed that the compulsory use of coin-operated dryers, which cost 20 cents a load, amounted to "a concealed $75,000 annual rent increase," and took their case to the city's federal rent director.[162] The women won, and the clotheslines remained. Parkmerced tenants joined the development's gardeners on the picket line in 1953, after Metropolitan terminated the groundskeepers' contract and replaced them with company employees.[163] They also formed the Committee of Parkmerced Residents, which resisted Metropolitan's attempts to keep the development self-contained by forming ties with nearby institutions. This included the newly opened San Francisco State University campus, located directly to the north of Parkmerced.

Resident ties to the campus and their participation in local and national politics proved fateful to the development and the insurance company. In 1968, committee members organized a "student strike support group" to aid students and faculty at the university during their historic five-month strike against the war in Vietnam and racial discrimination at home.[164] Metropolitan responded by swiftly issuing an eviction notice to Committee of Parkmerced Residents chairman Paul Trafficante and his family. Trafficante, a son of Sicilian immigrants who grew up in New York, had lived in the community since 1954. Claiming that the eviction was "punishment for political activity" and that it violated his right to free speech, the forty-eight-year-old carpet salesman gathered support from other Parkmerced residents and area human rights and tenant advocacy groups.[165] After the case received coverage in local news outlets, Metropolitan changed course and reversed the eviction.[166] Triumphant, Trafficante declared, "It reaffirms my belief that the right of dissent will be supported at the grassroots level."[167] This would not be his only fight against the insurance giant.

Less than a year after winning his eviction battle, Trafficante and other members of the Committee of Parkmerced Residents sued Metropolitan under Title VIII of the new 1968 Civil Rights Act, also known as the Fair Housing Act. The tenants, two Black and four white, alleged that the insurance company's discriminatory rental policies at Parkmerced were responsible for the fact that the development's population was 99 percent white. They argued that by refusing to grant tenancy to nonwhite applicants, the company had denied them "the benefits of living in an integrated community."[168] They also claimed that the company's policy had denied them opportunities in business and professional contexts because they had been stigmatized as residents of a "white ghetto."[169] The case, *Trafficante v. Metropolitan Life Insurance Company*, reached the United States Supreme Court in 1972. In a landmark decision, the court ruled against Metropolitan, setting a new precedent that significantly broadened the class of petitioners permitted to stand and challenge discrimination in housing and other aspects of American life.[170] Changing political sentiment—and the fact that over half of the plaintiffs in the case were white—no doubt helped secure this important victory in the fight against racial segregation in the United States. The refusal of tenants to be cowed by their insurance landlords, however, launched the process. Insurance companies' efforts to govern—even those enacted with the dedication and fervor of a company like Metropolitan—were not always successful.

Metropolitan responded to the suit by selling Parkmerced during the appeals process, a step it had already taken at Parkchester in 1968, after public pressure forced the company to integrate the community. The notorious real estate tycoons Harry and Leona Helmsley purchased both developments, along with others built by New York Life and New England Mutual. Known for their penchant for "flipping" properties (and evading taxes), the Helmsleys ceased maintaining the developments and converted several to condos, completing the process of privatization launched decades earlier by insurance investors. New York Life sold Lake Meadows to a private real estate firm in 1969; its parks were leveled and replaced by condos in the 1990s.[171] Metropolitan sold Riverton in 1973, just as the tax abatement on the development was set to expire. Without the concession, the company would have paid $575,000 in taxes on the property that year—a significant increase from the $77,000 it owed while the deal with the city was still in place.[172] Metropolitan insisted that the move had nothing to do with money. In an abrupt departure from the company's position three decades earlier, Sheila Klein Millen, a spokesperson for Metropolitan, explained the decision. "We're in the insurance business," she declared, "not the housing business."[173]

High management costs, conflicts with tenants, and the expiration of tax abatements led most other life insurers to sell their urban housing properties during the same period, closing a unique chapter in the history of both the insurance industry and America's cities. How should we understand this chapter? First, management practices adopted by insurance companies in their housing developments reveal the extent to which the industry engaged in a program of social governance beyond the provision of insurance. These practices can help us understand how companies like Metropolitan exported risk-based techniques and logics, developed for insurance, to other spheres of American life during the postwar period. Second, insurance urban housing projects privatized public space. Developments like Stuyvesant Town transferred public goods to private hands, setting and cementing a trend that would continue throughout the twentieth century. Finally, the life insurance industry's investments in urban housing increased racial inequalities in American housing. Segregation policies of the sort employed by insurance companies in midcentury urban housing developments reflected the rampant racism of the period—the social belief, based in subjective prejudice, that people of different races should live in separate spaces. But subjective prejudice alone cannot explain the systemic quality of racial segregation in postwar America. Insurance companies, as private investors, helped perpetuate patterns of racial discrimination in housing, but they also helped amplify and extend those patterns by infusing debates over segregation with the seemingly objective language of risk. Drawing on the power accorded to them as holders of capital in short supply, insurers successfully, for a time, evaded public pressure and diminished the ability of democratic institutions to effectively challenge racial segregation and discrimination.

The partnerships insurance companies developed with state and city governments, designed to alleviate the midcentury housing crisis, effectively dissolved legal restrictions on insurance investments in real estate that had existed for half a century. This change in regulation opened the door for insurance companies hoping to invest in commercial and not just residential venues. In a 1956 study on insurance investment strategies, the business administration professor Harold Snider suggested that the industry had *strategically* pressed for housing legislation as a way of gaining legal access to more lucrative commercial properties. "Insurance companies were always primarily interested in investing in commercial real estate," Snider argued, "even though the legislation was enacted primarily to permit construction of housing projects."[174] Still eager for new investment outlets but weary of bad publicity, conflicts with tenants, and management costs associated with urban housing, insurers set their sights on commercial properties in the rapidly expanding suburbs.

4

"A Mighty Pump": Financing Suburbanization

In 1964, *Fortune* magazine published a feature story about the postwar investment activities of the Prudential Life Insurance Company. Prudential, the article declared, was a "mighty pump":

> a kind of universal power plant, vast of maw and spout, breathing in and breathing out. Its function is the collection and redistribution of people's savings. As the giant mechanism pumps away, there are few U.S. businesses—or few U.S. citizens, in fact—that escape the effect of either its updraft or its downdraft.[1]

This description of the insurance company as a "pump" was apt, as was the suggestion that few Americans could escape the impacts of decisions made by its investment staff. By 1964 Prudential had become the third-largest private company in the world, and was pumping $2.4 billion into the nation's economy every year.[2] Though *Fortune* focused on Prudential, the press regularly described the entire life insurance industry in a similar fashion during the postwar years. In 1957, *Time* reported almost as breathlessly as *Fortune* on the industry's ability to spread its vast wealth. "With nearly $100 billion in assets," the magazine marveled, "U.S. insurance companies are the nation's greatest reservoir of private capital, the dispensers of investments that have an incalculable impact on the U.S. economy."[3] Business analysts joined the chorus. The economist James Walter singled out the insurance industry as one of the most important economic actors in the United States. "By virtue of the size of aggregate fund flows available for investment," he argued in 1962, "life companies exert a significant impact upon the economy."[4] These commenters were very much aware of a fact that many Americans have long forgotten: the insurance industry was a major player in the postwar economy, and the decisions it made helped shape the nation's economic, social, and spatial development.

This chapter examines those decisions and their impacts on postwar suburbanization in the United States. Chapter 3 traced the role insurance companies played in tearing down and rebuilding American cities during the 1940s, arguing that insurers deepened racial and class-based inequalities as they privatized urban space. By the 1950s, the industry's capacity to transform the built environment had expanded far beyond the enclosed walls of housing developments like Stuyvesant Town. As insurers moved away from troublesome investments in urban housing, they turned their attention to the suburbs, fueling growth of the periphery through massive investments in housing tracts, home loans, shopping centers, and office spaces. This move had deep consequences for the national process of suburbanization, and for the industry itself. Insurance leaders embraced their new role as promoters of national economic growth and development, boldly declaring, "Private enterprise can do the job!"[5] The billions that insurance companies pumped into suburban ventures helped increase their revenue, build their workforce, and expand their social and political power. Those billions also made the industry a key participant in transforming the living arrangements, consumption patterns, and workspaces of millions of Americans.

The insurance industry's role in financing suburbanization has been largely overlooked in historical scholarship.[6] Historians have paid far more attention to the federal government as the primary driver of suburban development. Scholars have illustrated, for example, how government-backed VA and FHA home loans, combined with the federally financed national highway system, set the stage for suburban growth.[7] They have also revealed the extent to which civil defense planners during the Cold War shaped federal policies to privilege "dispersal" of the nation's industrial production and human population.[8] Finally, historians have documented and analyzed the ideological commitment, universally embraced and endorsed by leaders of government, to the privately housed nuclear family as the ideal organizational unit of American society.[9]

The government, however, did not act alone in promoting suburbanization. Private capital, and especially insurance capital, supplied the funds for millions of government-backed VA and FHA mortgages. Companies like Prudential financed the developers who built Levittowns and hundreds of suburban tracts like them across the country. They also financed nearly every suburban shopping center built in the United States during the 1950s and 1960s. Insurance was the first industry to leave the cities and set up shop in the suburbs, launching a trend in the late 1940s and leading an exodus as an innovator of suburban workplace construction, design, and management in the 1950s and 1960s. Private insurers financed turnpikes, bridges, factories, and pipelines—all of which fueled suburban growth. They performed these feats in partnership with government, all the while nurturing a deep and enduring commitment to compete with the state and restrict its expansion. Insurers pursued goals that were not the same as those of government, and they used their power as financial intermediaries and direct investors in the suburbs to achieve them. Government may have set the terms of postwar suburbanization in the United States, but the process was carried out and shaped by powerful corporate actors who sought control over their investments in countless ways.

Becoming a Pump: Structural Change and Suburban Mortgage Lending

In 1952, the legal scholars Haughton Bell and Harold Fraine launched a study of the insurance industry investment climate. Noting that life insurance policyholders made up approximately 55 percent of the United States population, Bell and Fraine sought to analyze the impacts of the industry's investments on policyholders, whose money was being spent, and on the general public, who would inevitably feel the effects of the industry's investment decisions.[10] "Changes have taken place," they reported, "and are still taking place, both in the laws governing the investment of life insurance funds, and in the practices of the companies in making such investments."[11] The changes Bell and Fraine referred to would transform the insurance industry, and American cities and suburbs, in the 1950s and 1960s.

As discussed in chapter 3, New York amended its insurance codes in the 1940s, a decision made by regulators eager to solve the state's housing crisis with private capital. Other states quickly replicated New York's laws—a process that became standard practice over the course of the twentieth century. Though originally intended to spur investment in urban housing, amendments to state insurance codes gradually opened up a wide variety of other venues to insurance dollars. For example, by 1947 numerous states had passed laws permitting companies to acquire income-producing real estate, and by 1952 such laws had become universal.[12] Over the course of the early 1950s, state regulators gradually raised the percentage of total assets insurance companies were allowed to invest in real estate, eventually settling on 5–6 percent. By the mid-1950s, many states had also removed prohibitions on insurance investments in oil and gas production and common stocks—investment that had long been considered "too risky" for an industry entrusted with the savings of millions of policyholders.[13] Bell and Fraine identified the insurance industry as the causal force behind this unprecedented and accelerated legal change, noting that insurance leaders and their professional organizations had been actively lobbying state legislators to alter laws since the mid-1940s.[14] "The efforts by the life insurance companies to liberalize their investment statutes," the legal scholars concluded, "have been responsible for numerous amendments chipping away at statutory restrictions on corporate obligations."[15]

Why were insurers so eager to change the laws that protected their policyholders and had successfully shielded the industry from financial disaster only decades earlier during the Great Depression? The answer is fear. Though sales rose steadily in the late 1940s and early 1950s, industry analysts charged with facing the future's risks had identified a series of problems that posed potentially disastrous threats to the industry. To begin, the cost of doing business was rising. Despite the ILI's dedicated efforts, inflation continued to cause problems for long-term investors like insurance companies. To make matters worse, wildly fluctuating inflation rates in the 1940s made future costs unpredictable. Industry analysts worried, too, about what they called "social change." The movement of large numbers of married women and mothers into the paid workforce (a development that organizations like the ILI studied carefully) threatened to chip away at the primary social impetus for life insurance purchases: financial protection for widows and orphans. Competition from mutual funds and savings and loan associations also vexed insurers, and competition from government terrified them. In a 1957 interview with Prudential president Carrol Shanks, for example, *Time* magazine reported that "growing public desire for more security threatens his company with a new competitor far stronger than any within the industry: the U.S. Government itself, which is steadily expanding Social Security and other federal welfare programs."[16]

In response to this threat—a central concern for the industry since the mid-1930s—Prudential's president laid out a plan. "Insurance men must change their thinking," Shanks argued, and called on his colleagues in the business to seek out "new and exciting approaches" to investment and selling.[17] "We must give complete coverage," he asserted, "such complete coverage that there is no legitimate demand from the public for Government intervention."[18] To boost sales, however, the price of insurance would need to come down. "Companies have not been able to give policyholders the cheaper insurance everyone wants and expects," Shanks explained. "The only immediate solution to the problem is for the industry to increase the return it gets on its investments."[19] To do so would mean using "all the tricks in the financial bag," including the pursuit of investment outlets that had long been prohibited.[20] Laws would have to be changed, along with the conservative mentalities of most insurance investors, who favored government bonds and other safe but low-yield outlets.[21] Shanks promised other leaders of the industry that a new approach to investing would work as a hedge against "government encroachment," and warned that the price of failure would be devastating. "The stakes are high," he declared solemnly, "and the greatest stake of all is the preservation of our free capitalistic system."[22]

A vocal critic of both government and attempts to regulate his business, Shanks led by example, transforming his company into a pump over the course of the 1950s. He began by moving Prudential's investment dollars out of bonds and into high-yield residential and commercial mortgages. By 1956, Prudential had put 43 percent of its assets into mortgages that paid interest rates of over 5 percent. That was roughly 20 percent more than other major insurers like Metropolitan, Hancock, and Equitable, who continued to focus on bonds.[23] These companies followed Prudential's lead, slowly but surely, and by the end of the decade, life insurers had become the largest institutional holders of mortgage debts in the nation.[24] The majority of these loans went to new homeowners in the rapidly expanding suburbs. By 1966, life insurance company holdings of single-family home mortgages totaled $12 billion.[25] Prudential led the industry here as well, jumping early into risk-free, government-backed VA and FHA mortgages. As early as 1945, the company had already poured $178 million into FHA loans.[26]

To complement this mortgage-lending activity, Prudential took advantage of new laws that allowed insurance companies to build and finance housing. The company constructed several suburban apartment complexes and single-family housing developments. It also channeled millions of dollars to developers of suburban housing tracts in states across the country. Prudential financed some of the largest and most iconic of these projects, including the 17,500-house Lakewood development, outside Los Angeles, and the 16,000-house Levittown development, outside Philadelphia. As the historian Thomas Hanchett has argued, Prudential actively courted and pursued relationships with prolific suburban homebuilders like the Levitts. This allowed the company to "supply mortgages to buyers in an entire subdivision" while streamlining appraisals and reducing paperwork.[27]

Under Shanks's leadership, Prudential also inaugurated an industry-wide process of decentralization, setting up regional home offices and branch locations at sites across the nation during the late 1940s and early 1950s. Decentralization offered numerous advantages. First, it eased pressure on the labor market in Newark, the company's headquarters, where executives had been complaining for years that clerical workers were in short supply.[28] It also helped boost sales and, as *Fortune* reported, "quickened service, built local prestige, and expedited the development of executive personnel."[29] More than anything, decentralization helped the company expand its massive investment efforts. Prudential's Commercial and Industrial Loan Department, launched in 1956, placed representatives in each of the company's regional home offices, where they coordinated investment strategy with executives at the Newark headquarters.[30] The economist James Walter praised Prudential's move, claiming it offered "the most comprehensive organizational response to the question of investment of assets."[31] Other companies followed along the decentralization path, including Metropolitan. Distracted by its large investments in urban housing, the company was slow to move to government-backed VA and FHA home loans.[32] It also lacked the suburban strategy of the aggressive Shanks, which involved commercial as well as residential building and lending. Though Metropolitan swiftly decentralized to compete, it lost the mantle of industry leader. That mantle passed to Prudential, the "mighty pump," in the 1950s.

Structural changes to insurance law and industry organization had important impacts on the process of postwar suburbanization, and especially mortgage financing for single-family homes. Decentralization allowed insurers to become national lenders, setting them apart from other financial intermediaries. By 1961, a whopping 96 percent of the loans held by life insurance companies were made by firms that were national lenders; this compares to 11 percent of dedicated mortgage companies, 9 percent of commercial banks, and 7 percent of mutual savings banks.[33] Lending nationally allowed insurance companies to serve wide areas and follow new housing construction. It also enabled companies like Prudential to buy mortgages in any part of the country, easily shifting funds from regions that were growing slowly to ones that were growing quickly. The result was an acceleration of suburbanization, as well as the production of a national lending climate that was far more stable and uniform than it would have been if the industry hadn't followed Prudential and jumped full steam into the mortgage market. As one financial analyst put it in 1976, insurance lending on a national scale "rapidly served to narrow regional differences in mortgage interest rates."[34]

Of course, the national character of suburbanization also grew out of the federal government's historic decision to subsidize home loans. Programs like the FHA made new housing in the suburbs affordable for millions of white, middle-class Americans. These programs also helped keep suburban home-ownership out of reach for millions of others.[35] Well-documented discriminatory language, embedded in FHA underwriting manuals, excluded nonwhite neighborhoods and would-be homeowners from the program. This language also promoted racial segregation in housing by insisting on "compatibility among neighborhood occupants" as a prerequisite for government subsidy.[36] Federal policy encouraged white homeownership while barring racial minorities from suburban communities.

Life insurers, as the largest institutional holders of FHA mortgage loans, became important participants in this exclusionary process. The government received no complaints from insurance lenders when it made new suburban home loans for white Americans risk-free investments. It should come as no surprise that the same industry that vigorously resisted attempts to integrate urban housing, and whose leadership proclaimed "Negroes and whites don't mix," supported discriminatory federal policies.[37] This support was not coerced, nor did federal policies give birth to the insurance industry's long-held belief that nonwhite policyholders, borrowers, neighborhoods, and enterprises were "bad risks."[38] The FHA was a voluntary program, and postwar insurance companies could have easily invested their dollars in nonsuburban, nonwhite housing and neighborhoods. They chose not to. A detailed 1974 study of postwar mortgage lending in Chicago, produced by the political scientist Karen Orren, illustrates this point. After analyzing decades of data on lending in Chicago, Orren found that Black sections of the city were "virtually cut off from life insurance mortgage funds" in the 1950s.[39] Other American cities received similar treatment from the nation's largest source of private capital. This destructive pattern of urban disinvestment was not the product of government policy alone.

"Fifth Avenue Moved to Millburn": Investing in Suburban Shopping Centers

The changes to law and corporate structure that helped transform the insurance industry into a pump in the 1950s made mortgage lending for single-family homes more uniform, accelerated the pace of residential suburbanization as a national process, and deepened the discriminatory impacts of federal housing programs on suburbs and cities alike. Though much of the industry's suburban investment activity focused on residential mortgages, insurance companies also invested heavily in commercial real estate during the postwar years. Large firms poured millions into commercial and retail ventures, helping the insurance industry become the largest financier of shopping centers in the United States during the boom years of the 1950s and 1960s. Though most companies focused on supplying mortgage funds to shopping mall developers, some opted to build and manage their own commercial properties in the expanding suburbs. As both builders and financiers, insurance companies exercised significant control over their investments, playing an active role in determining the design, location, and tenant mix of new shopping emporiums. This control—and the strict guidelines insurance lenders set for developers—helped standardize the American retail landscape during the postwar years, with disastrous consequences for independent and local businesses as well as downtown shopping districts.

As soon as laws allowed them to do so, insurance companies began moving their investment dollars into income-producing real estate. The rise of commercial investment by the industry in the early 1950s was swift and it was steep. In 1947, when many states began relaxing regulations, insurance investment in commercial real estate amounted to only $219 million. By 1954, it had increased to over $1 billion.[40] Between 1950 and 1975, life insurance companies held over 30 percent of the total mortgage debt on all income-producing commercial properties in the United States. This made the industry the largest holder of such mortgages in the nation.[41] The new commercial commitments of insurance companies included large manufacturing plants, distribution warehouses, office buildings, and retail facilities. Combined with the industry's substantial investments in infrastructure—insurers had financed 70 percent of the nation's natural gas pipelines by 1958, and contributed millions to turnpikes, bridges, and dams—these commercial ventures gave substance to the claims made by insurance leaders that their industry was a vital economic pump responsible for providing "the basic enterprises essential to man."[42]

Of the industry's many commercial commitments, shopping centers stand out for their popularity among insurance investors—retail facilities made up more than half the industry's commercial investments during the 1950s and 1960s—and for their impact on postwar suburban development.[43] The suburban housing boom that the industry helped fund created demand for easy access to consumer goods in the expanding periphery. Insurers eagerly stepped in to feed this demand with investment dollars, shifting capital from housing to commercial properties early on in the suburbanization process. By 1951, retail stores and shopping centers constituted the largest category of life insurance commercial mortgage commitments.[44] Massachusetts Mutual and Connecticut General led the industry in this move to retail financing. The two firms chose to forgo the bonanza on residential lending and instead focused their energies on shopping centers, aggressively seeking out new retail investment opportunities at the periphery during the early years of the 1950s. Together, Massachusetts Mutual and Connecticut General held $525 million in mortgage loans on more than 225 shopping centers by the end of the decade.[45] The three largest life insurers—Metropolitan, Prudential, and Equitable—had joined the rush by the early 1960s, collectively investing more

than $500 million in shopping malls in 1962 alone. The industry's interest
in consumer retail properties increased steadily over the next half decade.
In just two years, between 1960 and 1962, insurers increased their investments in shopping centers by $900 million, with their stake in these ventures
reaching over $2 billion by 1963.[46] This wave of insurance industry invest-
ment increased the pace of what many commenters have called "the malling
of America."[47] Insurance financing, which occurred on a national level, also
helped stabilize and standardize that process.

The industry's decision to invest in shopping centers in the 1950s and
1960s grew out of number of factors. Past experience with retail, though limited, served as one early impetus. Several of the urban housing developments
built by insurance companies in the 1940s included commercial properties
that performed extremely well. Metropolitan, for example, leased out space in
its Bronx Parkchester development to roughly two hundred commercial tenants, each of which paid the company a percentage of gross earnings. Those
earnings were significant. Parkchester's movie theater netted $75,000 per year
in the late 1940s, and the development's Macy's department store did more
business per square foot than the flagship Macy's in downtown Manhattan.[48]
The success of these early experiments no doubt contributed to the industry's
belief that commercial real estate was a good investment. Mortgages on large
shopping centers, which took time to build and develop, also appealed to an
industry that specialized in long-term lending. More than anything, though,
insurers turned to shopping centers because they offered high returns. The
interest rates on shopping center loans rose steadily over the course of the
postwar era, reaching roughly 5.5 percent in 1955 and hitting rates as high as
6.5 percent in the early 1960s. This made them some of the best-performing
investments in the portfolios of insurance companies—far better than bonds,
or even residential mortgages.[49]

DEVELOPING EXPERTISE THROUGH DIRECT OWNERSHIP

Shopping center investments were still new in the early 1950s, however, and
insurers moved cautiously into the field. Direct ownership of retail properties
offered one approach to managing the risk of new and unfamiliar commercial investments. Several insurance companies built their own shopping centers in the early to mid-1950s—a move that allowed them to closely monitor
and control their investments while also gaining experience in the development, management, and promotion of retail space. Pacific Mutual, a large
Los Angeles–based life company, became one of the first insurance firms
to take this route. The company spent roughly $4 million on the ten-acre

Norwalk Square shopping center, billed as "the most complete metropolitan-style shopping center in the country" when the project was announced in 1950.[50] Norwalk, just southeast of Los Angeles, was one of the fastest-growing residential regions in the nation. Between 1949 and 1950 alone, more than ten thousand new homes were built in the area, making Norwalk a particularly attractive location for a new shopping center.[51] In planning the facility, Pacific Mutual considered population growth in the region as well as other factors, including "character of location, operation costs, lease arrangements, types of tenant, and future development opportunities."[52] The company also depended on the willingness of local government to support the project. This support allowed Pacific Mutual to arrange for the two highways leading up to the new center to be widened, which accommodated increased traffic into and out of the facility.[53]

Almost as soon as Norwalk Square opened, Pacific Mutual made plans to expand it. The same year the facility opened, in 1952, the insurance company acquired five acres of land adjoining the site and began making additions. Completed in 1957, these included several new stores, a post office, and 270 parking spaces to add to the existing 1,075 spaces at the original site.[54] This pattern of continual growth became a common feature of shopping centers in the 1950s. Like Pacific Mutual, other insurers also insisted on facilities that were built for expansion. This insistence was based on the theory that new shopping centers did more than simply follow suburban housing development—they also propelled future growth. This "catalyst theory" proved accurate in the case of Norwalk Square. The population of the region tripled after the new shopping center opened, leading one analyst to claim that the area "developed around the center planned, built, and operated by Pacific Mutual."[55] The insurance company took pride in its role as community builder. At the opening ceremonies for the new shopping mecca, Pacific Mutual unveiled a plaque, installed at the center of the facility, to mark the occasion. It read: "Undertaken in behalf of the company's half-million policy-holders as an investment in American enterprise to serve the people of Norwalk and southeastern Los Angeles County."[56] Pacific Mutual pursued similar themes in its advertising, claiming that construction of the modern shopping center represented the company's commitment to "a tradition of enterprise" and typified its "vigorous role in the continuing development of the West."[57] The Norwalk Square shopping center thus became a useful advertisement for the company, and for "free enterprise," as well as a lucrative new source of income.

Like Pacific Mutual, Prudential built its own mall in the 1950s in hopes of exercising direct control over its investment and gaining experience in commercial property development and management. For the location of its first foray into shopping center investment, Prudential chose Millburn, New Jersey, fifteen miles east of Newark. The company had purchased 135 acres in Millburn in 1949 during a heated legal battle with the city of Newark over taxation of its business. The insurance giant claimed that the city's taxes were "excessive" and threatened to leave Newark and develop the Millburn site into a new suburban headquarters. This threat—which would have led to the loss of crucial revenue and thousands of jobs—intimidated the city into cutting the company's tax burden nearly in half.[58] Satisfied, Prudential kept its head-quarters in Newark and converted a large portion of the Millburn property into an upscale residential community, described by the *New York Times* as "an unusual colony" of luxury homes.[59] The company announced a year later that it would develop the remaining fifty-two acres of the Millburn property into a shopping center, and set to work planning what would become Short Hills Mall.

Unlike Pacific Mutual, Prudential struggled to gain the support of local government as it planned its new retail facility. The new upscale housing built by the insurance company in the early 1950s only increased the prestige of the swank residential region, memorialized in Philip Roth's 1959 novella, *Goodbye, Columbus*, as the epitome of suburban class and upward mobility.[60] Concerned that a shopping center would alter the "character" of their quiet, elegant community, leaders of Millburn Township refused to rezone the land, already owned by Prudential, for commercial use. No stranger to legal battles, Prudential responded by suing the township. After enduring two years of threats and negotiation, Millburn finally caved. The township agreed to rezone the area if Prudential dropped the lawsuit and promised to include only "high types" of consumer outlets in the new center. The insurance company was more than happy to comply with this request, having already planned an "upscale" facility, and immediately began construction of the new shopping center, billed by Prudential as "Fifth Avenue moved to Millburn."[61]

Prudential took special care in selecting tenants for its new shopping center, rejecting "cheap variety stores" in favor of "the highest possible grade tenants" with proven track records in thriving downtown districts.[62] In materials advertising space at the facility, the company eagerly shared the results of detailed research it had conducted on the region, noting that "the more than 750,000 residents of the area have an estimated after-tax income of more than $2.5 billion, with retail spending estimated at $1.5 billion."[63] These materials described the mall as "strategically located for easy accessibility" and promised that the "suburban Fifth Avenue" atmosphere would attract consumers from Manhattan and all over the state.[64] Prudential eventually decided on

Bonwit Teller and B. Altman Company—luxury department stores associated with the opulence of downtown—to anchor the facility. Prudential granted both stores three-story structures, situated so they would be visible to passing traffic on nearby highways. The company added other high-end shops to the shaded, campus-like mall. Set on two levels, it included four air-conditioned buildings connected by sidewalks, stairways, and escalators.[65]

Though legal battles delayed construction of the mall, when it finally opened in 1961, Short Hills was celebrated as "one of the finest centers in the nation."[66] *Architectural Record* gave the facility a positive review, applauding the "unique character" of the mall and Prudential's commitment to quality: "quality of design and construction; quality of stores and shops—the list of tenants reads like a miniature Fifth Avenue Association; and quality of customers from the prosperous suburban countryside nearby."[67] Prudential expanded Short Hills several times over the next decade. Millburn Township continued to resist the insurance company, fighting Prudential over every expansion to the facility.[68] By the end of the 1960s, however, the shopping center had become the economic center of the area. When Prudential requested a massive expansion to enclose the mall in the mid-1970s—a step deemed necessary to compete with downtown and other centers that had opened in the region—local residents had little choice but to accept. "Can the taxpayers of Millburn Township afford to see the Mall at Short Hills fail?" asked one local journalist.[69] Though not all municipalities developed oppositional relationships with the shopping centers located within their borders, most eventually became dependent on them, as Millburn did, for jobs, tax revenue, and communal space.[70]

SHOPPING CENTER FINANCING AND THE STANDARDIZATION OF THE CONSUMER LANDSCAPE

Both Pacific Mutual and Prudential emphasized the "metropolitan" or "downtown" qualities of their suburban shopping centers. Both protected their investments by carefully selecting tenants. Both companies also went on to finance other centers, drawing on the experience they gained from designing and developing their own facilities.[71] Though Norwalk Square, Short Hills Mall, and other shopping centers directly owned by insurance companies succeeded, most insurers opted to conserve resources and manpower by financing, rather than owning and operating, commercial spaces. This did not mean, however, that insurers played a less active role in managing and protecting their investments. The architect Victor Gruen, hailed as the "father of the mall" for his influential work in building some of the most iconic American shopping centers, claimed that insurance companies, as "the primary source of financing for most shopping center developments," were "deeply involved in their construction and planning."[72] Indeed, as financiers, insurance companies exercised significant control over design and development of their shopping center investments. One of the primary ways companies did so was by setting strict guidelines for developers who hoped to receive their backing.

Insurance dollars may have been plentiful, but companies did not make them easy to come by. Before developers could receive financing from an insurance company, insurers required them to enlist the services of independent research organizations, tasked with determining the number and growth of households in a proposed shopping center location, the distribution of income among those households, the rate and direction of population growth in the area, and the population density within driving range of any proposed site.[73] Insurance companies financed only highly accessible centers with access to highways and feeder streets. Before funding a project, companies required evidence that developers had considered traffic flow, and insisted that centers feature both frontage and visual exposure on main approach routes. Many insurance lenders also demanded information from developers about topography and soil composition, quality of water and sewage systems, availability of land to allow for expansion, and availability of alternative sites nearby that might serve as future locations for competitor facilities.[74] Insurance companies generally financed only those projects located far enough away from downtown shopping districts or other retail centers to draw a significant population without competition. As one investment analyst put it, "If the area is already overstored, then the insurance company will be likely to reject the loan regardless of who the tenants are."[75] This demand pushed malls, and the growth that accompanied them, farther and farther away from cities.

Insurance lenders insisted that suburban centers should compete with, not complement, downtown business districts. For this reason, they required developers seeking financing to include as many "proven" downtown retailers with "established market acceptance" as possible. Insurers demanded that regional or national chains with "triple-A" credit standings occupy, at minimum, 70 percent of a shopping facility's space, and make up no less than 60 percent of its tenants.[76] Insurance financiers also exercised control over design and construction, creating strict guidelines concerning lighting, layout, pedestrian circulation, and parking. Insurance lenders required developers to ensure that service and delivery traffic was separated from consumer traffic. Most insurers also assisted developers in selecting architects and contractors, and nearly all of them had the final say concerning the timing and pace of the construction process, including whether or not it took place in phases.[77] Risk-averse insurance lenders insisted on architects, contractors, design lay-outs, and retailers that had proven successful, either downtown or in already existing shopping centers. What worked at one site was presumed to work at the next, and developers that failed to follow the strict rules set by insurance companies did not gain access to insurance investment dollars.

By the mid-1950s, insurer control over shopping center financing had largely standardized the field, cementing patterns in design, construction, and tenant mix in centers across the nation. Some commenters saw the ac-tive role played by insurance investors in mall development as positive and useful. The business analyst Harold Snider argued in 1956, for example, that life insurers, because of their long-term interest in commercial properties, did more to maintain and protect their investments than other financiers.[78] Snider also claimed that the insurance industry's central role in shopping center financing helped stabilize the real estate market because insurers were less likely than other kinds of investors to be affected by "market fluctua-tions."[79] Not everyone agreed that the industry's new influence over commer-cial space was beneficial, however. Independent and local retailers, unable to achieve the national credit rankings demanded by insurance investors, com-plained that the industry's strict financing guidelines prevented them from competing in the new suburban consumer economy. Denied access to space in the suburban shopping emporiums that were rapidly displacing downtown districts, and fearful for their survival, the nation's small retailers turned to the government for help.

In response to growing pressure from independent retailers and their ad-vocates, the United States Senate Subcommittee on Retailing, Distribution, and Fair Trade Practices, part of the Select Committee on Small Business, agreed to hold a series of hearings in 1959 on "alleged discriminatory treat-ment of small businesses" in shopping centers. William Sabbag, one of several business owners invited to testify at the hearings, captured the plight of small, local, and independent retailers. Sabbag had served as president of Economy 5 and 10 Stores, a locally owned chain of six variety stores that had operated in Jacksonville, Florida, for more than twenty-five years. "It is our firm belief that properly developed shopping centers are the answer to a public demand that shopping be made convenient," Sabbag testified, "but we are further con-vinced that local merchants must operate in the centers if [those merchants] are to survive." Noting that his company had been rejected by six suburban shopping centers in the Jacksonville area, Sabbag complained that his busi-ness, and others like it, had been systematically denied the chance to grow with their communities. Sabbag added that the "strategic locations" of new suburban shopping centers had caused existing stores in established locations downtown to "close their doors because of lack of customers." Worried that "small businessmen will be frozen out for good," Sabbag urged the assembled legislators to act. Speaking for other local and independent merchants, Sabbag concluded, "We do not believe that the concentration of all business into the hands of a few large corporations is a healthy goal for our country."[80]

The Senate committee invited mall developers as well as business owners to serve as witnesses at the hearings. Several of these figures confirmed Sabbag's testimony, but insisted that the alleged discriminatory treatment was not their fault. Many admitted that they excluded small businesses from their centers or charged them rents up to ten times higher than those reserved for large department stores and other companies with national credit rankings. They claimed that they did so, however, because insurance financiers forced them to. Financing guidelines set by the insurance industry privileged large chains to such an extent that most were allowed to rent space in shopping centers for practically nothing. Speaking in defense of his field, one experienced developer reported he had been "told time after time" by representatives of major life insurance companies that "no matter what your value is; no matter what your economic forecast is; no matter how good things look," insurers would only back projects with "guaranteed leases to major chains." Other developers agreed, testifying that insurance company lending policy discriminated against small businesses in shopping centers. "Unless a developer is willing to be courageous or foolish," one developer contended, "he is forced to exclude good local merchants and take practically all AAA chains."[81]

Even some insurance representatives agreed that financing guidelines designed to project their companies' investments had created a problem. "I think our own insurance industry, which has furnished most of the money for center development, has been guilty of doing many things it shouldn't do," Bruce Hayden, secretary of Mortgage and Real Estate for Connecticut General, conceded. "My own opinion, which I know will be considered heresy by most life insurance lending officers," Hayden added, "is that we have done our developers a great disservice by our emphasis on high percentage chain store leasing."[82] Other insurers disagreed, fiercely defending their lending policies. Prudential vice president John Jewett offered the standard industry response to charges of discrimination against small retailers, claiming that insurers had simply protected their investments by objectively managing risk. "Most shopping centers are located in untried, suburban areas, and their success will not be known for several years," Jewett explained. "In view of the unproven future of the average new center, many lenders require certain safe-guards."[83] James Rouse, president of a large mortgage banking firm that worked closely with life insurance investors, agreed with Jewett. Rouse testified that he didn't see a problem with the current state of affairs, and suggested that if small businesses couldn't compete, they should be allowed to fail. "This is a phenomenon of our times," Rouse declared. "It is a characteristic of business."[84]

This laissez-faire approach concerned the Minnesota senator Hubert Humphrey, who sat on the committee and penned the official report following the hearings. Moved by the testimonies of independent merchants and small business owners, the senator worried that "the personal qualities" that once guaranteed success in the "American free enterprise system" had been rapidly replaced "by the sole and arbitrary criterion of net worth: naked economic power." Humphrey urged action and suggested an "FHA for retailers" that would supply government-guaranteed lease bonds to businesses unable to meet the AAA requirement demanded by insurance lenders. The assembled insurance representatives objected to this plan, arguing that "government intervention" would lead to "control and regimentation." Humphrey's fellow senators also rejected his plan but promised to study the issue further. The final report from the committee concluded that shopping centers were in the process of displacing downtown business districts, and that "the outlook for independent tenants in those shopping centers, and in other prime locations, [was] not bright." Though the report found that small businesses had been treated unfairly by a system driven by "the unusually conservative demands of one industry," it offered no solutions to the problem.[85]

By 1961, with complaints from small retailers still rolling in, the federal Small Business Administration (SBA) announced an amendment to its regulations at the urging of Humphrey and the Subcommittee on Retailing. The amendment, designed to "offset discrimination against small retailers forced upon them by the lending policies of major institutional sources of financing," allowed the SBA to offer loans to local development companies that agreed to offer space for small businesses in their shopping centers.[86] Hopeful that this solution "held promise" for "competent, independent businesses which now seek shopping-center space in vain," the government stepped aside to allow the free market to function.[87] A far cry from the "FHA for retailers" requested by Humphrey, the SBA loan plan had little impact on mall financing, as few developers took advantage of the voluntary program. Indeed, five years after the SBA announced the amendment, the plight of small businesses had only worsened. In his 1966 study of shopping center financing, Robert Foster found that "in most merchandise fields, independents continue to be conspicuously absent from shopping centers."[88]

Changes to laws that allowed insurance companies to invest in income-producing property directly shaped the development of suburban shopping centers in the United States, the downtown districts forced to compete with them, and the small and independent businesses that struggled to survive in the rapidly changing consumer economy. Over the course of the 1950s, insurance companies developed expertise in shopping center design and management that could be easily transported from one site to the next. As national lenders, they readily shifted investment dollars to parts of the country that were growing the fastest and that offered the highest returns. This increased the pace of the "malling of America" and produced a standardized consumer landscape that was national in scope. Investments in shopping centers offered a valuable new source of revenue for insurance companies. Crucially, they also created an exclusionary and standardized consumer economy and a built environment rooted in unsustainable growth. By the mid-1960s, the shopping center market had become saturated and many insurers began looking for new investment outlets. Still eager to invest in lucrative ventures, insurance companies turned their attention to the new and uncharted territory of suburban work.

"Insurance Sets a Pattern": Office Design and the Suburbanization of White-Collar Work

Insurance office construction picked up pace during the postwar years as the growing industry sought to expand its workforce and make long-term investments in future growth. The industry's move to workplace building on the periphery launched a trend in the late 1940s that eventually led to an exodus in the 1950s and 1960s. Influential new insurance offices—like Connecticut General's sprawling headquarters, built in Bloomfield, Connecticut, in the mid-1950s—served as models for other companies and popularized the now-ubiquitous "suburban corporate campus" form. Insurance leaders played a central role in designing and determining the shape of their new workplaces, pursuing the same desire for "total control" exhibited by companies like Metropolitan in urban housing. This commitment to control extended beyond office construction and design to include employee management and governance. By the mid-1960s, the industry's interest in suburban workplaces had expanded beyond their own offices. Having already committed billions of dollars to residential and commercial ventures in the suburbs, insurance companies turned toward investments in industrial parks, corporate campuses, and other workplaces on the periphery. This wave of workplace financing—and the industry's own move to the suburbs—aggravated already existing patterns of urban disinvestment, pulling tax revenue and jobs out of cities.

THE INSURANCE OFFICE DECENTRALIZES

Insurance office buildings have long held symbolic power. During the late nineteenth and early twentieth centuries, the industry's first period of massive growth, large insurance firms constructed imposing office buildings in urban centers, leading the corporate turn to monumental architecture. The world's first steel-frame skyscraper, built in Chicago in 1885, for example, was an insurance office.[89] By the first decade of the twentieth century, some of the largest and most commanding buildings in the nation housed insurance companies, securing a highly visible presence for the industry in the skylines of American cities. Insurance office buildings served important functions, beyond the obvious necessity of providing a workplace for employees. Like other financial institutions that did not sell tangible products, insurance companies faced the problem of visual obscurity. Large, impressive buildings symbolized stability and security while increasing visibility for companies by working as advertisements in themselves. Metropolitan's "Tower of Light" in midtown Manhattan, for example, became the tallest building in the nation when it was completed in 1909 and the first in the world to reach fifty stories. The company integrated the building into its advertising, adopting it as the company's primary logo in the 1910s. The tower quickly became synonymous with the insurance giant and became so iconic that it featured prominently in the popular fiction of the early twentieth century, as well as the New York skyline.[90] Large office buildings also brought in additional revenue for insurance companies that leased space in their facilities to other organizations.[91]

Decreased building during the Depression and World War II—the same conditions that created the midcentury housing crisis—also produced a shortage of office space in American cities. This was no small setback for rapidly expanding corporations. The size of corporate staffs in the US doubled between 1942 and 1952, and the bulk of these new employees performed white-collar work.[92] Insurance, riding the wave of the postwar economic boom, expanded faster than many other industries. As early as the mid-1940s, several of the largest insurers had outgrown their urban headquarters. Cities still held sway for these companies, many of which had existed for a century and had formed corporate identities that were deeply entwined with their lavish home office buildings and the cities that housed them. For industry leaders looking to expand operations but remain headquartered in cities, decentralization offered a compelling solution to the problem of limited space. Prudential, which opted to keep its headquarters in Newark but distribute staff to newly built workplaces in sites across the nation, offers one example of growth through decentralization.

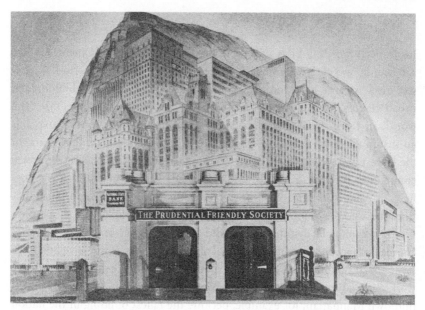

FIGURE 4.1. Postcard depicting Prudential's regional home offices, built in cities across the nation during the 1950s. Decentralization allowed companies like Prudential to invest on a national scale and become important shapers of the national economy. (Prudential Insurance Company of America, promotional postcard, c. 1958, private possession of the author.)

The company's decentralization process—what Prudential president Carroll Shanks called "breaking the whole thing up"—launched in 1946. Over the course of the next ten years, the company built seven regional home offices, spending $10 million on a towering Los Angeles office, another $10 million on an office in downtown Houston, $40 million for a forty-one-story Chicago home office, and $100 million on the massive "Prudential Center" and Northeastern home office in Boston's Back Bay.[93] Prudential also built offices in downtown Minneapolis, Jacksonville, and Toronto. Like insurance offices constructed at the turn of the century, these new structures served symbolic as well as pragmatic functions. *Fortune* reported that Prudential's wave of office construction helped "stamp its image" on the faces of cities, and the company proudly showcased its new buildings in promotional materials.[94] A postcard produced by Prudential in the late 1950s, for example, depicts illustrations of the company's seven regional home office buildings, nestled together under the protection of the company's symbol, the rock of Gibraltar (see fig. 4.1). Images like this one worked as advertisements for the company while also underscoring the national, and not simply regional, stature of the company and its contributions to the national economy.

Though Prudential chose to build large regional offices in cities, it began moving dozens of smaller branch offices to suburban locations in the late 1940s and early 1950s. The company also scattered its divisional units throughout its home state of New Jersey, selecting suburban locations for new offices devoted to statistical processing, group insurance, and computing.[95] The decision to disperse divisional staffs to the periphery accelerated the pace of suburbanization in the state. Other insurers followed a similar path during the early 1950s. New York Life, for example, moved its Arizona branch office to a suburban area outside Phoenix in 1952. That same year, the company also moved its Madison, Wisconsin, branch office out of town, where employees complained of "heavy traffic flow," to a "quiet street" in the surrounding suburbs.[96] Equitable and the Hartford-based Phoenix Mutual made similar moves.[97] In cities across the country, insurance companies began moving branches out of central business districts and relocating them to growing residential areas on the urban edge. These pioneering ventures in the early 1950s performed well, spurring interest in suburban locations from other insurers and other industries.

"AN EFFICIENT WHITE-COLLAR PLANT":
CONNECTICUT GENERAL AND THE DESIGN OF CONTROL

Moving branches or divisions to the suburbs was one thing, but transporting a company's headquarters was another. The Connecticut General Life Insurance Company became one of the first major corporations in the United States to make this pathbreaking move.[98] Drawing on a study conducted in 1947, which showed that the company would outgrow its downtown Hartford headquarters within a decade, forward-looking Connecticut General leadership launched an extensive research program to determine the shape, size, style, and location of a new building. After three years of study and "considered reasoning," the company decided in 1950 on "advanced design" and the "spaciousness and permanency" of a suburban location.[99] The company's president, Frazar Wilde, justified the unprecedented decision. "What acreage does is to permit future expansion," he explained, "and to provide employee facilities, especially parking, on a basis which is normally not possible in a more central location."[100] Claiming that a move to the periphery represented an expression of "faith in the future," Wilde oversaw the purchase of three hundred acres in Bloomfield, Connecticut, a rural area five miles outside Hartford, and then dove into planning.[101]

Wilde formed several committees in charge of researching leading architects, architectural styles, and the "use of modern materials and functional

efficiency" in recently constructed buildings around the world.[102] The committees eventually selected Skidmore, Owings, and Merrill (SOM), a firm led
by the architect Gordon Bunshaft, to construct the company's new headquarters. An extensive planning period followed, throughout which Wilde and
other Connecticut General staff members led the decision-making process.
Bunshaft and the architects at SOM endured more than five hundred meetings with Connecticut General representatives over the next five years.[103] Reflecting on his experiences with the insurance company after completing the
facility, Bunshaft recalled, "I don't think we've ever worked more closely with
a client, or had a more demanding one."[104] Wilde insisted on personally approving nearly every aspect of the project, engaging in heated battles with
SOM—some of which lasted for years—over details ranging from flooring
materials to the size and location of the executive suite. This obsessive med-
dling led one observer to wonder whether it was "an economical use of time
for an executive to ponder, as Wilde did, what type of material should be used
for the drawstrings on the venetian blinds."[105] Though surprising to some,
Connecticut General's desire to exercise direct control over its investment
was standard practice for insurance companies during this period. Wilde and
his colleagues also understood that a suburban location was a daring choice
for a corporate headquarters. Through research, planning, and active participation in the design process, Connecticut General's leaders sought to ensure
that their company's new headquarters made a statement, serving as an "exceptional" new model and "a clarion call for change in corporate building."[106]

In this endeavor Connecticut General succeeded wildly. The new headquarters won several awards when it opened in 1957, and was selected as one
of the top ten "Buildings in America's Future" by the prestigious American
Institute of Architects.[107] Many commenters focused on the modern design
of the new building—a sleek, three-story glass and steel structure described
by *Architectural Forum* as "a masterpiece of sumptuousness" rooted in "financial and artistic economy."[108] *Fortune* called the building "glittering" and applauded its "functionalism and beauty."[109] Other commenters focused on the
site's landscaping and unorthodox country setting. The long private road that
led to the building, accessible through an impressive steel gate, was trimmed
with immaculately clipped hedges and surrounded by an expansive lawn dot-
ted with willows and abstract sculptures created by the landscape architect
Isamu Noguchi (see fig. 4.2). *Architectural Forum* described the site as "precision in pastorale—beautifully crafted in design, new, with new dignity."[110]
The *New Yorker* writer Anthony Bailey compared the setting to a Consta-
ble painting, and Connecticut General to "an eighteenth-century English

FIGURE 4.2. Isamu Noguchi's *Family* sculpture group (facing), one of several contemporary artworks commissioned by the Connecticut General Insurance Company for its Bloomfield, Connecticut, headquarters (rear), completed in 1957. Connecticut General was one of the first major corporations in the United States to relocate from the city to the suburbs. (Ezra Stoller, © Esto.)

nobleman making sure that the country house he was building, and the park that surrounded it, were as distinguished as could be."[111] The less loquacious *Saturday Evening Post* simply noted with approval that the facility looked a lot like a country club.[112]

Though many praised Connecticut General's choice of location for its new headquarters, a move to the suburbs was not without challenges. The problem of attracting and retaining employees accustomed to working downtown, for example, worried Connecticut General leadership. Bustling Hartford, just a few miles away, housed dozens of other insurance companies, and Connecticut General executives feared that workers would choose employment at other firms located in the more convenient city center. This concern was especially troubling for a company that, like all insurers, relied heavily on female clerical labor. Of Connecticut General's roughly 2,500 employees, 1,600 were women, and 1,200 of those workers were unmarried high school graduates in their late teens and early twenties.[113] "There are various problems attached to having women as nearly three-quarters of a total staff of twenty-five hundred," explained Henry Dawes, director of personnel for the company. "They get married and pregnant and have husbands who move to distant places. They like to go shopping during their lunch hours, buy strange sandwiches in delicatessens, and take courses in German language or Spanish literature."[114] When choosing a location for the new headquarters, Dawes and other managers at Connecticut General worried that young female workers might not take kindly to spending their days surrounded by rolling fields. One journalist imagined the "typical feminine reaction" to working outside the city: "Bloomfield? Why there are cows out there!"[115]

To address this concern, the company designed its new headquarters to offer many of the services and conveniences of the city. The new facility included a library, theater, gym, cafeteria and soda fountain, card and game rooms, a book and record library, medical services, six bowling alleys, and outdoor tennis and volleyball courts.[116] It also offered amenities geared specifically toward female employees, including a beauty salon and a large dress and novelty shop, described by the New Yorker's Bailey as "interestingly stocked with cosmetics, children's clothes, good china, etc., and always full at lunch hour."[117] Bailey marveled at the company's commitment to both employee satisfaction and efficient management. "This latter-day version of the mill village company store makes a profit," he noted approvingly.[118] These amenities ultimately proved successful in attracting workers. After making the move to the new facility in 1957, the company received so many job applications that it had to maintain a waiting list.[119] Design and planning had also solved the problem of employee turnover, which shrank by 80 percent after the move.[120] Dawes additionally claimed that absence periods for employees at Connecticut General dropped after relocation to the new space. "Our business is growing faster than that of other companies," he boasted, "but so is our productivity per worker—we've only added 5 percent to our clerical force while other large companies have added 15 percent."[121]

This kind of efficiency was designed into the building. The aggressively horizontal structure had been planned in consultation with "efficiency experts" to serve the unique needs of an insurance company. Of these needs, "flow" was deemed particularly crucial. As one Connecticut General official explained, paperwork shuffled between various departments "flowed much more rapidly and smoothly on a horizontal pattern" rather than piling up vertically, "as was necessary in a city skyscraper."[122] To facilitate flow, design teams left the floors of the new headquarters entirely open, free of pillars or posts. Open floors and a movable partition system (custom-designed by SOM for Connecticut General) allowed for more efficient processing of policies. An innovative suspended ceiling grid, also designed for the building, contained lighting and an air-conditioning-and-distribution system that increased circulation while free-ing up space that might otherwise be taken up by fans or standing lamps. Even the furniture in the building was designed for peak flow: designers working for the company placed each of the thirty-seven different types of desk, tailor-made for the building, "in a precise position that was determined after serious study and consultation on the problems of space and efficiency."[123]

Factory comparisons abounded in discussions of the new workplace. Bunshaft, who went on to design several other prominent insurance build-ings, described the Connecticut General headquarters as a "factory of mov-ing paper" that required special attention to the efficient flow of documents and the human workforce.[124] Wilde proudly called the new building "an ef-ficient white-collar plant."[125] Even the workers themselves embraced factory metaphors. "You might say we have a five-girl assembly line," one clerk ex-plained, describing her precisely positioned workstation and the repetitive tasks she and her colleagues performed there.[126]

The factory-like nature of the new space extended to the management of workers. Connecticut General coordinated worker tasks with a commitment to efficiency that paralleled that of the most fervent turn-of-the-century Tay-lorists. As early adopters of "human resource" theory, which championed management-worker cooperation, Connecticut General leaders took a step beyond older forms of worker control by encouraging employees to play an active role in their own governance.[127] Every aspect of the new headquarters—from the numerous amenities to the shape and position of desks—had been de-signed to increase productivity through participation on the part of workers, an approach to management that targeted psychological as well as physiological processes. Company managers recorded a significant increase in worker pro-ductivity after the move to the new headquarters, and enthusiastically reported that employees came to the office earlier and stayed later. Managers also claimed that workers were "more articulate" and "dressed better" in the new, modern surroundings.[128] Some even wore clothing that "harmonized" with the brightly colored wall panels surrounding their work stations.[129] "The effects have been both physical and psychological," personnel director Dawes declared.[130]

To illustrate the "educational effect" of the new space and its ability to encourage self-governance, Dawes recounted the case of a young secretary whose performance on company-administered personality tests changed drastically after moving to the new facility.[131] While working at the old Hart-ford building, the secretary's test results revealed a personality that was "eas-ily discouraged, inhibited, moody, nervous, and submissive." After working at the Bloomfield headquarters for three years, her test results registered as "even-tempered, self-confident, cheerful, imaginative, and sociable." When asked by management to reflect on this change in a "self-appraisal," the secretary observed, "I guess it's done things for me to work in a place where sometimes I catch sight of a pheasant in the woods, and where I can look out over my desk and see swans on a pond."[132] Connecticut General representatives repeated stories like this one, which emphasized the transformation of workers themselves and not merely their performance on the job. Careful attention to workplace design, it would seem, had produced more productive workers capable of efficiently governing and improving themselves.

Not all employees reacted to the new workplace and management techniques as cheerfully as company leaders suggested, however. One clerk claimed nervously in an interview that the building "imposed its own discipline, making one feel that one's desk should be tidy at night."[133] Another said she missed meeting up with friends who didn't work for the company during lunch breaks in the city. Other workers disliked the music, selected carefully by management, that played over the building's intercommunication system for twelve minutes every hour. "I resent it as much as if somebody suddenly turned on a television full blast while I was trying to read," one secretary grumbled.[134] Though managers reported "improved team spirit in practically all departments," some workers bristled at the company's insistence that they refer to themselves as "members of the Connecticut General Family."[135] Still others, noting the highly gendered nature of the workplace hierarchy, thought women in the company should have more say in commanding day-to-day operations. "It's still a man's world, though we outnumber them more than three to one," one clerk complained to a journalist. "They make the rules."[136]

An unsettling sense of constant observation also permeated the brightly lit, modern workplace. Though visitors to the facility applauded the "feeling of informal spaciousness" produced by the facility's open-floor design, that same openness made it easier for managers to closely watch workers throughout the day.[137] Female employees admitted that they "dressed better" in the new building, for example, just as company leaders claimed. When interviewed about this phenomenon, however, the workers explained that they did so because they were "always on display."[138] This feeling of being watched continuously, the *Saturday Evening Post* reported, led to the pursuit of "trimmer figures" among the female staff. Dieting and weight loss became so popular at the new headquarters, according to the *Post*, that Connecticut General decided to hang a chart in the cafeteria listing the number of calories contained within each dish.[139] These developments did not register as problems for company leaders, who saw only improvements to their workforce. Members of the press reporting on the company's impressive new suburban facility were only slightly more judicious. Most applauded Connecticut General's ability to design a building that "took the people who work within it into account."[140] At least one journalist, however, wondered whether "in the long run, it would be a good thing to work inside a masterpiece."[141]

Just as Connecticut General's president had hoped, his exceptional new headquarters changed the nature of corporate building, serving as an influential model for other companies. The adjustable partition system designed specifically for the Bloomfield facility, for example, went into mass production shortly after its debut at the suburban site. A precursor to now-ubiquitous workplace cubicles, the flexible new walling system was dubbed the "C.G. Partition."[142] The new building's innovative suspended ceiling grid, which contained lighting and air-distribution systems, was also replicated on a wide scale.[143] The grid allowed for open floors and the efficient circulation of employees and workflow—desirable features for insurance companies and other corporations that specialized in white-collar work. Though Connecticut General's expansive facility featured glass walls and views of the idyllic countryside, other corporate office builders discovered quickly that the new ceiling grid eliminated the need for windows as a source of ventilation and light. This, they found, increased worker efficiency and the autonomy of new office spaces, which could now be completely shut off from exterior environments. The new corporate commitment to circulation and "flow" was thus extended to the very air employees breathed.

Connecticut General's embrace of "total design" and the company's strict control of the aesthetic character of its office also proved influential. When planning a move to the edge of Des Moines, Iowa, in the early 1960s, executives at the American Republic Insurance Company studied Connecticut General closely. After touring the Bloomfield site, American Republic president Watson Powell Jr. decided that he, too, wanted a modernist "clerical factory" and swiftly hired Bunshaft and the SOM team to build it.[144] The new American Republic headquarters, a rectangular glass and concrete structure, opened in 1965. The facility included many of the same features as the Bloomfield building, including an open-floor design and a suspended ceiling grid. Captivated by Connecticut General's interior decor and sculptural elements, Powell opted to decorate his own headquarters with modern furniture, custom-designed for the facility, and original artwork created by cutting-edge, contemporary artists. A serial portrait by Andy Warhol of company founder Watson Powell Sr. became one of the crowning works of the company's impressive art collection (see fig. 4.3). Titled *The American Man*, the portrait is typical of the artist's serialized screen prints, which depict people as commodities and are often described as "machinelike" and "impersonal."[145] Powell thought the

FIGURE 4.3. Photograph of American Republic president Watson Powell Jr., seated in front of Andy Warhol's 1964 *The American Man*, a serial portrait of the company's founder, Watson Powell Sr. Insurance companies became important collectors of contemporary art in the 1960s and led the fields of corporate office design and management. (Henry Groskinsky, "American Republic Insurance Co. Art Collection & Architecture," *Life*, 1966, © Time Inc.)

piece perfect for his insurance company's new headquarters, and surrounded it with more than a hundred artworks by contemporary artists, including installations by Claes Oldenburg, Joan Miró, and Charles Hinman, tapestries by Le Corbusier, and a Calder sculpture for the courtyard.[146]

American Republic executives studied Connecticut General's approach to management as well as the company's aesthetic strategy. Like Wilde, Powell believed that office design could increase the efficiency of employees while also "improving" workers themselves. Employees at American Republic's new headquarters were barred from displaying personal items in their workspaces, required to remove all items from desks before leaving each night, and reprimanded if they moved chairs or other furniture from preselected spots. Powell argued that "strict control" of the office environment freed employees from "meaningless petty considerations" while helping them "blend into the organization."[147] Enforced contemplation of contemporary art facilitated this process, according to the insurance executive, while also "liberating" the minds of employees as they performed "automated, machinelike" tasks.[148] "We were not surprised when most of our people first failed to enthusiastically hail the unfamiliar art that surrounded them," Powell admitted. "The 'taste' for contemporary art must be developed and conditioned," he explained. "It requires a change in attitude resulting from an imposed educational process."[149]

Though American Republic's modern new building received praise and awards, the company's efforts to aesthetically "condition" employees raised some eyebrows. In a *Life* magazine feature story about American Republic, the journalist Chris Welles criticized executives like Powell for setting "rigid rules" about office aesthetics, and for imposing on workers "the tyranny of dictated décor."[150] Perhaps responding to Powell's claim that contemporary art "shocks the unwashed into extending their horizons," Welles accused the insurance executive of embracing "a snobbish view of the average worker as an esthetic child needing discipline from more sophisticated superiors to route his actions along approved channels."[151] Though at least one journalist expressed skepticism, Powell proudly defended the new building, new art, and new order in his office. The executive boasted that business volume "increased by 47%" after moving into the new space, and claimed, like Connecticut General's leaders, that employees changed their working habits, coming to the office earlier and staying later. "Our people look different; they *dress* differently," Powell beamed. "The increase in efficiency has been just terrific."[152]

Other insurance companies also followed Connecticut General's lead, relocating to the suburbs and employing internationally renowned architects to design their new headquarters. The College Life Insurance Company, for example, began plotting a move to the outskirts of Indianapolis in the early 1960s and hired Kevin Roche and John Dinkeloo to construct their new facility. Completed in 1967, the College Life Insurance headquarters featured three eleven-story pyramids occupying the 160-acre core of a 640-acre campus. In a glowing review of the complex, the architecture critic William Marlin praised the combination of these elements and marveled at the ability of the structures to "establish a spatial effect whereby people and objects dissolve into one another, and whereby interior and exterior become reflections of each other."[153] Though Marlin was referring to the architecture of the new site, the same language could have easily described the management goals and strategies of worker control adopted by insurance executives. Like Connecticut General's suburban headquarters, the College Life facility offered a wide range of amenities designed to draw employees from the city and increase their efficiency on the job. Along with the central pyramid structures, the campus also became home to a manmade lake, a dinner theater, apartment units, smaller one-story office buildings, and a shopping center.[154]

By the late 1960s, a growing number of insurance companies had moved their headquarters to the suburbs. Like the skyscrapers of an earlier era, these corporate estates became symbols of the companies that built them. As embodiments of economic, social, and spatial order, they reflected the goals of the industry and the new role it hoped to serve in American life. The meticulously designed workspaces of new insurance offices mirrored the industry's commitment, encouraged by investment strategists like Shanks, to the efficient circulation and "flow" of capital. Their modernist architecture and suburban locations exuded newness and optimism, while also promising predictability—real estate values in the cities fluctuated over time, but suburban properties resisted swings in the market. As the architectural historian Louise Mozingo has argued, "The suburbs were predictable, spacious, segregated, specialized, quiet, new, and easy to traverse . . . a promising state of affairs to corporations bent on expansion."[155] The bucolic quality of these new workplaces (many included ponds, sprawling lawns, and sculpture gardens) prompted comparisons to turn-of-the-century urban parks developed by socially minded landscape designers like Frederick Law Olmsted. Postwar insurance campuses differed from these earlier, democratic forms in crucial ways, however. Gated and securitized, suburban corporate landscapes were private spaces designed for control. Extensive press coverage of these new sites, combined with promotional efforts by the companies that built them, helped popularize the cutting-edge design and management techniques adopted by insurance executives in the 1950s and 1960s. Ultimately, the industry's move to the periphery did more than "set a pattern," as *Architectural Forum* declared in 1957.[156] It also cemented the economic power of suburban regions and revolutionized the management of white-collar work.

"CORPORATE COUNTRY": EXPANDING INVESTMENTS IN WORKPLACE SUBURBANIZATION

Insurance companies didn't only build workplaces in the suburbs for their own uses; they also financed and developed offices and other worksites along the urban edge for other industries. In 1951, retail stores and shopping centers constituted the largest category of commercial mortgage commitments held by the insurance industry. By 1970, office buildings—the great majority of which were located in the suburbs—had replaced them.[157] Insurance investors became particularly influential leaders in financing and building a new and uniquely American suburban form, the "office park," which began popping up with increasing frequency in the countryside outside urban centers in the 1960s. Occupied by not one but several businesses, these spaces offered flexibility, room for expansion, and an opportunity for managers to more closely supervise labor. Mozingo argues that by the end of the 1960s, suburban office parks had become centers of international, not just American, managerial capitalism: "integral parts of peripheral expansion around the globe."[158]

The insurance industry's first attempts to build and finance large office complexes began in cities during the late 1940s. The top-three firm Equitable served as an early leader in this kind of investment. While Metropolitan was busy clearing New York's working-class population to make way for white middle-class housing, Equitable was clearing slums in Pittsburgh to make way for white-collar workspace. Equitable poured millions into downtown Pittsburg to create the Point Park office center, described in 1949 as "one of the finest business districts in America."[159] A handful of other companies followed Equitable, building corporate complexes of their own in cities during the 1950s and 1960s. The Prudential Center, for example, opened in 1964 and housed a massive shopping center as well as extensive office space, remaking the Back Bay district just east of downtown Boston.[160] These large projects became locally significant and provide evidence of a continuing interest in urban building on the part of some major insurance companies. The industry's move to offices and other corporate spaces on the periphery was already well underway by the mid-1960s, however. The suburbs, not the cities, represented the future of work.

Noting the success of its Bloomfield headquarters, Connecticut General began financing and developing other suburban workspaces in the mid-1960s. These included "Executive Park" outside Atlanta, which opened in 1967, and a thousand-acre industrial center in Columbia, Maryland, which became home to a General Electric appliance plant and managerial facility that same year. Connecticut General also built a $45 million office complex in the suburbs near Chicago's O'Hare Airport and a massive commercial campus, located outside Newton, Massachusetts, in 1968. The Newton campus straddled the Massachusetts Turnpike and included a hotel and shopping center. By the end of the decade, Connecticut General proudly reported that it was investing $2 million in the American economy every day. The bulk of that capital was directed at "corporate estate ventures" on the periphery.[161]

Prudential turned increasingly to similar investments. The company's urban building, though significant, was eventually eclipsed by its suburban commitments. Prudential began investing in workplaces outside of cities in the late 1950s, building several suburban office parks in states around the country. These included the Uptown Wilshire Center outside Los Angeles, the Texas Medical Center outside Houston, and the suburban Stanford Research Institute in Menlo Park, California.[162] Prudential built some of its largest suburban office projects in its own home state of New Jersey in the 1960s and 1970s. The company spent a decade developing four hundred acres outside Parsippany–Troy Hills, about an hour east of Manhattan, for example, into a sprawling corporate campus, which company marketers advertised as "an exceptional real estate opportunity" in a "suburban environment with urban access."[163] The insurance giant built similar projects in the Madison and Chatham townships, and in Essex County's Roseland.[164] By the end of the 1970s, Prudential had developed large swaths of the state's countryside into corporate campuses, office parks, and industrial centers. In promotional materials selling space at these sites, the company proudly proclaimed of the Jersey suburbs, "This is corporate country!"[165] Indeed, by the end of the century, the investment dollars of the state's largest insurer had made New Jersey the nation's leader in workplace suburbanization.

Not all insurers moved their branches and headquarters to the suburbs, but many did, and because insurance companies were some of the largest employers in the country, this move proved significant and influential. The relocation of insurance offices led to a relocation of white-collar work. From their secluded estates in the countryside, insurance executives helped popularize new forms of corporate design and workplace management. What's more, by building and financing suburban campuses and office parks for other industries, insurers extended their already substantial contribution to spatial privatization beyond urban centers and into the periphery. Though suburbs are commonly associated with residential segregation, the investments of large insurance companies made them sites of worker segregation as well. The new landscape of suburban labor sorted workers from different industries into discreet zones, separating them from larger political communities and from one another. By the end of the twentieth century, suburbs had displaced downtown districts as the primary location of office space in the United States.[166] Insurance investment dollars drove this development, just as they drove the standardization of shopping centers and the rapid pace and discriminatory impact of residential suburbanization.

Notably, the same federal programs that enticed insurance lenders into the residential mortgage market and other suburban ventures also aided the industry in its bid to compete with government and limit its expansion. Just as Prudential's president Shanks promised, the pursuit of lucrative new investments in the suburbs increased insurance revenue. This allowed companies to lower the rates they charged for policies. More and cheaper private insurance may not have halted the expansion of Social Security (the government expanded the program several times during the 1950s), but it did buoy the industry and keep it in the game. The flurry of insurance investment activity during the postwar years boosted esteem for insurers, drawing celebratory accounts like the *Fortune* "mighty pump" feature. It also enabled companies to claim that the primary function of their industry was investment in the nation's growth—what one analyst in the late 1950s called the chief "sociological responsibility" of the industry.[167] When asked about the major problems facing the insurance business in 1957, for example, Shanks responded that, after "government encroachment," the biggest challenge for the industry was "how to get more savings into insurance to supply the loans for the expanding US."[168] The two challenges were connected. By identifying the efficient circulation of capital as the principal task of insurance companies, industry leaders like Shanks added fuel to their case against government expansion. The industry's rallying cry, "Private enterprise can do the job," was thus extended in the 1950s and 1960s to encompass nation building and stewardship of the national economy, as well as the provision of economic security.

Through a successful strategy in its bid to compete with government, the insurance industry's turn to the suburbs led to devastating consequences for America's cities. As white, middle-class Americans fled the nation's urban centers, vital tax dollars left with them. Insurance investment strategies during the 1950s and 1960s intensified this pattern. It mattered when the nation's largest source of private capital—and largest employer of white-collar workers—moved its investment dollars and jobs to the suburbs. Disinvestment in cities led to decline, and by the end of the 1960s many Americans were talking about an "urban crisis." The nature of that crisis, and the responses it elicited from government, the insurance industry, and social activists, is the subject of chapter 5.

PART III

Defending Discrimination

5

"Communities without Hope": Urban Crisis and Insurance Redlining

Impoverished by years of disinvestment, many cities in the United States fell into disrepair and decline in the 1960s. Deeply entrenched patterns of residential segregation, combined with the flight of tax revenue, jobs, and investment capital to the suburbs, left cities—and their primarily nonwhite residents—without vital economic resources. Deteriorating conditions, discriminatory policing, and the slow pace of social and political change led to frustration and desperation in many urban communities. Tensions exploded during the middle years of the 1960s, as a wave of urban uprisings shook the nation. Between 1965 and 1967, hundreds of rebellions broke out in cities across the United States, beginning with the Watts neighborhood of Los Angeles in the summer of 1965. Violent clashes between Watts residents and police, who instigated much of the violence, lasted for five days and resulted in the deaths of thirty-four people and thousands of injuries. Newark, Detroit, and other cities followed. Over the next two years, more than two hundred uprisings broke out in thirty-five states, leading to hundreds of deaths. Horrified by the increasingly violent nature of what was commonly referred to as the "urban crisis," Americans turned to the federal government in search of explanations and a response.

That response came in July 1967, when President Lyndon Johnson launched the National Advisory Commission on Civil Disorders and charged its members with explaining the uprisings and offering recommendations to prevent future unrest. The group, known informally as the Kerner Commission, published its findings seven months later. The report concluded that the nation was "moving toward two societies, one black, one white—separate and unequal." Without action, it warned, the nation would fall further into a "system of apartheid" and more violence would be inevitable.[1] Less than a month after the report's release, the assassination of Dr. Martin Luther King Jr. sparked more than two hundred new uprisings in thirty-six states. Johnson, who had opted to ignore the Kerner Commission's findings, faced intense criticism. Under growing pressure to act, he dove into efforts to pass the Fair Housing Act—a bill designed to end racial discrimination in housing that had languished in committees for two years. Congress passed the act less than a week after King's murder, securing a major victory for civil rights proponents. Johnson also moved to speed the repair of cities damaged in the uprisings, authorizing the President's National Advisory Panel on Insurance in Riot-Affected Areas, popularly known as the Hughes Panel.

Unlike the Kerner Commission, the Hughes Panel set out to address recovery from the urban uprisings, not their causes. The withdrawal of insurance companies from "riot-affected" neighborhoods created an obvious roadblock on the path to rebuilding, and the primary goal of the panel was to identify strategies for making insurance available to regions that had been devastated by civil unrest. Despite its focus on recovery, the Hughes investigation, once launched, made shocking discoveries surrounding the underlying causes of urban decline. The panel's findings revealed that insurance unavailability was not simply an unfortunate byproduct of the uprisings that rocked American cities in the mid-1960s, as many had assumed before the investigation. Evidence instead suggested that lack of access to insurance had played a significant role in *creating* many of the conditions that had led to the disturbances. A survey conducted by the Hughes Panel of three thousand homeowners and businesses in six major cities found that 30 percent of homeowners and 40 percent of business owners faced serious insurance problems. The investigation revealed that these problems—either prohibitively high premiums or total unavailability of insurance coverage—existed in cities throughout the nation. What's more, the panel discovered that lack of access to insurance had plagued urban communities for decades, playing a central role in producing the condition analysts referred to as "blight."[2] The urban crisis, it seemed, had begun as an insurance crisis.

The realization that inequalities in insurance provision had fed urban decline and unrest set off a wave of concern and activism. At the heart of this activism, and the panel's findings, stood the notion that insurance served a vital function in modern American life. As the Hughes Panel reported:

> Without insurance, banks and other financial institutions will not, and cannot make loans. New houses cannot be built. Existing houses cannot be repaired. New businesses cannot be started. Existing ones cannot expand, or even survive. Thus, without insurance an area deteriorates. Its services, goods,

and jobs, the lifeline of the city, diminish. Communities without insurance are communities without hope.[3]

With these words, the panel revealed both the essential nature of insurance and the disastrous impacts of its unequal distribution. The insurance era had arrived, but not all Americans had been granted access to its promise.

If insurance was, in fact, as important as the Hughes Panel suggested, how did a situation arise in which large portions of the American population could not obtain it? To answer this question, activists and regulators turned their attention to property and casualty insurance providers. Investigations into these fields found evidence of discrimination in the methods homeowners, fire, auto, small business, and other property and casualty firms used to market insurance and manage claims. Activists found evidence of discrimination in underwriting as well, including prohibitions against insuring residents of nonwhite neighborhoods in the fields of homeowners and business insurance. They also uncovered evidence of rating structures in the field of auto insurance that charged nonwhite urban policyholders significantly higher rates than white suburbanites. Critics of the industry embraced the term *redlining*—a reference to the practice of drawing a red line on a map around neighborhoods considered "too risky" to attract investment, or services like insurance. Though this term eventually became associated with the racist practices of federal programs like the FHA, which relied on color-coded maps to determine which regions would be granted government housing subsidies, it was popularized in the late 1960s and 1970s by critics of insurance, who set out of combat discrimination perpetrated by private institutions as well as public ones.[4]

Redlining was not the only explanation offered by activists and regulators for the decline of American cities and the impoverishment of their residents. Another powerful argument cited disinvestment—the withdrawal of investment capital from cities, and its subsequent relocation to the suburbs. This argument, like charges of redlining, targeted the insurance industry directly. Life insurers, guardians of one of the nation's largest sources of private capital, had *also* played a role in creating the urban crisis. Relaxation of investment regulations during the 1940s and 1950s allowed insurance companies to invest heavily in suburban housing developments, shopping malls, and office spaces. Life insurers pulled a substantial portion of the capital for these projects out of urban areas, making the industry a key player in aggravating— and at times leading—the trend toward urban disinvestment. The movement of insurance dollars from the cities to the suburbs struck a damning blow to urban communities across the country. As the consequences of those investment decisions became clear, life insurers, like property and casualty insurers, became the focus of intense criticism and charges of discrimination.

Reponses to the urban crisis during the late 1960s and 1970s thus created a crisis of a different nature for the insurance industry. As Americans turned to government to solve the urban crisis, many insurers feared the return of public desire for universal insurance programs capable of serving the most vulnerable and insecure members of society. The 1965 passage of Medicare and Medicaid—public programs launched as part of Johnson's vision for a "Great Society"—suggested that Americans were willing to support new government insurance initiatives. Would these kinds of programs proliferate and eventually replace private insurance? In a 1966 study announcing a "long-term crisis" for private insurance, the business professor Richard Farmer predicted that they would. "Increasingly Americans appear to recognize insurance as a total social notion, rather than as something belonging exclusively to the middle classes," he argued. "One can predict that social insurance schemes will continue to grow steadily to cover still more of life's increasingly complex risks." Farmer concluded his assessment with a prophecy that captured the attention of insurance industry leaders. "There is a growing social attitude that people really are interdependent, and that one's misfortunes are not his alone," he declared. "If society really is responsible for individuals, public programs will be devised to cover the problems."[5] Perhaps without knowing it, Farmer had identified the central conflict at the heart of the battle to define and control the insurance era.

Fear of the providential state—a driving force that had structured the actions of insurance leaders throughout the postwar era—thus returned in the late 1960s with an urgency and intensity unseen since the 1930s. The prospect of containing government expansion, however, no longer seemed tenable for many private insurers. As the depth and complexity of the problems facing American cities became apparent, more and more insurers began to wonder if a less active state was even desirable. The insurance industry's response to the urban crisis, and to charges of discrimination, reflected this change in thinking. As life and property insurers scrambled to mount a defense of their industry, they drew from strategies they had developed over the course of the postwar era—with two important exceptions. Insurance leaders no longer called for a diminished state, and instead advocated for "public-private partnerships," like those developed through Medicare and Medicaid, in which government became an insurer of last resort that took charge of risks private industry could not profitably manage. Gone, too, were claims from insurance leaders that they governed through a paternalistic desire to protect and care for Americans. Retreating to the cold abstraction of statistical equations, insurance leaders abandoned associations with moral authority cultivated over the course of a century, and instead staked the future of their industry on claims of objectivity, fairness, and the efficient management of risk.

This chapter examines the responses to the urban crisis offered by life and property casualty insurers, as well as their responses to charges of discrimination leveled by social activists. The first part of the chapter traces the history of the five-year, $2 billion Urban Investment Program launched by the life insurance industry in 1967. The second part examines the legal and rhetorical defense of risk-rating practices developed by property and casualty insurers in reaction to charges of discrimination and redlining. Though neither response solved the urban crisis, together they offered a path forward for the beleaguered insurance industry, helping it weather the storm of social unrest that threatened to dismantle the nation's privatized insurance system in the late 1960s and 1970s.

The Life Insurance Urban Investment Program

Public relations experts at the ILI had been predicting a "long term crisis" for years by the mid-1960s. Pollsters and other analysts hired by the institute had identified disturbing social and political trends that promised to wreak havoc on the industry: a growing number of institutions competing for the nations' savings; declining faith in the nuclear family, and along with it, the moral imperative for breadwinners to provide for dependents; and calls from new social movements for the industry to more equitably distribute coverage and investment dollars. Discussions of the coming crisis became common at industry conferences throughout the 1960s. Rumors that economists working for government were calling for the absorption of the insurance business and its assets into the Social Security system circulated widely, and many top lawyers for the industry believed that federal regulation was inevitable. When Dr. Martin Luther King Jr. and twenty of the largest civil rights organizations in the nation instituted a boycott of Metropolitan in 1966, arguing that the company's investment practices discriminated against Black Americans, insurance leaders knew that the long-predicted crisis had arrived.[6]

The industry moved quickly. Late in 1966, James Bentley, president of the National Association of Insurance Commissioners, reported to the ILI that proposals had been introduced in Congress to nationalize auto insurance—a move that would endanger the private status of the entire industry. Bentley warned that 1967 would be the "last time around" for the life insurance industry to address the growing tempest of criticism "on a voluntary basis."[7] He suggested that a "pledge" from life insurers to invest in the nation's cities—one significant enough that it "couldn't be ignored by public officials"—might go a long way toward generating goodwill and staving off federal regulation.[8] The ILI jumped on Bentley's proposal and began making plans for an unprecedented financing program that would channel a total of one billion life insurance dollars into American cities. After consulting with government officials and securing guarantees for federal loan insurance on potential urban investments, the ILI presented the plan, still rough around the edges, to the American Life Convention (the annual gathering of the nation's life insurers).[9] The convention unanimously approved the plan, and dubbed it the Urban Investment Program (UIP).

This decision was made in the summer of 1967, during some of the worst months of urban uprisings. Though leaders of several large life insurance firms had followed Connecticut General and relocated their offices to the suburbs in the 1950s and 1960s, many retained their historic urban headquarters and witnessed firsthand the devastation and destruction unfolding in the nation's cities. Orville Beal, president of Prudential, watched the Central Ward of Newark burn from the window of his office in the company's downtown headquarters. Shaken, Beal became a vocal proponent of industry efforts to address the urban crisis, and volunteered to serve as a leader of the UIP's Planning Committee. Experiences like Beal's no doubt contributed to the conviction, shared by most members of the committee, that urgent action was necessary. They dove into planning immediately.[10]

The group determined first that a united industry front was essential. To encourage participation in the voluntary program, they set the contributions of individual firms on a percent basis of total company assets. This allowed larger companies to take on the brunt of the $1 billion commitment while still making it appear that the industry as a whole was responsible for the UIP—a crucial move if the goal of avoiding new regulations was to be achieved. The committee also determined that the program needed focus in order to guarantee that the industry's efforts made a noticeable contribution to urban problems. In deliberations, committee members considered a number of sites of intervention that might serve as a focus for industry resources, including "slum conditions, air pollution, transportation issues, civil disorders, and the need for better employment, education, and job training."[11] All agreed that while jobs and education were a top priority, the life insurance business was best positioned to contribute to the cities in the field of housing finance. After announcing that the industry's $1 billion pledge would focus on housing, Beal and the committee moved next to form a clearinghouse, responsible for putting companies in touch with government officials and other groups that might assist in placing loans in "blighted" urban neighborhoods across the nation. Finally, the committee directed the ILI to take charge of public relations. The institute would draw on its experience and resources to generate interest in the program, both within the industry and in public forums.

By September 1967, a total of 161 life insurance companies had agreed to participate in the UIP's $1 billion pledge. Beal and the committee felt confident that the program, though still vague, was ready to launch. The ILI contacted Metropolitan head Gilbert Fitzhugh, a close friend of President Lyndon Johnson. In private conversations, Fitzhugh convinced Johnson of the virtues of the program, and both agreed that an announcement at the White House would be a fitting way to ensure its success.[12] Beal, Fitzhugh, and a number of other industry leaders joined Johnson on the White House lawn late in September 1967. There, in front of a gathering of representatives from the press, Johnson announced the UIP, calling it "a historic contribution to the country" on the part of private enterprise.[13] Noting the complexity and depth of the urban crisis, he called on other industries to join the nation's life insurers in offering solutions. "What the government does really is only the beginning," Johnson declared. "Private efforts are not just essential to success—they are central to success."[14]

The announcement received front-page coverage in the *New York Times*, the *Washington Post*, and a number of other major news outlets. Nearly every story neglected to mention that the insurance industry had played a major role, through disinvestment, in creating the urban problems it now set out to solve. *Time* noted briefly that the UIP would bring "private enterprise into an area it has traditionally shunned," but applauded the program and called it "important beyond all accounting."[15] The overwhelmingly positive press coverage pleased leaders of the life insurance industry immensely. So, too, did the ringing endorsement offered by the president of the United States. The UIP had not even begun, and it had already succeeded in its primary goal of attracting the goodwill of government. Whether or not the UIP would succeed in its secondary objective—ameliorating the problems of the nation's deteriorating cities—was yet to be seen.

INSTITUTING THE UIP

Many details of the UIP had not been ironed out when it launched late in 1967—a situation that forced leaders of the program to become on-the-fly problem solvers. The UIP was primarily a public relations campaign, and some of the earliest problems arose in that field. The White House announcement had attracted good press, but analysts at the ILI quickly realized that public awareness of the program, though desirable, could also cause problems. The institute argued that investments in "high risk" urban loans might be seen as "unscrupulous" and attract protests from policyholders, whose savings were on the line. To contain this danger, UIP organizers agreed that loss of return on investments would not be an option, and quietly informed participant companies that all loans through the program should be made at market rates. The UIP, they insisted, would not be a "giveaway," and companies would continue to profit, perhaps just slightly less than usual, under the banner of "enlightened self-interest."[16]

The question of how to discuss the program in public once it was underway had also not been settled. Some thought the UIP presented an opportunity to extoll the virtues of private enterprise and criticize government, an old tack that had produced dividends in the past. One executive, for example, argued that the ILI should depict federal programs as "unable to cope" with the problems of cities.[17] Americans should be reminded, he argued, that private enterprise was "the sinew and strength of America, and the most *realistic* element in our society."[18] Other insurance leaders thought this approach might backfire—if the program failed to make an impact, the industry would be forced to take the blame. With this in mind, UIP organizers decided to depict the program as tangible support for government policies already in place, a supplement to larger national efforts, not a solution. Beal and other insurance leaders began referring to government as a "partner," and the industry's efforts to help the cities as acts of "collaboration" between the state and private enterprise. Metropolitan's vice president of economics, Charles Moeller, for example, called the UIP "a prime illustration of private capital taking the initiative, and at the same time cooperating with government."[19] This move toward partnership and away from antagonism in regards to the state—a significant shift in industry positioning—remains one of the more lasting legacies of the UIP.

Once essential public relations questions had been settled, organizers of the UIP turned to deal with the many problems associated with making actual investments in long-neglected urban centers. To ensure that the program directed resources to areas in need, eligibility standards for the UIP stipulated that investments "benefit those residing in the core areas" or "persons moving from the core."[20] Beyond these requirements, UIP organizers left standards vague and flexible. Any city could qualify, though UIP organizers emphasized the importance of making the program a national effort and asked firms to finance projects in a variety of regions. All UIP investments constituted individual company loans. Contrary to the impression made in industry advertising of the program, there was no "pool" of money. Though the UIP Planning Committee offered advising, lending officers at participant companies made the final decisions about where to invest. Despite the flexibility of UIP eligibility standards, those decisions proved difficult for a number of reasons.

Public relations experts at the ILI originally encouraged references to government agencies as "partners" as a way of avoiding blame for potential failures. UIP participant companies quickly realized, however, the necessity of working with federal agencies as they sought out investment opportunities. The UIP mandate to invest at market rates under conditions that would not lead to losses or policyholder protest, for example, restricted lending options and made government FHA insurance essential. The federal Rent Supplement Program (RSP), under which poor families paid one-fourth of their gross income for rent on FHA-insured apartments and the federal government paid the remaining balance, quickly became a popular venue for UIP funds. Introduced by Johnson in 1965, the program was in danger of failing by 1967 due to lack of financing. Insurance dollars saved the RSP and helped provide housing for thousands of low-income families in urban centers. This real example of collaboration between private insurance and government became one of the few success stories of the UIP.

Life insurers looking to invest in low-income urban housing discovered quickly that, beyond the RSP, few FHA-insured investment opportunities existed in deteriorating urban neighborhoods. After years of restricting their mortgage-lending and home-financing efforts to suburban regions—where FHA backing was plentiful—some life insurance lenders expressed surprise upon learning that the FHA did not offer insurance in most urban centers. In an accurate but remarkably hypocritical assessment, life insurers accused the federal government of redlining. "For many years the FHA had excluded blighted areas from its insurance program on the theory that it would be imprudent to insure housing mortgages in deteriorating areas," an appraisal of the UIP, produced by the ILI, explained.[21] Though life insurers found this policy reasonable—"the FHA, after all, was primarily an insurance mechanism not a social mechanism," the ILI noted—UIP organizers realized that lack of government insurance in "blighted" areas would doom their investment program.[22] In hopes of saving the UIP, Beal and other life insurance executives lobbied leaders at the FHA and encouraged them to change the policy. These efforts were successful. The FHA announced late in 1967 that it would extend government-subsidized insurance to single-family mortgages in "blighted" urban areas, ending thirty years of discriminatory, and deeply damaging, federal housing policy. The life insurance industry proudly took credit for the change. "The Urban Investment Program gave impetus to the new policy," the ILI boasted.[23]

With FHA backing in place, the UIP picked up pace. By August 1968, roughly $600 million had been lent by UIP participants in 215 cities across the country. California received $76 million, $64 million went to Texas, $57 million to Illinois, and $46 million to New York State. Michigan, New Jersey, and Ohio each received roughly $30 million in loans from insurance firms, and Florida and Tennessee received roughly $25 million.[24] By the conclusion of the program's first year, participant companies had financed forty-two thousand units of federally insured multifamily housing in urban centers. As interest rates rose over the fixed FHA ceiling late in 1968, however, the cost to insurance lenders also rose, and the pace of investment slowed.[25] UIP organizers, concerned that investments in urban housing could no longer be made at a profit, considered their options. Before the first billion had been dispersed, they decided to extend the program but focus on other, hopefully more lucrative, fields in need of financing.

The decision to launch a second billion-dollar pledge came late in 1968. Beal and other leaders of the largest life insurance companies led the charge, arguing that the program had achieved positive but potentially fleeting results in the sphere of public relations. The industry announced its intention to focus on creating jobs and building "minority enterprises" with a second billion-dollar pledge to the new president, Richard Nixon, in April 1969. Nixon welcomed the industry's commitment but offered little by way of fanfare. Much to the disappointment of industry leaders, the announcement also received little coverage in the press. The New York Times carried the story briefly on page 44 of its late city edition; major magazines and television networks ignored the announcement entirely.[26]

To compensate for the lack of press, the ILI produced several full-page ads that ran nationally in 156 newspapers and twenty-one major magazines.[27] The campaign emphasized the accomplishments of the UIP during its first round and adopted a tone that might best be described as optimistic humility. "While knowing that it doesn't really fill the whole need," one ad read, "the life insurance business regards [the second billion-dollar pledge], like the first billion, as an investment in its own future" (see fig. 5.1). The ILI employed rhetoric encouraged by UIP organizers in the campaign, citing "enlightened self-interest" as the motivating factor for the industry's new commitment to urban financing. "In a businesslike way, our business is investing in its own future," another ad declared.[28] Every ad in the series carefully noted that before the UIP, "capital had not been available to the cities on reasonable terms, due to risk and location"—a clear attempt counter charges of discrimination like those leveled by Dr. King and other civil rights leaders only three years earlier.[29] The institute also published and distributed two booklets, titled Whose Crisis? . . . Yours, and The Cities . . . Your Challenge Too.[30] As these titles suggest, the messages conveyed by the booklets were consistent with

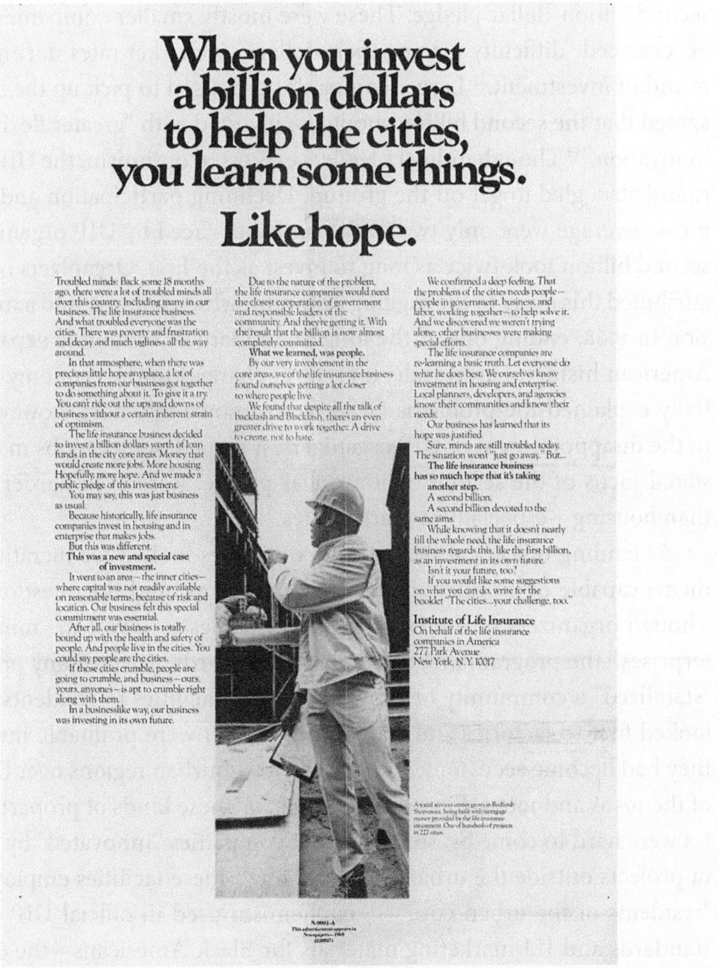

FIGURE 5.1. Institute of Life Insurance advertisement promoting the industry's 1967–1972 Urban Investment Program. The ILI created advertisements like this one to attract public support for the program and stave off government regulation of the industry. (ILI, "When You Invest a Billion Dollars to Help the Cities, You Learn Some Things. Like Hope," 1969, J. Walter Thompson Company, Domestic Advertisements Collection, David M. Rubenstein Rare Book & Manuscript Library, Duke University.)

those of other life insurance marketing efforts from the era, which emphasized individual responsibility and personal initiative in solving social problems. In hopes of attracting participants for the second billion-dollar pledge, the ILI also produced a half-hour color film titled *A Chance to Build* and distributed it to life insurance companies across the nation.[31]

Despite these efforts, enthusiasm for the UIP within the industry declined. Of the original 161 participants, fifty chose not to partake in the second billion-dollar pledge. These were mostly smaller companies that had experienced "difficulty placing their dollars" at market rates during the first round of investment.[32] Larger companies promised to pick up the slack, and agreed that the second billion should be invested with "greater flexibility and innovation."[33] Though industry leaders expressed optimism, the UIP's second round struggled to get off the ground. Declining participation and minimal press coverage were only two of the problems faced by UIP organizers. The second billion took twice as long to invest as the first. Organizers of the UIP attributed this delay to the sagging economy, which entered into a mild recession in 1968, ending one of the longest and largest economic expansions in American history. Large-scale, long-term changes to the economy only partially explained the problems faced by insurance investors, however. Much to the disappointment of UIP organizers, it turned out that jobs in cities, the stated focus of the second billion-dollar pledge, were even harder to create than housing—especially at market rates.

As lending officers at participant companies looked for lucrative investments capable of producing jobs, they tiptoed around the question of race. Though organizers of the UIP urged companies to invest in "minority enterprises," the program's vague eligibility standards accepted any project that "stabilized" a community or provided service facilities to residents. Insurers looked first to factories and warehouses, which were profitable investments they had become accustomed to making in suburban regions over the course of the 1950s and 1960s. Financing options for these kinds of properties in cities were hard to come by, so participant companies "innovated" by investing in projects outside the urban center. Though these facilities employed some "residents of the urban core"—a euphemism used in official UIP eligibility standards and ILI marketing materials for Black Americans—the owners of industrial properties financed by the UIP were primarily white. Investments in medical facilities, another popular UIP venue, followed a similar pattern. Karen Orren, a political scientist who cataloged the investment of UIP funds in Chicago, found that over 75 percent of the medical clinics and 85 percent of the nursing homes financed by the UIP in the city were white-owned.[34]

UIP investments in commercial and retail projects also overwhelmingly benefited whites. A large proportion of second-round UIP investments, for example, went to white-owned shopping centers located at the edges of cities. Though some of these centers included Black-owned businesses, most devoted the bulk of their space to large national chains—a product of financing guidelines put in place years earlier by life insurers.[35] Commercial investments that did focus on the "urban core" tended to reinforce long-standing racial divisions and inequalities in employment. One major financing effort in Chicago, for example, helped

repair a supermarket in the city's South Side that had been damaged in the uprisings. The supermarket, owned by whites, employed only white workers. "We
helped the community in an important way by providing that facility," declared
a lending officer of the insurance company that provided the loan.[36]

As investments outside city centers and in white-owned facilities became
increasingly common, UIP organizers encouraged participant companies to
finance Black businesses in the urban core. One effort to do so offered financing to a Black-owned development company, which used UIP funds to take
over an abandoned supermarket in Trenton. The shop went out of business
in less than two years, unable to compete with chain stores located in nearby
suburban shopping centers. Program leaders attributed this and other failures
like it to "the gap between hope and the economic realities of the inner city."[37]
No mention was made of the decades-long suburban investment strategy of
the life insurance industry, or the systematic assault on small businesses that
its shopping center financing model had consciously put into place in the
1950s and early 1960s. Still eager to fulfill the goal of supporting "minority
enterprises," insurers turned to the federal government in hopes of receiving
assistance. The organizers of the UIP urged the Small Business Administration to adopt an FHA-style insurance program for small businesses in cities.
A similar program had been floated in Senate hearings by Hubert Humphrey
a decade earlier, but life insurers helped defeat it.[38]

Unlike the FHA, which had cooperated with UIP organizers during the
first round of investment, the Small Business Association declined to change
its policies. Other efforts to attract assistance from government also faltered
as federal priorities shifted and Nixon's "war on crime" replaced Johnson's
"war on poverty." Insurers were quick to blame the new administration for
failing to open investment channels and support the UIP's efforts in cities.[39]
No attempts were made, however, to account for the role the industry itself
had played in creating the conditions it now found objectionable. UIP organizers instead attributed the "scarcity of realistically viable loan opportunities" for small, urban businesses to lack of government cooperation and "the
fundamental facts of urban life."[40]

Other industry justifications for the UIP's struggles targeted the communities and people the program had purportedly been designed to serve.
"There are disturbing trends in this country which tend seriously to weaken
the resolution and reaction of many Americans in their confrontation with
life," noted a top executive at Metropolitan, who attributed the impoverishment of urban communities to an absence of "responsibility and discipline."[41]
"What's really needed," a mortgage officer for a different insurance company
argued, "is to change their whole family structure, and we can't do that."[42] In

a discussion of loan defaults, which affected roughly 10 percent of all UIP investments, a New England Life representative argued that the insurance industry's efforts to invest in the cities were "well-meaning but premature," because "more training and experience was needed before a great many Black businessmen could compete effectively."[43] Interviews with industry workers conducted by Orren in her study of the UIP in Chicago revealed deeply racist attitudes that clashed with the "enlightened" rhetoric of ILI publicity materials. "We find these people still living in the jungle," one anonymous insurance representative quipped, "and if I took those people and put them along the Lake Shore, the Lake Shore would become a jungle."[44]

It is not surprising, given statements like these, that many Black city residents did not welcome life insurance financiers into their communities or wholeheartedly embrace the UIP. Longtime residents of neighborhoods targeted for UIP loans no doubt remembered the insurance industry's participation in destructive slum-clearance programs just twenty years earlier. Those programs, which produced segregated housing developments like Stuyvesant Town, led to intense resistance and created lingering resentment toward the industry. Though the UIP claimed to intervene in a different spirit, several of the projects financed through the program offered a reprise of earlier insurance urban renewal efforts. Protests erupted, for example, during construction of a UIP-financed housing complex in Brooklyn's Bedford–Stuyvesant neighborhood. Developers condemned and razed the homes of residents of the area, then neglected to relocate them to adequate housing.[45] For people who had lived through slum-clearance projects in the 1940s and 1950s, this updated version of urban renewal did not appear any different. To make matters worse, many UIP company participants chose not to involve community groups when planning projects. Industry representatives were nonetheless surprised to encounter disdain and distrust when entering urban communities. In some cases, local residents physically ejected insurance mortgage appraisers out of neighborhoods. One company resorted to hiring a local gang to guard the construction site of a housing project that had been repeatedly vandalized.[46] In response to these acts of resistance, one frustrated insurance loan officer remarked, "When someone is looking for a supply of capital, don't beat the supplier over the head with a sledge hammer. We're as sensitive as the next guy to being beat up or thrown down the stairs."[47]

THE "QUIET RETREAT"

Poor relations with urban communities, lack of government cooperation, and difficulties finding profitable investment outlets dampened enthusiasm

for the UIP among the nation's life insurers. In October 1972, before the en-
tirety of the second billion had been invested, the UIP's organizers quietly announced that the program would be discontinued. To replace the UIP, industry leaders established the Clearinghouse on Corporate Social Responsibility
to assist individual companies interested in "socially responsible" investment
programs, including those geared toward cities. Industry-wide efforts to
address the urban crisis, however, ceased. In a *Business and Society Review*
article, "The Insurance Industry's Quiet Retreat," Eugene Epstein criticized
insurers for "pulling out of the ghetto" and suggested that the entire UIP had
been a publicity-generating mechanism designed to maintain the industry's
autonomy over its investment decisions.[48] The article quoted the director of
the new clearinghouse, Stanley Karson, as declaring "People are still poor,
but poverty has become a stale issue."[49] Karson later denied making the statement, but the fact that the UIP's second round had produced diminishing
returns in prestige and goodwill was no secret.[50]

Industry leaders responded to Epstein's criticism by insisting that they had
discontinued the UIP because it had succeeded in accomplishing its goals.
If the primary goal of the program was to help American cities, this claim
was specious at best. Though insurance leaders criticized government agencies for failing to cooperate with UIP objectives, many openly supported the
new Republican administration and welcomed its resistance to both social
activism and investment as a solution to urban problems. Declining pressure
from government to distribute industry assets more equitably meant that a
program like the UIP was no longer necessary from a business standpoint.
Electoral politics did not lead inevitably to the discontinuation of the UIP, but
the chances that the federal government would seek to regulate insurance investment practices were much lower under Nixon than they had been under
Johnson. If the life insurance industry truly hoped to prove its commitment
to helping cities, 1972 would have been the year to do it. Its "quiet retreat"
instead signaled other motives.

How should we assess the UIP, a program widely hailed as an unparalleled
effort on the part of private enterprise to invest in solving social problems?
To begin, the program was not without precedent. Though the UIP did usher
in an era of "corporate social responsibility"—a now-ubiquitous term that
was virtually unheard of in the late 1960s—the pursuit of business objectives
through public service initiatives was not a new strategy for the insurance
industry. What differentiated the UIP from earlier efforts in the spheres of
public health and safety was not its stated social motives, or even its public-
facing nature. If anything, the UIP stands out instead for its lack of planning,
arbitrary execution, and outright failures. The bumbling UIP was a surprising

move for an industry that took pride in making sound predictions and facing the future's risks with confidence. The astonishment expressed by many insurers when they encountered resistance in urban communities, or when they could not find profitable outlets for their investment dollars, is striking. The fact that an industry willing to invest billions on terms that were only marginally profitable could not do so suggests that the economic problems facing America's cities in the late 1960s and early 1970s were far deeper than even insurance leaders expected. Though its organizers feigned optimism, calling the UIP "on the whole, successful," a sense of failure permeated discussions of the program within the industry during its last few years. As the final report on the UIP, produced by the clearinghouse, admitted, "However large the life insurance business is, its resources and expertise are dwarfed by the magnitude of the needs of the urban centers."[51]

This newfound humility no doubt contributed to the willingness of life insurers to look to government as a partner. Insurers had worked with government agencies in the past, accepting generous land grants and tax breaks during their first attempts at urban renewal in the late 1940s and early 1950s, and relying on FHA backing to secure a profitable suburban investment strategy in the 1950s and early 1960s. Through the UIP, however, industry leaders appear to have recognized, perhaps for the first time, the limits of a thoroughly privatized insurance era. Some problems, some risks, are simply too pressing and too great to be managed at a profit by private enterprise. As the director of mortgage lending for one of the few Black-owned UIP participant companies put it, "The really hard core [urban] areas? They need a subsidy. Either a decrease in the cost of a home, like mobile homes, or a subsidized interest rate, say a point or two, or subsidized equity money. We've subsidized wheat farmers and cotton farmers, why not people [in urban centers]?"[52] Recognizing the limits of privatize industry's ability to solve social problems did not mean turning over control to public entities or embracing socialized risk sharing across the board. From the late 1960s onward, however, insurers willingly endorsed government efforts to take on the risks that private industry could not profitably manage. The question of which risks and problems should be addressed through private means, and which deserve collective or public solutions, remains a topic of debate in the United States well into the twenty-first century.

What impact did the UIP have in cities? Upon the program's completion, participating companies had financed one hundred thousand housing units, forty nursing homes, and two industrial parks. Insurers also invested roughly $11 million in hospital construction and millions more in commercial properties and "job training and service facilities."[53] Organizers of the program boasted that it had "created or maintained" between forty thousand and fifty thousand jobs as well, though evidence suggests that a great number of these jobs fell under the difficult-to-measure "retained" category.[54] The good done by these dollars, which would have gone elsewhere without the UIP, should be recognized. The program's many flaws, however, also deserve attention. The mandate to invest at market rates meant that UIP funds rarely went to the parts of cities that needed them most. Already revitalizing or gentrifying neighborhoods received the bulk of UIP funding, and many of the new housing units financed by the program served middle-income and in some cases high-income residents. Owners of projects that received UIP loans were overwhelmingly white, and while some participant companies invested in minority-owned businesses, no attempts were made to integrate all-white neighborhoods or invest in long-term ways in nonwhite communities. Few insurance investors involved community groups in decisions about UIP projects, and the racist attitudes expressed by some industry representatives fueled distrust and resentment. The implementation of the UIP ultimately failed cities in countless ways, but the program's greatest failure of all grew out of its conception, not its execution. Designed to preempt meaningful public initiatives, the UIP prevented or stalled real efforts to solve the urban crisis and improve the lives of some of the nation's most impoverished and vulnerable citizens.

By industry standards, however, the program succeeded. As Eugene Epstein argued in his critical *Business and Society Review* article, the UIP was, indeed, a public relations program strategically designed to protect the life insurance industry's investment autonomy. Orren, one of few scholars to study the program's on-the-ground impact, agreed. In her astute 1974 analysis of the UIP, she argued that "social impulses are more likely to materialize into money and bricks when industry officials perceive a threat to their autonomous control over life company assets, and this links social responsibility to other, political purposes."[55] Those "political purposes" clearly involved pending regulation. Between 1965 and 1972, states across the nation launched nineteen unsuccessful attempts to enact mandatory insurance reinvestment legislation. These proposals would have required insurance companies to reinvest up to 75 percent of the premiums collected from a state's residents and businesses back into the localities from which they originated.[56] Insurers had depicted premium payments as tax-like investments that served the larger good for decades, and the proposed investment laws would have given truth to those claims. Goodwill generated by the UIP almost certainly contributed to the failure of proposed investment laws. It also helped diminish the federal government's interest in seizing regulation of the industry. Just as its organizers hoped, the UIP provided tangible evidence that life insurers were willing to voluntarily invest in "socially responsible" ways without the force of law requiring them to do so. The amount invested, $2 billion, may seem like a lot, but in 1967 that number represented two-thirds of 1 percent of the industry's assets.[57] As a price to pay for substantial political gain, $2 billion was a bargain.

Of the many problems life insurance companies encountered when attempting to make profitable investments in cities, one stands out as particularly revealing. Over and over again, industry representatives bemoaned the "lack of fire and extended insurance coverage" in "blighted" neighborhoods.[58] It wasn't just discriminatory federal programs like the FHA that hampered urban investment, UIP organizers realized. Redlining perpetrated by colleagues in the property and casualty insurance industry also presented a major roadblock for life insurers and other financiers willing to invest in struggling urban neighborhoods. Though life insurers succeeded in convincing the FHA to offer insurance subsidies in urban regions—a move deemed necessary to save the UIP—they did little to encourage private property insurance companies (many of which were subsidiaries of life firms) to change their discriminatory policies. That task fell to social activists, who mounted campaigns across the country in hopes of attracting public attention to insurance redlining and, ultimately, abolishing the practice.

The Discovery of Insurance Redlining

Charges of discrimination leveled at life insurers focused primarily on the industry's investment decisions, which privileged white, suburban regions over urban neighborhoods populated primarily by people of color. Charges of discrimination leveled at property and casualty insurers addressed a different but related problem. By denying residents of minority neighborhoods access to essential forms of coverage—like fire, homeowners, or auto insurance— property insurers prevented entire communities from securing mortgage loans, repairing and protecting property, building wealth, and participating in economically necessary activities like driving.

The Hughes Panel revealed the devastating consequences of insurance unavailability in cities, but it did not come to any conclusions concerning what had caused this serious problem. Why couldn't urban residents get insurance? In attempting to answer this pivotal question, urban analysts and activists proposed two distinct but related explanations. The first explanation cited overt racial discrimination on the part of insurance sales agents, marketers, underwriters, and, in some cases, executives. The second argument evoked the disparate impact (rather than discriminatory intent) of the risk classifications on which insurance access decisions were based. Race played an important role in both explanations, but the question of whether or not property and casualty insurers discriminated directly became a sticking point in debates over how to fix the problem. Was insurance redlining the result of blatant racial discrimination? Or were other factors at work? Should the industry be punished for violating civil rights laws? Or should it be offered incentives to distribute insurance coverage more equitably?

Though insurance redlining first received national attention during the late 1960s, it was not a new phenomenon. Civil rights organizations like the NAACP had been aware of discriminatory insurance practices for years. In the early 1940s, Thurgood Marshall, then a young lawyer for the NAACP, applied for auto insurance from the Travelers insurance company and was rejected. When Marshall issued a complaint to the company, a Travelers representative explained that his place of residence, Harlem, made his vehicle "too risky" to insure because of "traffic congestion," and insisted that the company's refusal to offer coverage had nothing to do with race.[59] Marshall, who eventually became a justice of the United States Supreme Court, began studying race-based insurance discrimination in auto and other fields, and even reached out to friends at the American Civil Liberties Union for assistance in tracking the problem. Though Marshall originally hoped to pursue litigation, he eventually moved on, concluding, "It is practically impossible to work out a court case because the insurance is usually refused on some technical ground."[60]

The insurance industry's response to complaints like Marshall's changed little over the next three decades. Property and casualty firms continued to deny insurance to nonwhite Americans, and they continued to defend those decisions on what Marshall called "technical ground," using supposedly impartial categories like congestion, crime rates, and age of buildings to justify discriminatory policies. The insurance industry's stance may not have changed, but the law eventually did. The Fair Housing Act of 1968, passed by Congress following the assassination of Dr. Martin Luther King Jr., prohibited discrimination based on race, religion, national origin, or sex in the sale, rental, and financing of housing. Though the language of the act did not mention insurance directly, many civil rights leaders felt confident that its broad prohibitions against racial discrimination would force insurance companies to provide homeowners and other forms of insurance coverage long denied to nonwhite Americans. Without this coverage, as the Hughes Panel noted, consumers could not secure mortgage loans and thus could not become homeowners—a situation clearly covered by the Fair Housing Act.

The insurance industry's response to the act set a pattern that would continue throughout the twentieth century and into the twenty-first. Claiming special status that exempted their industry from federal law, property insurers argued that the Fair Housing Act did not apply to their business and refused to change their policies. Insurance leaders based this claim on the state-based regulatory structure put in place by the passage of the McCarran–Ferguson Act in 1945. That act exempts the insurance industry from any federal law or act of Congress that threatens to "impair, invalidate, or supersede" existing state laws.[61] In response to this claim, civil rights lawyers and other critics of industry policies launched a decades-long battle to prove that (1) the Fair Housing Act does, in fact, apply to insurance, and (2) the McCarran–Ferguson Act does not exempt insurance companies from compliance with federal prohibitions against discrimination. As this battle raged in the courts, activists hoping to curtail insurance redlining considered their options.[62] To secure equal access to insurance, they would need to either abolish McCarran–Ferguson or mount campaigns in every state.

State-based activism posed several problems. Under McCarran–Ferguson, insurance companies actively "played" states against one another—states that passed legislation unwelcome by the industry faced the withdrawal of insurance companies to other states with more favorable laws.[63] Progressive insurance reforms passed by Wisconsin in 1958, for example, instigated the flight of twenty-three companies to nearby states, leading to substantial losses in jobs, investment capital, and tax revenue.[64] Hoping to provide a favorable business climate, many states imitated others that passed laws advantageous to the industry.[65] When New York passed the redevelopment law that allowed insurance companies to build housing complexes like Stuyvesant Town, for example, most other states in the nation quickly followed suit. To complicate matters further, representatives of the insurance industry made up the bulk of state regulatory bodies. Though this situation could lead to obvious conflicts of interest, insurance leaders and legislators defended the composition of regulatory bodies by citing the "technical demands" associated with insurance regulation. As one Illinois House committee member put it in 1974, "Insurance is technical as hell. We need somebody on [the regulatory committees] who has some vague idea of what's going on."[66]

Despite these challenges, anti-redlining activists forged ahead in their quest for equal access to insurance. Their efforts to solve the problem through state regulation, however, achieved only limited success. In response to activist pressure, regulators in Illinois considered adding redlining restrictions to state codes on numerous occasions throughout the early 1970s. In response to pending bills, several insurers withdrew from the state, including Parliament

Insurance Company, which provided the majority of the homeowners' policies in Chicago's North Side.[67] Illinois and other states did eventually pass
anti-redlining measures, but few of these new laws contained strong policing
mechanisms, and most were easy to evade. Insurance companies that faced
racial discrimination charges under state anti-redlining laws could cite any
number of legal justifications for not insuring specific properties, including
"age of residences," "traffic congestion," and other criteria unrelated to race.
Like Thurgood Marshall before them, anti-redlining activists in the 1970s
faced a "technical" wall that protected insurance companies from public efforts to change their practices.

SETTING THE TERMS OF THE DISCRIMINATION DEBATE: RISK VERSUS RACE

Insurers in all fields of the business agreed that federal regulation would damage the industry. Desperate to defend McCarran–Ferguson but unwilling to
overhaul profitable underwriting and risk-rating policies, property and casualty insurers bolstered their legal defense of redlining with a rhetorical argument that emphasized the objectivity and efficiency of their risk classification
structures. Moving early to set the terms of the debate over discrimination,
insurance companies insisted that they based underwriting decisions, which
determined price and availability of insurance, on risk, not race. As C. Robert Hall, vice president of the National Association of Independent Insurers,
insisted, "The insurance industry refrains from moral pronouncements. We
measure risk as accurately as we can, applying experience and objective criteria refined for more than two centuries. We leave it to others to speak of
discrimination and other such moral terms."[68]

Anti-redlining activists contested this stance, but not its framing. Convinced that overt discrimination was at play, activists accepted the objective,
apolitical nature of underwriting decisions based on risk, but insisted that
insurance companies secretly relied on subjective factors, particularly race,
when setting rates. As one critic of the industry wrote in 1970, "Contrary to
the insurance industry's claim that the unavailability of property insurance in
the ghetto is the result of risk/loss experience, race is the real factor that insurance companies use to set rates and terms or to deny insurance protection
altogether."[69] To expose the fallacy of insurer claims—and hold companies
liable under state laws that required evidence of intentional discrimination—
activists turned to research and social scientific methods in hopes of generating empirical data capable of contesting the industry's "risk, not race" stance.
By the mid-1970s, calls from critics of insurance for data supportive of their

own "race, not risk" argument had become common. "While the public controversy has raged, there has been virtually no empirical research directed to
resolving the underlying issues," one redlining analyst complained in 1978.[70]
These calls were eventually answered as activists dove into internal industry
literature, launched undercover investigations, and developed new methods,
like blind testing, in hopes of generating data capable of proving the industry's subjective bias.[71]

Critics looking for evidence of blatant racism in the insurance industry
experienced very little trouble finding it. A survey of insurance textbooks
conducted by one set of activists in 1979, for example, found that many included references to "morally objectionable neighborhoods," and warned
against insuring "demographically changing" areas.[72] Undercover investigations and interviews with industry workers produced more damning findings. In a tape-recorded conversation cited often in anti-redlining studies and
organizing materials, a Milwaukee sales manager for the American Family
Insurance Company admonished an agent:

> Your persistency went down the shitter. . . . Very honestly, I think you write
> too many blacks. . . . You gotta sell to good, solid premium-paying white peo-
> ple. . . . The only way you're going to correct your persistency is to get away
> from the blacks.[73]

Similar examples of racism within the industry could be found across the
country. In 1978, Harold Summers, the chief actuary of the New York State Insurance Department, justified redlining thusly: "Take Harlem, for example—
they don't need any insurance because they don't have anything of value to
insure."[74] This kind of obvious, overt racism generated calls for increased objectivity in insurance practice. Activists demanded that companies discon-
tinue use of "subjective and arbitrary" underwriting categories and instead
rely only on "statistically valid" criteria.[75]

As research commenced, critics of redlining turned to methods like blind
testing and detailed comparisons of insurance rates in different regions. They
found wide discrepancies in insurance availability and pricing that could not
be explained by objective criteria alone. Redlining critics used this research
to call into question the impartiality of insurance risk classifications and to
attract support for new underwriting guidelines based on accurate, authentic
data. Activists noted, for example, that "age of residence" was not a valid predictor of risk and hence should be understood as a subjective underwriting
category subject to fair housing legislation. The idea that city streets were
more congested than suburban ones—a justification for redlining offered by
many auto insurers—was similarly criticized for its subjectivity. Most of the

cars in urban areas, activists argued, actually belonged to suburban residents who drove into cities to work during daylight hours. The problem of "congestion" thus affected suburban and urban car owners equally, redlining critics argued, and should therefore not disproportionally affect the rates for premiums of urban residents.[76]

The activist strategy of questioning the industry's objectivity quickly developed into a game of cat and mouse. Insurance representatives cited statistical evidence to defend their decisions to restrict insurance availability in certain areas, and their critics responded with accusations of subjective practice—the use of biased classification categories that served as a proxy for race. In the stalemate that ensued, insurance companies continued to evade charges of discrimination and sidestep attempts to police anti-redlining laws. As activists noted, the success of the industry on this front had much to do with the dearth of legislation designed to monitor underwriting decisions made by insurance firms. As late as 1995, only four states (Illinois, Minnesota, Missouri, and Wisconsin) required geographic disclosure of policies at all, and those states required disclosure only on an aggregate zip-code level.[77] Without access to crucial industry data, critics had no way of challenging it.

Control of potentially damaging data played an important role in helping insurers evade charges of racial discrimination. Yet the industry's success in defending its practices also grew out of the rhetoric adopted by its critics. In turning the redlining problem into a question of accuracy and objectivity, activists unwittingly embraced the logic of their opponents. Anti-redlining activists did not, for example, call for the insurance industry to abandon risk classification systems that used place of residence as a category. Instead, they argued that insurers had used incorrect and inaccurate data to measure risk. By calling for newer, more accurate statistics, critics essentially confirmed the industry claim that objectivity could be achieved through risk rating, underscoring the usefulness and desirability of classifications based on the (supposedly objective) notion of risk.

Other strategies adopted by insurance critics led to similar problems. One particularly troubling argument advanced by activists in hopes of curtailing redlining cited the concept of "moral hazard"—an industry term that refers to the effects of being insured on individual behavior. Activists noted, for example, that many Black Americans had been systematically denied access to suburban housing and thus had no choice but to reside in urban centers. Pointing to this lack of choice, they claimed that the use of "arbitrary" risk classifications based on factors individuals could not change might prove harmful to the insurance industry itself. Individuals subject to arbitrary insurance pricing and coverage, activists warned, might lose the impetus to protect their property and gain a justification for fraudulent activity, including "arson for profit."[78] As Gregory Squires (one of the most prolific redlining analysts of the era) and colleagues argued in 1979, "One clear negative consequence of using territorial classifications . . . is that such a practice provides no incentives for customers to try to reduce losses."[79]

Insurance companies had claimed for decades that charging individuals different rates according to their projected exposure to risk helped condition those individuals to act more responsibly. This justification for risk classification schemes relied on the belief that people held financially accountable for their behavior would be less likely to act in risky ways. The idea that people needed insurance-based incentives to make them behave responsibly might seem cynical, but it went largely unchallenged throughout the postwar era and became a bulwark in insurers' defense of risk rating. In claiming that "arbitrary" risk classifications did not sufficiently promote conscious efforts to reduce loss and might even encourage fraud, critics of insurance inadvertently bolstered the industry's own defense of risk classification as a system. What's more, by embracing a moral hazard argument, activists reinforced an understanding of insurance as a governing technology necessary for the production of good, responsible, risk-averse citizens.

The ease with which insurers evaded redlining laws led many activists to seek alternate, and ultimately unsuccessful, strategies in their battle to equalize access to insurance and improve the lives of urban residents. By the late 1970s, many insurance critics began calling on the industry to voluntarily cease redlining and reinvest in "blighted" neighborhoods—a kind of UIP for property insurers. Some companies, either in the name of public relations or to avoid potentially costly lawsuits, invested millions of dollars in urban areas through participation in "community reinvestment" programs.[80] The Illinois-based property insurance company Allstate, for example, created a Department of Urban Affairs in the late 1970s and launched a widely celebrated urban investment program, designed to "create jobs in urban communities by providing expansion capital to minority businesses."[81]

This strategy, however, did not succeed in ending redlining or improving the lives of impoverished city residents. Instead, property and casualty industry "community reinvestment" programs simply replicated the failures of the life insurance industry's UIP. Companies that voluntarily reinvested in urban communities encouraged gentrification and promoted the relocation of long-term, low-income residents in order to "make room" for higher-income families and commercial spaces. Reinvestment efforts by property insurers, like the UIP before them, did not involve local communities and overwhelmingly benefited whites. Looking back in the mid-1990s, two decades after the creation of these "community reinvestment" programs, Squires criticized them as profit-making mechanisms for "the same insurance institutions that previously redlined neighborhoods . . . then profited from the financing of housing projects for higher income families and new commercial ventures."[82]

FAIR PLANS: CORPORATE RISK SHARING
AND THE CREATION OF TWO INSURANCE MARKETS

As attempts to end insurance redlining through the stick of regulation faltered, inequalities in insurance access continued to plague American cities. In an effort to solve insurance access problems in urban centers, activists and government leaders turned to incentives for the industry. Drawing on recommendations offered by the Hughes Panel, the federal government launched a net program designed to "catch" individuals and communities deemed "too risky" to insure by private companies. The Fair Access to Insurance Requirements (FAIR) program, instituted under the Urban Property Protection and Reinsurance Act of 1968, attempted to increase insurance availability by creating a shared market for "high-risk" property insurance in urban areas. Though supported by the federal government and subsidized by taxpayers, FAIR programs were not federally mandated—insurers and states could choose to participate on a voluntary basis. To encourage participation, the federal government promised to sell "riot reinsurance" to companies that took part in state-based FAIR programs. This reinsurance, sold through the Department of Housing and Urban Development, reimbursed insurance companies for any substantial losses caused by "riots and civil disorders" in urban centers where FAIR policies were sold.[83]

Although public in name, private insurance companies managed FAIR plans and used internal criteria to determine which insurance applicants would be selected for private coverage and which would be relegated to the "public," high-risk market. Participant companies agreed to share the cost of losses incurred under the program, paying for claims made by FAIR policyholders from a collective pool. This practice protected individual companies from shouldering the burden of insuring "bad risks" on their own. Notably, it also violated the free market principles endorsed for decades by industry leaders. Throughout the postwar era, insurance executives had shunned public insurance programs, and all forms of collective risk sharing, as socialism. These same leaders abandoned market-based principles and willingly accepted collective risk sharing *within* the industry when it benefited their business.

The federal government required that companies participating in the FAIR program make insurance accessible to all "responsible" property owners, regardless of the section of a city in which they lived. The government did not, however, stipulate specific rates or levels of coverage for FAIR policies. For this reason, FAIR plans uniformly provided less coverage, at higher premiums, and on worse terms than those offered on the private market. In Minnesota, FAIR rates were, on average, 25 percent higher than private ones; in Wisconsin, rates were 35 percent higher; in New York, the state that witnessed the most extreme discrepancies, FAIR rates reached as high as 250 percent higher than private rates.[84] One Brooklyn resident, dropped by a private provider in 1977, for example, saw her property insurance premiums rise from $60 to $583 a year under her new FAIR plan.[85] In addition to charging much higher premiums, FAIR policies generally offered only fire and vandalism, or "malicious mischief," coverage—a far cry from the extensive "umbrella" coverage offered by private homeowners policies. FAIR policyholders also reported much slower service when they placed claims, and were typically denied access to premium payment plans.[86] Efforts to correct inequalities in FAIR rates through legislative means achieved only limited success. The 1978 Holtzman Amendment, named for the redlining critic and New York Representative Elizabeth Holtzman, required equalization of private and public coverage, but was easily evaded by insurance companies, many of which chose to withdraw from voluntary FAIR plans after passage of the amendment.[87]

The inequalities that characterized public and private coverage led to criticism, but the insurance industry stood its ground, arguing that high rates for FAIR policies reflected the principles of "actuarial fairness," a new term embraced by the industry in the mid-1970s. Insurers depicted "actuarial fairness" as a necessary and valuable governing principle that prevented "good risks" from subsidizing "bad" ones. New York's FAIR manager, Richard Bruckner, expressed this view succinctly in 1977. "The bad risks should be made to pay," he quipped. "Nobody wants to pay for somebody else's insurance."[88] This clear attempt to mask the collective nature of risk spreading reflected a strategy the industry would turn to increasingly during the final decades of the twentieth century. By advancing the notion that some individuals and communities "deserved" to pay less for security than others, industry representatives infused their market-based underwriting decisions with a moral claim to fairness and perpetuated already existing disparities in wealth and status among Americans.

The creation of separate and unequal insurance markets, like "community reinvestment" programs, did not solve insurance access problems in American's cities. In fact, the control exercised by private insurers over FAIR plans often made these problems worse. By the late-1970s, insurance redlining had become a setback for a growing number of Americans, including those not living in traditionally low-income or minority neighborhoods. Under FAIR, property insurers began the practice of "advance redlining," which relegated "changing" neighborhoods to public markets in anticipation of demographic shifts.[89] This strategy ultimately affected more and more white consumers and communities as patterns of urban renewal and gentrification put higher-income populations in the path of insurance redlining. Residents of "rejuve-nated" and gentrifying neighborhoods in urban areas found that proximity to low-income districts increased their chance of being redlined into inferior public markets. As one "well to do" resident of Brooklyn's Park Slope, shocked at being refused access to the private property insurance market, declared in 1979, "If it could happen to me, it could happen to anyone."[90]

Although poor, nonwhite populations made up the vast majority of insur-ance redlining victims throughout the 1970s, the addition of small numbers of higher-income individuals to the ranks of the redlined toward the end of the decade reinvigorated public concern and drew mainstream media atten-tion to the problem. Notably, the upper- and middle-class property owners redlined into FAIR markets resorted to many of the same problematic argu-ments embraced by earlier critics of insurance redlining. Many, for example, cited the "inaccuracy" of industry calculations.[91] Interested more in regain-ing access to private markets than in challenging the basic principles of risk classification, these new redlining targets did not question the existence of inferior public programs like FAIR or the ethics of geographically dividing entire communities into "good" and "bad" risk pools. Instead, they sought to dissociate themselves from the "truly bad" risks that were thought to "belong" in the public market and insisted, as did earlier activists, that inaccurate cal-culations had placed them on the wrong side of the divide.[92]

By the end of the 1970s, the urban crisis—and the discriminatory insurance practices that helped create it—had not been remedied. Life insurers suc-ceeded in attracting enough government goodwill through the UIP to pre-vent passage of new laws that would force them to surrender control of their investment decisions. The UIP did not, however, repair the damage done to American cities by decades of disinvestment on the part of the industry. Af-ter discontinuation of the UIP, large life insurance companies continued to invest selectively in urban centers in the name of corporate social responsi-bility, and to preempt government initiatives through voluntary action. Like the UIP and later community reinvestment programs launched by property and casualty insurers, these projects did little to improve the condition of impoverished communities. More often than not, they helped blaze a path of gentrification that pushed low-income individuals and families out of long-time residences.

The property insurance industry's response to urban crisis and charges of redlining also failed to solve urban problems or end racial disparities in insurance access. The industry's successful dissemination of "risk versus race" discourse ultimately helped to blind Americans to the structural inequalities baked into insurance classification systems. Anti-redlining activists criticized the subjective, discriminatory practices of insurance companies, but they largely accepted the industry's claim that some people should pay more for insurance coverage than others, that "good risks" and "bad risks" exist as real entities in the world. During debates over redlining in the 1970s, both insurance companies and their critics argued that risk, if measured objectively, reflected a reality removed from political calculations. Few commenters from the period recognized the complicity of this stance with the justifications for redlining offered by private insurance providers. In 1983, however—several years after the most heated public debates over urban redlining—the legal theorist Regina Austin noted the problematic nature of many anti-redlining arguments, especially those based on the accuracy of risk-based classifications:

> Analysis reveals that accuracy either cannot be defined in a neutral, apolitical consensual fashion, or must be balanced against, and sometimes give way to, competing non-neutral considerations through a blatantly political process. . . . The predictive accuracy of the classification system and its political acceptability are thus inextricably bound.[93]

In pointing to the political nature of actuarial calculations and the impossibility of "accurate" or "objective" insurance risk classifications, Austin set herself apart from other redlining analysts. Her rare call to politicize risk itself represented a new approach to insurance discrimination, one that called for democratic participation in determining how best to distribute insurance and other vital social resources. Two decades into the twenty-first century, this approach has yet to find a wide audience.

Nonetheless, by the 1980s, debates over insurance risk rating—what Austin termed the "classification controversy"—had expanded beyond urban redlining and property and casualty insurance.[94] A new group of activists emerged during this period with new strategies for reforming and regulating the industry, and with new arguments that challenged the classification systems used by insurers to price and measure risk.

6

The Unisex Insurance Debate and the Triumph
of Actuarial Fairness

The 1970s was a decade of sweeping women's activism in the United States. The feminist movement reached its highest levels of participation during this era and achieved some of its most significant gains. Along with overhauling a host of deeply rooted cultural beliefs concerning appropriate roles for women and men, activists won important legal protections in reproductive and health matters, in the workplace, in education, and in other realms of social and political life. Despite the pace and extent of these transformations, some institutions failed to respond to the changing roles of American women and resisted their demands for equality. Looking back in 1977 on a decade of women's activism, United States Representative Yvonne Brathwaite Burke identified insurance as one such institution, an industry that lagged behind others:

> Despite the significant changes in the law prohibiting sex discrimination, there remain a number of areas in which women have made little progress in gaining equality. The insurance industry, because of its unique characteristics, remains a bastion of sex-based practices, which are deleterious to women. . . . There remains a need for instruments of change to engender a more widespread awareness of the insurance practices which discriminate against women.[1]

The "unique characteristics" Brathwaite Burke cited referred to the insurance industry's widespread use of sex as a risk classification category.[2] Insurance companies in all fields used sex to set rates and determine access to insurance products. The "sex-based practices" Brathwaite Burke cited referred to the equally widespread discriminatory treatment many women encountered in their interactions with industry representatives. Responding to calls like

Brathwaite Burke's, feminist activists turned their attention to insurance in the mid-1970s, identifying both sex-based risk classifications and sex-based industry practices as impediments to the achievement of social and economic equality for American women.

These activists joined an already extensive movement, launched in the 1960s, that sought to combat insurance discrimination. As discussed in chapter 5, insurance redlining became the subject of far-reaching social and legal activism following the urban uprisings of the late 1960s. Critics of redlining succeeded in attracting public attention to insurance discrimination but failed to secure legislation capable of changing industry practices or equalizing access to private insurance coverage. Feminist activists brought new energy, and new resources, to the movement against insurance discrimination. Building on methods developed by redlining critics, they conducted extensive research that uncovered rampant bias within the industry. They also launched grassroots organizing efforts and drew on existing political networks, developed over the course of the 1970s, to raise awareness of inequalities in insurance provision. Most important, feminist activists introduced new approaches to legislation, eventually turning to federal regulation as a means of combatting insurance discrimination.

As the women's movement shifted its focus to insurance, industry leaders struggled to contain the fallout and were forced to develop new strategies to defend their practices and resist unwanted regulation. Insurers had weathered the storm of late-1960s unrest, but now they faced a new and unpreceded challenge: a highly organized national movement with deep political resources and a widely accepted ideological platform. Feminist demands for social and economic equality threatened to fundamentally transform insurance practice, and no criticism hit the industry harder than claims from women's activists that actuarial risk classifications—seen by many as the very basis of private insurance systems—were themselves discriminatory.

This chapter explores public debates between the insurance industry and feminist activists during a period of profound social and political change in the United States. It begins in the mid-1970s and ends in 1983, a year that marked a turning point in public opinion against attempts to reform insurance industry classification structures, and the defeat of efforts launched by the women's movement to pass federal sex-blind, or "unisex," insurance legislation. While feminist activism from this period has been studied extensively, the challenges the women's movement posed to private insurance have not.[3] Yet debates between insurers and feminist activists during this era mark an important moment in the history of both the insurance industry and

American social activism. Criticism of insurance risk classifications based on "immutable" characteristics like sex sparked intense public debate over the relationship between actuarial systems and social order and justice. This criticism called into question the role of risk in constituting communities and the value of using statistical knowledge about populations as a means of distributing costs and benefits to individuals. The terms of these debates, and the strategies embraced by both sides, also reflected important changes in the meanings of fairness and equality in American life.

In their exchanges with the insurance industry, feminist activists deepened their understanding of the structural and economic forces that fed social inequality, and they responded by embracing bold legislative measures as paths to social change. Powerful liberal feminist groups like the National Organization for Women (NOW) led the charge in debates with the industry over insurance discrimination. Their efforts culminated in the early 1980s with the proposal of two federal bills—one in the House and one in the Senate—that would mandate unisex insurance access and pricing on the private market.[4] Both the insurance industry and large segments of the American population, however, resisted antidiscrimination insurance legislation. This opposition, and the resulting failure of feminists to reform insurance classification structures in the early 1980s, should not be understood as *only* the products of backlash against social movements or of the persistence of prejudice in American life.[5] Insurers grounded their widely accepted defense of risk classification systems in objective, statistical terms, and bolstered their case with market-based logics and an ideological claim to fairness.

This stance demands analysis. The public nature of the insurance discrimination debates in the late 1970s and early 1980s helped disseminate and popularize the notion of "actuarial fairness"—the pillar of the industry's defense of sex-based classification structures. Actuarial fairness (an ideological construct developed by the insurance industry) refers to the notion that individuals should pay for their own risks and not the risks of others. This understanding of fairness has become deeply embedded in American life since the conclusion of the unisex insurance debates. Examining the contexts in which actuarial fairness emerged and gained purchase in public discourse can help us understand why attempts to reform and regulate the insurance industry faltered during the final decades of the twentieth century. Perhaps more important, it might also help us make sense of the role played by private industry in fostering social fragmentation—the sense that Americans should be responsible for themselves and not for one another—and the long-term decline in public support for collective approaches to managing risk.

Origins of the Insurance Discrimination Debate

Leaders of the insurance industry have argued for the past half century that critics of their practices do not adequately grasp the nature of risk rating or its function within an insurance context. To combat this stance, and to better understand the challenges feminist activism posed to the insurance industry during the 1970s and 1980s, it is useful to review how risk classification systems work, and to outline the various strategies private insurance institutions have deployed over the course of the twentieth century to defend them.

By the postwar era, most insurance companies determined cost and availability of coverage by creating groups composed of individuals who were thought to share similar levels of risk exposure. Risk classification was the process used to create these insurance groups, or risk pools. First adopted systematically by insurance firms in the mid-nineteenth century, risk classification helped insurance companies assess and identify the probability of exposure to risk, or loss potential, of individual insurance consumers.[6] Once loss potential had been calculated, insurance companies grouped consumers into aggregate pools with others who shared a similar classification of projected risk. Notably, these aggregates did not reflect internal ties or shared experiences of members. Instead, insurers created risk pools by grouping individuals according to their proximity along a probabilistic curve that statistically charted a distribution of potential, abstract risks.

Classifying risk is an uncertain business. The kinds of data that insurance firms employed to do so changed over the course of the twentieth century as information about different populations became available through surveillance and other data-gathering efforts, and as social acceptance of various classification categories shifted. Drawing on new medical studies that showed a correlation between body type and longevity, for example, life insurance actuaries in the early twentieth century introduced the category of "build" to height and weight in classifications designed to chart mortality risk.[7] By the 1950s, in response to the threat of civil rights legislation, life insurers voluntarily removed race, a category used throughout the nineteenth century in similar calculations, from most actuarial tables.[8] Auto and homeowners insurance providers added a host of new categories to their risk-rating systems during that decade. Under new classification structures developed during the 1950s, property and casualty insurers sorted divorced and unmarried policyholders, considered "less stable" than married ones, into specialized pools. The creation of separate risk pools for suburban and urban residents—the subject of anti-redlining activism—also became common during the postwar years. As these examples suggest, the categories insurance companies used to create risk classifications throughout the twentieth century reflected changing political trends and social values, and not simply objective realities.

Insurers portrayed their calculations as objective and "scientific" to the general public, but within the industry, risk classifications were known to be, by their very nature, speculative. It simply cannot be proven conclusively or objectively who should pay how much to participate in a given insurance pool. All risk classifications are imprecise, but imprecision is necessary in order to preserve the risk-spreading function of insurance. Even if it were possible to create a perfect system of prediction, knowing the exact risk faced by each insured individual would effectively place every person in their own unique risk pool, negating the risk-spreading function and making everyone self-insured.[9] Recognizing these contingencies, insurance representatives argued throughout the second half of the twentieth century that broad groupings such as sex made the best classification categories because they could be fairly accurate (though never perfect) while still allowing for the spreading of risk across populations. Under this system, companies charged women and men different rates for different coverage. Women, for example, paid lower premiums for life insurance than men, because women, *as a group*, lived longer and cost less to insure over time. Following the same logic, insurers charged women higher premiums for health and disability insurance, because statistics showed that women, *as a group*, accessed medical services more frequently than men.

The use of broad group characteristics to sort and classify individuals—and determine their access to resources—violated deeply held social values cemented in the United States over the course of the twentieth century. A widespread belief that individuals should determine their own fates, for example, made safeguarding equality of opportunity and equal access to social resources central goals for American legal and political institutions throughout the postwar period. It is not surprising, given these commitments, that resistance emerged to practices that linked insurance pricing and availability to group factors over which individuals had little control. A person identified by an insurance company as a member of a "high-risk" group, for example, was forced to claim financial responsibility for that status within a risk classification framework, whether they "deserved" that status or not. "Low-risk" group membership, on the other hand, made one eligible for all the benefits of that group status, whether deserved or not.[10] If assessed on an individual rather than group basis, the immutable risk classifications used by insurance companies clearly discriminated against individuals in a process that violated the ideology of social equality. This stance became the platform on which feminist activists staged their critique of insurance risk classifications in the 1970s and early 1980s.

Risk classification and risk pooling allowed insurance companies to profit and compete in a market economy. The rapid growth of the industry after World War II led to fierce competition among various firms. Identifying and segregating insurance applicants likely to incur losses and make claims allowed companies to reduce the average cost of premiums charged for policies. Charging a lower price for insurance attracted more customers. If a competing company accepted the "bad risks" rejected by another insurance provider, that company might be forced to pay out more claims, increase the cost of premiums, and eventually lose business. Risk classification thus served an important function within the industry: it protected the assets and competitive positions of individual firms. Insurers argued that risk classification enhanced competition, and that competition benefited consumers because it lowered the average price of insurance premiums. Industry representatives also noted that reliance on difficult or costly-to-measure risk characteristics required more company resources and would ultimately lead to higher premiums for consumers. The use of "easily identifiable" group characteristics as classification categories, according to industry logic, thus served the public by controlling insurance costs across the board.[11]

When forced to defend problematic classification categories like geographic location or sex, insurers often turned to economic factors, and particularly efficiency and cost effectiveness. The industry's desire to be seen as a beneficent "public servant," however, required its representatives to offer less commercial justifications for risk-based rating as well. In debates with civil rights and feminist activists, for example, industry leaders and their supporters relied heavily on two rhetorical devices to validate their classification structures: "moral hazard" and "adverse selection." Insurers claimed that risk classification helped offset moral hazard—the notion that individuals take more risks when someone else bears the costs. Risk classification, they argued, could combat this potentiality by offering incentives to those who accounted for, and made efforts to lower, their exposure to risk. An insured car owner, by this logic, was impelled to drive more safely because she knew she would be placed in a "high-risk" pool (and pay higher premiums) if she received numerous speeding tickets or crashed her vehicle.

Insurers also claimed that risk pooling protected against adverse selection— the tendency of those who were likely to need insurance to buy it, while those less likely to need coverage opted out. By classifying risk, insurance providers could identify consumers with low loss potential and entice them to purchase policies with offers of cheaper premiums and better coverage than consumers with high loss potential, who were either denied coverage or forced to pay more. Though both moral hazard and adverse selection refer primarily to situations that negatively impact the *providers* of insurance products, postwar insurers successfully deployed these concepts to justify not only the proprietary pooling of risks (and the exclusion of some individuals from coverage), but also the notion that risk classification served a social good by incentivizing individual responsibility and loss prevention.[12]

The various strategies insurers used to defend risk rating over the course of the postwar era—claims of objectivity, market-based arguments citing economic necessity, and the principles of moral hazard and adverse selection—surfaced regularly in debates over insurance discrimination with feminists in the 1970s and early 1980s. As activists tackled each argument, they came face-to-face with an industry that accused them of not understanding their subject matter. Industry representatives regularly cited the grueling technicality of insurance practice in debates with feminists over discrimination. Defenders of the industry accused women who attempted to change insurance regulation—by calling for a federal framework, or for more public input in determining industry practice—of failing to grasp the basic features and functions of insurance as a system. Despite these claims, feminist activists forged ahead, confronting the industry's deep rhetorical arsenal with a formidable ideological weapon of their own: the principle of equality.

The stakes of the insurance discrimination debate, for both activists and the industry, were high. Failure to leverage a widespread public commitment to equality in exchanges with the insurance industry promised to endanger future efforts on the part of feminists to reform other social and economic institutions. The insurance industry, for its part, also entered into debates over discrimination with much to lose. Increased public interest in underwriting practices and risk classification structures could have easily led to the repeal of McCarran–Fergusson and the introduction of federal regulation. These fears led the insurance industry to respond to feminists' charges of discrimination with the full force of its powerful lobby. The industry's success in defending its risk classification structures should be understood as a product of the substantial political and economic power private insurers had come to wield over the course of the postwar era. The losses incurred by feminist activists in the fight for unisex insurance, however, also grew out of those activists' failure to set the terms of the debate—and a much broader shift in public opinion, away from socially determined definitions of equality and toward an acceptance of a market-based definitions of actuarial fairness.

"Sex Discrimination in Its Most Blatant Form":
Feminist Activism against Insurance Discrimination

Like anti-redlining activists who fought similar battles during this era, women's activists focused their early arguments against the insurance industry on charges of discriminatory treatment. In search of empirical evidence of discrimination, members of women's organizations pored over insurance underwriting manuals, textbooks, company publications, and state laws. They also conducted extensive interviews with insurance executives, industry workers, and female insurance consumers. As they dove into research on the industry, feminists found what they had become accustomed to finding in earlier sites of activism: stereotypes depicting women as temporary workers, discussions of women as "untrustworthy" and likely to dissemble, a lingering sense that women were incapable of making financial decisions for themselves, and the persistent belief that women depended on male providers for their livelihoods.

Research conducted in 1977 by the DC-based Women's Equity Action League (WEAL), for example, revealed that many insurance representatives treated women as a homogenous group of nonworkers dependent on their husband's wages and employment benefits. These assumptions, WEAL argued, led to a number of overt discriminatory practices, including denial of disability insurance to women who worked at home, refusals to offer increased coverage in the event of marriage or the birth of a child (coverage commonly offered to men), and exemption of conditions unique to women, like pregnancy, from health and disability coverage. Insurance companies justified this particular practice on the grounds that pregnancy was a "voluntary" condition and therefore not eligible for coverage under disability policies. WEAL's research, however, revealed that many of the same insurance firms that refused to cover pregnancy offered extensive coverage for "voluntary" male procedures, like vasectomies.[13]

Other studies conducted by women's activists uncovered highly subjective, discriminatory language in industry literature. Underwriting manuals examined in 1976 by members of North Carolina's Task Force on Sex Discrimination in Insurance, for example, included numerous prohibitions against insuring unmarried individuals.[14] Prohibitions pertaining to divorced insurance applicants cited "change in lifestyle which may be productive of poor risk experience" and warned that "persons who are not married should be closely underwritten."[15] Prohibitions on single and divorced individuals, feminists argued, disproportionately affected unmarried women and single mothers—those women most in need of insurance protection. Activists also discovered that many underwriting materials addressed women specifically. In a 1973 congressional hearing on insurance discrimination, for example, Barbara Shack, assistant director of the New York Civil Liberties Union, cited a North American Reassurance Company manual from the early 1970s. The manual informed agents that "women's role in the commercial world is a provisional one—they work not from financial need but for personal convenience."[16] It also warned agents that women could not be trusted, and were likely to commit insurance fraud. "The subjective circumstances which create 'convenience' tend to change," the manual read, "and if a woman has disability coverage, the temptation exists to replace her earnings with an insurance income once work loses its attractiveness."[17] Feminists denounced the overt sexism of such claims and demanded that specific references to women as a "moral hazard risk" be removed from training materials and underwriting guidelines.

Feminists linked discriminatory language in industry literature to failures on the part of insurance companies to provide insurance coverage to women. Subjective prejudice, they argued, fed fears among sales agents and underwriters that women would abuse or defraud the insurance system and led directly to the industry's refusal to provide coverage advocated by women's activists but rarely offered by private insurers—including pregnancy, childbirth, and homemakers insurance. As activists dug further into industry literature, they publicized their findings. The feminist publication *Ms.* magazine, for example, ran several articles criticizing the industry throughout the 1970s.[18] These articles, along with "workshop guides" and other organizing materials produced by women's organizations, helped attract widespread public interest in insurance discrimination.

THE FEMINIST CRITIQUE OF SEX-BASED RISK CLASSIFICATIONS

Though documenting the discriminatory language in insurance literature and the discriminatory treatment of women by industry representatives remained a focus for feminist activists well into the 1980s, by the late 1970s the women's movement had shifted much of its energy to the more abstract question of the industry's use of sex as a risk classification. Arguments posed by critics of sex-based rating rested on the notion that women should not be treated differently from men in legal, political, economic, or other realms of American life. These claims, successful elsewhere, faltered in the sphere of insurance, a field that specialized in ascertaining and categorizing difference. Not only could the insurance industry claim discrimination as one of its fundamental principles, but insurers also argued that they discriminated for the public good, using fair and objective statistical evidence to do so. Hoping to call into question the objectivity of the industry, feminists responded to these claims by launching a public debate over the accuracy of statistical evidence used by insurers to classify and measure risk. Similar to earlier debates between insurers and anti-redlining activists over the validity of urban property and casualty ratings, the sex classification debate began with an assault on the authenticity, precision, and objective application of data used by insurers to measure risk.

Anti-redlining activists in the 1960s and 1970 had based their charges of discrimination in insurance on the claim that geographical location worked as a proxy for race in actuarial classifications. Unlike race, sex was used openly and extensively by private insurers as a category for classifying risk. NOW and other women's groups cited this discrepancy to call sex-based classifications into question, drawing comparisons between the industry's treatment of race and its treatment of sex. Noting that insurance companies had ceased using race as an underwriting category decades earlier, women's activists asked why companies were unwilling to cease treating sex as a class as well.[19] Drawing clear connections between racial and sexual discrimination, the authors of a workshop guide on sex discrimination in insurance proclaimed: "Race has also been used as a factor to classify risks, although custom now forbids this. It is interesting to note that the industry justified race as a classification factor on the same grounds that it presently defends sex; that is, that race as a factor was not discrimination because it was dictated entirely by actuarial findings."[20]

As feminists made comparisons between race and sex in their critique of insurance discrimination, industry supporters jumped at the chance to launch a divisive public debate over the nature of gender difference. Barbara Lautzenheiser, chair of the Committee for Fair Insurance Rates (an industry group formed with the explicit goal of combatting charges of sex discrimination), for example, challenged activists who aligned race and sex in their criticisms of risk classifications. "Mortality differences between whites and nonwhites have narrowed, and any remaining differences are still attributable to socioeconomic factors," she argued. "Sex, on the other hand, is an accurate predictor of mortality, and differences between sexes cannot be explained merely as lifestyle factors. . . . There is a wealth of scientific evidence that women are simply biologically superior to men."[21] Some feminists contested the essentialist approaches to sex and gender offered by insurance representatives like Lautzenheiser. Noting that recent changes in law, society, and culture had altered the lives of American women, they argued that differences between the sexes had decreased to such an extent that existing risk classification structures no longer captured lived realities. Others accepted the notion that essential differences existed between the sexes, but maintained that the industry's use of sex as a classification category violated social definitions of equality. Nearly all feminist critics of the industry agreed with Marsha Levick, executive director of NOW's Legal Defense Education Fund, who argued that the industry's use of sex-based classifications constituted "sex discrimination in its most blatant form."[22]

In their fight against the industry, feminist activists gravitated toward auto insurance and life insurance—two fields where sex played a primary role in setting rates. Auto insurance companies had relied for decades on three central underwriting categories: age, marital status, and sex. Insurance firms introduced age as an underwriting category in the early 1950s. This change reflected statistical findings, gathered through surveillance efforts discussed in chapter 2, that identified drivers under the age of twenty-five, and young men in particular, as a more likely to crash their vehicles and make claims. Companies added marital status and parenthood as criteria during the same period to differentiate these younger drivers. Drawing on the social belief that married people were more stable and responsible than their peers, insurers charged unmarried policyholders higher rates than married ones. Underwriters during this era also argued that unmarried, cohabiting couples (referred to in industry literature as "mingles") were irresponsible, and that divorcees were suspect drivers, claiming that "divorce generates emotional turmoil that may lead to problems on the road."[23] Auto insurers added sex to rating structures in the 1950s as well, charging men more than women for insurance coverage on the logic that women drove the family car less frequently and were subject to "the restraining influence of family responsibility or parental supervision."[24] Feminist activists cited these claims as evidence that the so-called "objective" calculations employed by insurers were, in fact, highly subjective and laden with prejudice. Classifications based on sex and marital status reflected outdated social beliefs, they argued, not objective realities or true differences between women and men.

Women as a group paid less on average than men for auto premiums—a fact that eventually harmed the feminist case against the industry. Activists nonetheless seized on auto insurers' subjective use of statistical data in order to call into question the accuracy and consistency of industry risk calculations. Levick, for example, asked why women paid less on auto insurance before the age of twenty-five but not in later life, if the industry's argument for charging women hinged on their overall lower mileage and accident rates. "If the industry were to better utilize mileage as a basis for setting premium rates," she argued, "women would in fact pay less throughout their lifetimes."[25] This critique succeeded in highlighting inconsistencies in the ways insurers wielded data. By suggesting that insurers should better utilize or collect more accurate data by sex, however, critics like Levick essentially confirmed the value of risk classification and the existence of a "statistical truth" about women as a group.

Debates over sex-based classifications in life insurance (where women also paid less on average than men) and annuities (where they paid more) took a similar tone. The question of longevity, cited often as "irrefutable" proof that women are biologically different from men, became a touchstone in public discussions of sex discrimination in insurance. Insurers justified discrepancies between annuity and life premiums for men and women on the grounds that women, as a group, live longer. Some feminists, however, disputed this claim, pointing to the lack of solid data on the *actual* mortality rates of women, and the haphazard ways in which existing data was applied in rate setting. "Life insurance rates are clearly not based on any principle reflecting true life expectancy differentials," argued Marcia Greenberger, an attorney for the National Women's Law Center. After comparing the rates of the ten largest insurance companies, Greenberger found that a standard policy would cost a forty-five-year-old woman anywhere from 8–67 percent less than it would cost a forty-five-year-old man, a statistical gap she argued offered proof of gross inconsistency in underwriting.[26]

Other women's activists disputed the claim that women live longer than men, arguing that longevity statistics reflected social, not biological, realities. The authors of a nationally distributed workshop guide on sex discrimination in insurance, for example, argued that no "actual data" existed on the life expectancies of men and women who "have been employed outside of the home most of their lives," and suggested the higher longevity rates attributed to all women were true only for those who did not work outside the home.[27] Still others argued that small numbers of "long-lived" women, rather than all women as a group, were responsible for skewing gender-based longevity statistics. Employing what became known as the "overlap theory," the president of WEAL, Mary Gray, reasoned:

> While the "average woman" dies later than the "average man," considerable overlap exists in the distribution of death ages. If at a single point in time we were to pick at random 1000 men age 65 and 1000 women age 65, and follow them through and observe their death ages, we would find an overlap of 84 percent. This means that we could match up 84 percent of the men with 84 percent of the women as having an identical year of death. This leaves 16 percent of the population, consisting of the 8 percent who are men who die relatively early, unmatched by women's deaths, and 8 percent who are women who die relatively late, whose deaths are unmatched by male deaths.[28]

The question, according to proponents of the overlap theory, was how to equitably distribute the financial burden of small numbers of long-lived women. Most feminist critics of insurance risk rating agreed that the principle of social equality demanded that policyholders of both sexes, not simply the shorter-lived women, should bear those costs.

Arguing under the banner of individual equality, many liberal feminists called on the insurance industry to voluntarily replace sex as an underwriting category with criteria based on nonimmutable behavioral conditions that individuals could control. "Rates should be based on appropriate criteria: driving record, smoker/non-smoker, high-stress job, etc. not on the gender of a person," argued Jacqueline Zachary, Connecticut coordinator for NOW.[29] Life insurers had been using data of this nature (and especially data related to policyholder smoking habits) for years. In the face of feminist criticism, however, industry representatives responded that behavioral classifications would be costly to measure and would require invasive surveillance of policyholders. Insurers also noted that such classifications were "subjective" and could change over time. A smoker might not always be a smoker, insurers claimed, but a woman? Well, presumably that wouldn't change.[30]

Feminists responded by claiming that even if women were always going to be women, what it means to be a woman, and the risks associated with that category, *do* change. On this platform, they called for refined classifications that reflected the new and changing roles of women in American life— their increasing presence in the workforce, and their embrace of traditionally "masculine" habits, behaviors, and lifestyles. Women might live longer "statistically" for social reasons, they argued, not biological ones. Women smoked and drank alcohol more than they had in the past; they drove more miles in their cars, and had fewer children. All these new factors, activists argued, might change women's risk portfolio as a group. Thus, more data was needed—data that wasn't so old and outdated. The National Commission on the Observance of International Women's Year, for example, argued that "recent, actuarially sound data be used to justify premiums and rates, rather than the decades-old, notoriously outmoded data that companies now use."[31] The commission, along with other women's groups, argued that insurers should use newer and more refined data that would allow them to measure women more carefully in order to better assess their "actual" risks. This stance, once again, confirmed the usefulness and virtues of sex as a classification category—so long as insurers used sex-based data objectively. Like earlier arguments embraced by anti-redlining activists, feminist calls for more behavioral data bolstered the industry's claim that insurance classifications served as a responsibilizing force necessary to protect against moral hazard.

THE TURN TO FEDERAL LEGISLATION

As feminists refined their arguments against sex-based classifications in debates with the insurance industry during the late 1970s, many women's organizations began calling for legislative solutions to insurance discrimination. Convinced that insurance companies would not voluntarily eliminate sex-based rating—and familiar with the industry's penchant for evading state laws—leaders of NOW, WEAL, and other large feminist organization opted to push for federal legislation. Two developments sparked this bold move. The first was the groundbreaking 1978 United States Supreme Court ruling in *City of Los Angeles Department of Water and Power v. Manhart,* a case generated out of years of feminist efforts to uncover and litigate instances of sex-based discrimination in the workplace.[32] The decision, argued under Title VII of the Civil Rights Act of 1964, prohibited employers from charging women and men different monthly premiums for pensions offered through group employer plans. Justice John Paul Stevens delivered the majority opinion in the case, concluding, "Practices that classify employees in terms of religion, race, or sex preserve traditional assumptions about groups, rather than thoughtful scrutiny of individuals."[33] The court's decision effectively prohibited the use of sex as a classification category in group employee benefits—a major win for critics of sex-based rating structures. Stevens was careful to note, however, that the ruling did not apply to private insurance or annuity policies sold outside the employment context, citing "the potential impact which changes in rules affecting insurance and pension plans may have on the economy."[34] Though only a partial victory, the *Manhart* ruling encouraged feminists to push for legislation that would extend beyond benefits offered through employer plans and bring about equal rates for individual policies sold on the private market.

The impending defeat of the Equal Rights Amendment (ERA) provided a second impetus that spurred women's activists to focus their energies on federal insurance legislation. The ERA had monopolized organizing efforts by the women's movement since its passage by the House and the Senate in 1972. In order to become law, the ERA needed to pass a ratification threshold of thirty-eight states before its expiration in 1979. Opposition to the ERA had mounted over the course of the 1970s, and by 1977 state ratifications had stalled, falling just three short of the required threshold. NOW and other women's groups successfully appealed to Congress, which granted the ERA an extension of several years. Despite massive lobbying efforts, countless rallies, fundraisers, pickets, and coordinated acts of civil disobedience on the part of women's activists, the ERA failed to achieve the three necessary state ratifications by the final deadline of June 1982.

The defeat of the ERA—the primary focus of feminist activism and organizing for a decade—was a devastating loss for the women's movement. Though historians typically credit the amendment's defeat to anti-feminist activists like Phyllis Schlafly and to a general rightward shift in American politics, many participants in the women's movement at the time, including leaders of NOW, placed the blame on "business interests," and on the insurance industry in particular. Feminist publications like *Ms.*, for example, published scathing attacks on "big business groups like insurance," whose "vested economic interests" in the outcome of the ERA led them to form "covert special interest groups" designed to defeat the amendment.[35] As the final deadline for the ERA approached, NOW purchased full-page advertisements criticizing the industry in the nation's largest newspapers, including the *New York Times*, the *Los Angeles Times*, and the *Washington Post*. These ads accused insurance leaders of "working to block attempts to prohibit sex discrimination" and behind-the-scenes lobbying to kill the ERA.[36] At a press conference held shortly after the ERA's expiration, the president of NOW, Eleanor Smeal, voiced an opinion that had become common among women's activists, claiming that "corporate influence" was behind "the male legislators who cast the final votes" in key states like Florida, Illinois, and North Carolina.[37] Smeal added that "corporate interests that profit from discrimination" contributed heavily to political campaigns of the amendment's opponents.[38]

The success of the *Manhart* decision and the failure of the ERA offered feminist activists hope regarding the prospects of legislation aimed specifically at insurance—and a grudge to settle with the industry. In January 1983, NOW and a handful of other women's organizations—"eager to re-heat the hot potato," as one conservative journalist put it—helped introduce to the House and the Senate two federal bills that would prohibit insurers in all fields of the industry from using sex-based classifications to calculate risk and price policies.[39] These "unisex" bills, deemed "the most hotly contested consumer and civil rights issue in years" by the *New York Times*, attracted allies across the political spectrum, drawing support from Democrats and Republicans alike—all eager to address what was called at the time the "gender-gap" problem by placing their names on a bill that supported women.[40] Proponents included women's, consumer, civil rights, and labor organizations. NOW was a particularly strong supporter of the bills and organized pickets of insurance company offices around the nation, where activists chanted the slogan, "Life, health, and auto insurance, too! Sex discrimination is bad for you!"[41] Like the ERA before them, both unisex bills were initially expected to pass with ease.

The Insurance Industry's Campaign against Unisex Insurance Legislation

Insurance leaders viewed feminist criticism of sex-based rating as a fleeting "compensatory crusade" following the loss of the ERA, and many assumed that the clamor would blow over in time.[42] When the House unisex insurance bill attracted 125 cosponsors upon its introduction to Congress, however, the industry panicked. Fearing an assault on the McCarran–Ferguson Act via the introduction of federal regulation, property and casualty insurance lobbyists in Washington quickly offered to compromise and assist in shaping the new legislation to avoid harm to the industry. After a group of life insurance executives vowed to fight the bills, however, this compromise was withdrawn, angering many congressional representatives.[43] Convinced they could defeat the bills, industry leaders swiftly mounted a skillfully developed public relations effort designed to sway public opinion against unisex insurance rating.

During the early months of 1983, individual companies joined forces with industry trade organizations and state insurance regulators in launching a national grassroots campaign opposing the bills.[44] Several companies, including GEICO, Nationwide, Cigna, and Aetna, turned to advanced direct-mailing technology (and their extensive consumer databases) to send millions of letters to policyholders, employees, and stockholders in targeted congressional districts, asking them to contact their representatives in opposition to the bills. The Travelers Indemnity Company sent letters to female policyholders, at the rate of twenty-three thousand a day, warning of increased premiums if the bills should pass. Trade organizations, including the Independent Insurance Agents and Brokers of America and the American Insurance Association—along with the two largest state regulatory associations, the National Association of Insurance Commissioners and the National Conference of Insurance Legislators—actively lobbied against the unisex bills on Capitol Hill. The American Council of Life Insurers (ACLI), an organization that absorbed the ILI in 1974 and represented 590 independent life insurance companies, distributed advertising kits to each of its member firms. These kits included sample full-page advertisements designed for publication in national and regional newspapers. The Aetna Life and Casualty Company published dozens of such notices in papers across the country, titled "Our Case for Sex Discrimination" (fig. 6.1). Drawing on a reserve of over $400,000 budgeted for anti-unisex advertisements alone, the ACLI published similar ads in twelve of the nation's largest newspapers. The ads read:

> Women live longer than men.
> Congress shouldn't penalize them because they do.
> A bill is moving through Congress that will force single men to buy maternity benefits for themselves in their health insurance.
> A bill is moving through Congress that will force most women to pay more for insurance. That's not *fair*.[45]

Our case for sex discrimination.

Sex no longer determines who, if anyone, wears the pants. So why, a lot of you are demanding, should it determine insurance rates?

Consider the nearly double crack-up rate of male drivers 25 and under versus female drivers 25 and under.

Suppose we at Ætna Life & Casualty ignored this statistical reality. Sister Sue would pay 40% more for auto insurance so Brother Bob could pay 20% less. Unfair!

Now let's sauce the gander. Say we had unisex insurance rates. Collective Bobs would more than chivalrously pay for collective Sues' annuities, since women live to collect longer. *Equally* unfair!

Accusations of Neanderthalism aside, Ætna simply isn't going to toss out cost differences based on criteria like sex and age when the results would be inequitable.

But we *do* have squads of experts studying the impact of changing life patterns on auto, life, and other insurance. And ongoing analysis has already eliminated some risk criteria and instituted others, including *factors you control personally.*

Example: We give young driver-training graduates an average 12.3% discount. And we now reduce individual life premiums for non-smokers.

That's fairer, we think, than changes that would make insurance *less* affordable for a lot of us — men and women alike.

Ætna wants insurance to be affordable.

FIGURE 6.1. Aetna Life and Casualty advertisement emphasizing the fairness of sex-based risk classifications as tools for pricing and determining access to insurance products. Insurance companies and industry professional organizations used marketing campaigns like this one to turn public opinion against legislation designed to prohibit sex discrimination in insurance. (Aetna Life and Casualty Insurance Company, "Our Case for Discrimination," 1983, private possession of author.)

In a study examining the industry's anti-unisex lobbying campaign, the consumer rights organization Common Cause estimated that these ACLI ads reached more than 5.6 million people.[46]

The industry's economic argument against unisex bills, laid out in widely distributed marketing materials, rested on two key factors: the cost of the legislation to American women, and its cost to the industry. Industry supporters pointed out that while women might benefit "abstractly or ideologically" from unisex insurance, they would "pay for these intangibles in cold cash."[47] The American Academy of Actuaries estimated that the bills would annually increase the national average cost of women's life insurance by $360 million and the cost of women's auto insurance premiums by $700 million, while rates for women's health and disability insurance would decrease only $69 million and $37 million, respectively.[48] Some feminists contested these figures. Others responded that they were willing to pay. As Johanna Mendelson, director of public policy for the American Association of University Women, claimed, "We may have to pay a price for equality, but it will eventually even itself out."[49]

Along with warning against the negative impacts of unisex legislation on female consumers, industry representatives also argued that the bills might bankrupt small companies and produce billions of dollars in debt for state and local government agencies. The Academy of Actuaries estimated that the administrative costs of complying with the bills could be as high as $1.3 billion.[50] The ACLI painted a more disastrous picture, warning that the unisex bills—which they claimed would require companies to equalize women's benefits to match men's—would immediately cost the industry $14.5 billion and bankrupt an untold number of firms.[51] Responding to these figures and fearing their implications for the national economy, one journalist echoed the sentiments expressed in Justice Stevens's opinion in the *Manhart* case, concluding, "The good reasons to eliminate sex discrimination in insurance do not justify reckless damage to the insurance industry."[52]

Insurance leaders did not rely solely on dire economic forecasts in their efforts to defeat the unisex bills. They also consistently returned to the concept of actuarial fairness in their speeches, interviews, direct mailings, and advertisements. The anti-unisex ads produced by Aetna and the ACLI provide examples of this trend. Both campaigns avoided discussion of equality and instead repeatedly emphasized fairness. Here and in other venues, insurers admitted they discriminated, but demanded that they did so *fairly*, in a way they claimed served the public good. Sex-blind classifications, supporters of the industry argued, were *unfair* because they would force both men and women to pay more than they should, to bear the cost of risks that were not their own.[53] To support this claim, defenders of sex-based rating turned often to the language of subsidy. "Once it becomes obvious that one group is subsidizing another, the free market won't support the policy anymore," insisted a representative of the ACLI. "Women shouldn't pay what amounts to a 7–8-year subsidy for men with a shorter life span. It's like charging someone with healthy life habits the same rates as an overweight, alcoholic, chainsmoking trapeze artist. It won't sell."[54] The widespread public acceptance of this rhetoric, which combined a market-based justification for discrimination with a critique of subsidy linked to fairness, remains one of the more lasting and profound legacies of the unisex insurance debate.

Industry lobbying efforts intensified as the bills neared consideration in the House and Senate, leading to charges of foul play by unisex insurance proponents. Oregon Senator Bob Packwood, a Republican and leading supporter of the bills, declared that he was "absolutely infuriated" by the industry's "inaccurate" publicity campaign. Barbara Bergmann, a University of Maryland professor of economics and former economic adviser to President John F. Kennedy, reminded voters and representatives that "the insurance industry does not come to this debate with a good record on women's issues." Berg-mann accused the industry of treating women with contempt, and warned the public to be wary of "a profit-making industry that attempts to portray itself as a truer champion of women's economic welfare than women's rights organizations." She added that insurers were "fighting to keep old ladies on low pensions."[55]

Despite such accusations, the insurance industry's warnings about the potentially catastrophic economic effects of the bills—and its portrayal of actuarial fairness as a social good—succeeded in tempering congressional enthusiasm for unisex legislation. The bills, given a "better than even" chance of passage by *Time* magazine in June 1983, were dead in the water by the end of the year.[56] In hopes of keeping public attention focused on sex discrimi-nation in insurance, NOW pursued lawsuits against individual companies throughout the 1980s. In 1987 the organization led a $21 million class action suit against Metropolitan, charging that the firm had violated New York's hu-man rights laws by using sex in setting rates. The appeals court ruled that the practice was justified. A year later, NOW lost a similar suit against Mutual of Omaha. Continuing efforts by feminists to pass unisex legislation in the states made little progress. In 1987 alone, twelve states considered unisex in-surance legislation, but none of these bills advanced beyond initial hearings. By the end of the decade, Massachusetts and Montana were the only states in the nation with unisex insurance laws in place. The Massachusetts law was repealed, with insurance industry backing, in 1991.[57] Though women's groups "appeared to have the strength of conviction to ensure an underwriting revo-lution," one industry analyst reflected in 1995, looking back at a decade of failed attempts to end sex-based insurance rating, "the reformers may have underestimated their opponents."[58]

The debate over sex discrimination and sex-based classifications in in-surance ended in much the same way as debates over insurance redlining in the 1960s and 1970s. Insurance critics in both cases succeeded in attract-ing substantial public attention to discrimination in insurance, but failed in establishing legislative frameworks capable of transforming industry un-derwriting practices. Both efforts to reform the nation's system of insurance provision failed in the face of vigorous resistance from private industry. No-tably, both movements against insurance discrimination also foundered on criticisms that activists leveled against risk classifications. Anti-redlining and anti-sex-discrimination activists challenged insurance risk classifications by calling into question their accuracy and objectivity and by demanding that *particular* classifications were unfair or unjust. Their failure to identify the measurement of risk itself as a political act prevented activists in the 1970s and 1980s from addressing the true root of discrimination in insurance: the actuarial logic itself.

Risk Classification and Collective Organization

The debate over unisex insurance initiated a sustained discussion in the public sphere about insurance risk classification. Throughout 1983, coverage of the bills and their potential impacts appeared in the pages of national and local newspapers, in major magazines, and on network television news segments. As Americans debated the value and costs of unisex insurance legislation, they encountered aspects of insurance practice rarely discussed in public venues. The conversation that ensued required Americans to assess the ability of private corporations to fairly distribute resources and determine who deserved security and how much they should pay for it. The industry's success in setting the terms of the debate over risk rating during this crucial moment of public awareness mattered immensely. Its campaign to defeat unisex insurance legislation revealed the tremendous power private insurers could wield, when motivated, over public opinion and policy. Perhaps more important, the public's acceptance of industry rhetoric also signaled a waning commitment to equality as a social good, and a growing acceptance of market-based definitions of fairness in American life.

While many unisex insurance proponents contested sex-based classifications on the grounds that they were old or inaccurate, others made arguments based on principle, not practice. For the liberal feminists who led debates with the industry, sex-based risk calculations violated the principles of equal opportunity and individual advancement. These feminists contended that risk classifications based on immutable characteristics reproduced already existing social hierarchies, and then projected them into the future. An individual identified by actuaries as a "bad risk" would not only have to bear that designation in the present, they would also be classed as a "bad risk" perpetually. The blindness of insurance classification to the constructed and changeable nature of gender, activists claimed, created and reinforced impediments to individual mobility and advancement.

This liberal, individual-centered argument echoed the decision of the US Supreme Court in the 1978 *Manhart* ruling, as well as a similar ruling by the court in July 1983. The court's decision in *Arizona Governing Committee v. Norris* prohibited employers from offering retirement plans that provided men and women with unequal benefits. Justice Thurgood Marshall delivered the majority opinion in the case. Himself a victim of insurance redlining,

Marshall had been interested in risk-based discrimination for decades. He concluded in his *Norris* opinion, "Even a true generalization about class cannot justify class-based treatment. An individual woman may not be paid lower monthly benefits simply because women as a class live longer than men."[59] The inability of feminist activists to find traction with this rhetoric when attempting to regulate insurance sold on the private market raises important questions about the ability of rights-based claims based on equality to compete with market-driven justifications for sorting groups and distributing resources. What's more, by enshrining the individual, feminist activists may have unintentionally called into question strategies used in other fields of legal activism that privileged group affiliation—and membership in legally defined "suspect classes"—as tools for achieving social advancement for women and minorities (affirmative action, for example).[60]

Feminist critics of insurance classification were caught in a bind—one that ensnared other liberal-oriented social activists during the final decades of the twentieth century as well.[61] In the insurance discrimination debates, critics of industry risk classifications were forced to either highlight the injustice of treating individuals on the basis of group status, or to bargain for a better position within an insurance context for women specifically as a group. Neither strategy called for the elimination of an insurance system that dictated, without public input, who received access to essential forms of security. Feminists also failed to directly challenge the industry's claim that actuarial fairness was possible or desirable. Once insurers were granted their own unique definition and claim to fairness, the application of social legislation in the name of equality became nearly impossible.

By the final decades of the twentieth century, private insurance had become a primary provider of economic security for most Americans. The only competitor was the state, which became an "insurer of last resort" through programs (often administered and controlled by private insurers) designed to "catch" those individuals and communities deemed "too risky" for participation in the private market. These public insurance mechanisms often provided inferior service and less coverage than private ones, at rates that were in some cases exorbitantly higher, as was the case with FAIR homeowners plans. The rise of separate and unequal insurance markets allowed a private, profit-driven industry to become largely responsible for controlling access to an essential service that many considered a basic right. Insurers used this leverage to avoid unwanted regulation, claiming that social legislation banning certain practices would be too costly and might lead to widespread insolvency—a "too important to regulate" argument, similar to the "too big to fail" rhetoric that permeated debates over how to solve the national banking crisis of 2008. Not surprisingly, in the face of these arguments, resistance to insurance industry practices became difficult.

But resistance to risk classification was impeded for other reasons too—ones more closely linked to the governing nature of insurance and actuarial systems. As Jonathan Simon has argued, risk classifications do not simply identify (or misidentify, as some activists argued) the world as it exists; they also actively construct that world, and they do so according to the interests of those who wield them.[62] Insurance systems that classify risk are inherently conservative in the sense that they preserve the status quo by maintaining the economic and social status levels held by individuals before a misfortunate event. Under risk classification systems, some people have to pay more than others to enter a risk pool, and others cannot enter at any price—thus, argues Tom Baker, "insurance institutions not only maintain status, they also assign it."[63] Risk classifications, in their emphasis on individual responsibility, help "persuade people that the purpose of insurance is individual protection and, accordingly, that the insurance group [or risk pool] is a collection of individuals without any responsibility to one another."[64] As Simon and Baker suggest, actuarial insurance systems wear an ideological veil that masks their collectivism: in the United States during the twentieth century, insurance, an inherently collectivist activity, effectively promulgated and reinforced atomized individualism.

This shrinking sense of responsibility to others was bolstered by the insurance industry's insistence in the 1970s and 1980s that its risk classification systems were "actuarially fair." Yet despite insurer claims of objectivity, "actuarial fairness" is at its heart a deeply subjective and moral concept, what Baker calls "a watered-down form of liberalism that privileges individual interests over the common good and that privileges, above all, the interests of insurance institutions organized on its terms."[65] Internal ties and external experience—the tools through which humans have formed groups for centuries—are useless to, and often attacked by, actuarial mechanisms. These mechanisms separate individuals from existing communities and solidarities and then reconstitute them in new, more passive, distributions.[66] As Simon argues, risk classification systems "diminish the potential for resistance by changing the representations through which we come into ourselves as collective subjects."[67]

Since the conclusion of the unisex insurance debates, the insurance industry has turned often to the rhetoric of actuarial fairness as a tool to defend classification structures against public critique. Deborah Hellman, for example, has examined the industry's successful claims in the late 1980s that denial of insurance coverage to victims of domestic abuse was "actuarially fair."[68]

Deborah Stone has studied similar developments in the realm of health insurance, where a belief that it was "morally wrong" to "pay for someone else's risks" had become widespread by the early 1990s.[69] Like moral hazard and adverse selection, the rhetoric of actuarial fairness has also moved beyond the insurance industry, finding application in fields as diverse as education, medicine, policing, and paroling—fields where actuarial classifications and the aggregate group formations they produce have been embraced widely.[70] The tort system in the United States also relies extensively on actuarial tables that price lives according to race and gender, leading to settlements that attach significantly lower value to Black and Brown lives than white ones.[71] Critics of the use of actuarial risk classification systems in these and other fields would be wise to examine and learn from past battles over insurance discrimination.

Beyond these practical concerns, the history of 1970s and 1980s debates over discrimination and risk classification matter because they illustrate well how disputes over insurance are often at the center of some of the most pressing social and political questions of our time. These debates revealed tensions in the ways Americans imagined the social commitments of private insurers, but also touched on concerns surrounding how society should be ordered and how its members should be cared for; how difference should be measured, and responsibility assessed. The tendency to relegate discussions of insurance to the realms of finance and economics has created a situation in which many of the moral and ethical questions insurance and its calculative techniques raise are subsumed under the so-called "objective" logic of the market. An understanding of insurance risk classification as apolitical and divorced from moral questions—the very understanding endorsed by insurers during the unisex debates—has become mainstream and very difficult to challenge, even today, when Americans are once again embroiled in debates over the relationship between insurance, actuarial practices, and social justice.

Imagining Insurance Futures

In 1914, on the eve of the First World War, the Harvard philosopher Josiah Royce celebrated the utopian promise of insurance. In an address delivered at the University of California at Berkeley, titled "War and Insurance," Royce welcomed what he called "the coming social order of the insurer"—a new system of global governance based on the model of mutual insurance. Borrowing from Charles Sanders Peirce's notion of "communities of interpretation," Royce imagined on the horizon a global "community of insurance" made up of all the nations of the world. Under this new system, Royce predicted, every nation would contribute to a large insurance pool overseen by an independent world body. This pool would not only insure the peoples of the world against future conflagrations, natural and manmade, it would also help bring them closer together by encouraging a spirit of interdependence and mutual aid. Royce's address predicted the rise of a utopian insurance era in the not-too-distant future, one he hoped would produce a "true community of mankind" by nourishing and encouraging "loyalty, social unity, and active charity as no other community of interpretation has ever done."[1]

Forty years later, the American science fiction author Frederik Pohl imagined a vastly different insurance future. In his 1955 novel, *Preferred Risk*, Pohl depicts a dystopian insurance era ruled by "The Company," a massive insurance firm that achieves total global domination, displacing state governments. "The Company" rises to power by distributing comprehensive insurance for everything imaginable: hunger, natural disasters, reproduction, and even war. It rules over humanity by refining every action and consequence down to a scale of precise probabilities, represented statistically in complex actuarial tables decipherable only by specially trained experts. Most subjects of "The Company" unquestioningly embrace the new era of peace and plenty brought about by the insurance of everything, despite being segregated—for life—into risk classes that dictate what they eat, where they live, how they work, and who they meet. Others, however, struggle to simply survive. A desperate group of outcasts, deemed "uninsurables," live miserably on the outskirts of society, shunned as deviants by those lucky enough to be classified as "preferred risks."[2]

Neither of these attempts to imagine an insurance future succeeded in predicting the insurance era that developed in the United States over the course of the twentieth century. Both, however, are useful for those who hope to understand the history of insurance in America. Taken together, these vastly different visions reveal the range of possibilities inherent in insurance as a system of social governance. Decades before sociologists and legal scholars coined the term *insurance as governance*, Royce emphasized insurance as a powerful form of social and political organization.[3] Believing that insurance was more than a risk-spreading mechanism, he argued that it could also function as a powerful kind of government, a form of association capable of shaping social understandings of responsibility and dictating relationships between individuals and groups. Like many intellectuals working and thinking at the dawn of the insurance era, Royce celebrated solidarity and collective risk sharing as central components of insurance, and imagined a future in which these social goods would reign supreme.

Royce failed to foresee on the horizon forces that would seek to diminish and contain the collective nature of insurance, to privatize the management of risk and the provision of security. Pohl, by contrast, saw the privatization of risk and security as the primary function of insurance—and placed it at the center of his own vision of an insurance future. Unlike Royce, Pohl ignored the solidaristic elements of risk sharing and instead imagined insurance as a "total institution" dedicated to the quantification and divisive segmentation of human life. Pohl did not predict the complex partnerships that developed during the second half of the twentieth century between private insurance providers and the state. But as a study of what an insurance era ruled by private industry might look like, *Preferred Risk* is eerily prescient. From the omnipresence of corporate-controlled statistical data and its entry into nearly every aspect of daily life, to the work of risk classification mechanisms in determining access to a wide range of social goods, to the sorry fates of those deemed "uninsurable," Pohl's vision of a dystopian future mirrors our own insurance era in striking ways.

Insurance in the Twenty-First Century

What happened to Royce's utopian vision of a "human community" structured around interdependence and mutual aid? Why did Americans stop

imagining insurance as a form of solidarity, a collective commitment to sharing risk? Why did the insurance era that developed in the United States over
the course of the twentieth century tend so often to privatize risk rather than
spread and socialize it? How did we arrive at a present that looks more like
Pohl's imagined future than Royce's? This book has offered a key to answering
these questions. By foregrounding the historical development of select segments of the private insurance industry in the United States, it has illustrated
how historical contexts shaped the ways Americans understood the meanings of insurance and security, and how the insurance industry itself helped
shape those contexts.

Two key themes have emerged in the course of this study that remain
particularly relevant to our understanding of insurance in the United States
in the twenty-first century: (1) the evolving relationship between the private
insurance industry and the state, and (2) the role of insurance institutions in
gathering and wielding data about individuals and groups. The pages that follow explore these themes, with an emphasis on how an understanding of the
past might help us imagine new insurance futures.

PRIVATE INSURANCE AND THE STATE

In 1937, the poet and insurance executive Wallace Stevens argued that the
federal government's new commitment to providing security for Americans,
ushered in by the New Deal, was the single greatest threat facing the private
insurance industry in the United States.[4] In the years that followed, private
insurers went to great lengths to stem the growth of the nascent American
welfare state. Fear of government intrusion into insurance practice—via competition in the market for security or through passage of unwanted regulation—remained deep-seated among industry leaders for much of the twentieth century.

Despite these fears, partnerships with government became increasingly
desirable for the industry as it grew rapidly during the postwar years. The
landmark 1965 passage of Medicare and Medicaid, the first major expansion of
the American welfare state since the 1930s, was even welcomed by many large
insurers. Insurance companies became the primary managers and coordina-
tors of medical services under these programs, which provided a government-
funded safety net designed to catch Americans deemed too risky for the private health insurance market. The burden of providing security for these "bad
risks" now fell to federal and state governments, leaving private insurance
companies with a consumer base less likely to make claims and less costly
to insure. This partnership, the lynchpin of America's public-private health

insurance system, did not challenge the viability or profits of the private insurance industry. In fact, as the historian Christy Ford Chapin argues, it helped legitimize the previously contested private insurance model, neutralizing (at least for a time) calls for universal insurance programs that would cover all Americans.[5]

Partnerships in which commercial insurers worked with or subcontracted for government became common by the 1970s. Laws requiring the purchase of private coverage before driving a car or buying a home, for example, granted the insurance industry immense power in shaping the lives of Americans and determining who had the ability to maintain property and build wealth.[6] Critics of these laws and other insurance practices faced serious obstacles, including a powerful insurance lobby and a state-based regulatory system that made reform on a national level nearly impossible. The 1945 McCarran–Fergusson Act cemented this state-based system, which exempted insurance from federal regulation, including most antitrust abuses.[7] The insurance industry has fought aggressively over the past seventy-five years to protect McCarran–Fergusson—a major reason social movements led by civil rights and feminist activists in in the 1970s and early 1980s failed to achieve substantial and lasting reform on the federal level.

Consumer activists working at the state level, however, did eventually succeed in passing strong insurance regulations during the final years of the twentieth century. In California, a consumer movement supported by Ralph Nader successfully oversaw the passage of Proposition 103 in 1988. The new law required property and casualty insurers to scale back premiums by 20 percent and to seek approval from the California Department of Insurance before setting rates. These reforms made California the most regulated insurance state in the nation, and saved consumers of auto insurance in the state over $100 billion between 1989 and 2013.[8]

While other states have attempted to pass similar reforms since the late 1980s, no state has succeeded in establishing regulations as far reaching as those in California—a reminder of the limitations inherent in a state-based regulatory system. Increased pressure from insurance lobbyists no doubt contributed to the inability of activists in other states to follow California's lead. After the passage of Proposition 103, the industry organized nationally to prevent passage of similar legislation in other states, hiring specialized public relations firms and calling on local officials to reject new calls for regulation.[9]

Notably, while insurance critics in California succeeded in lowering average premiums across the state, their efforts did not eradicate the racial divide in insurance access and pricing that persists across the nation to this day. A groundbreaking *ProPublica* study found in 2018 that California drivers who resided in minority neighborhoods still paid over 10 percent more for auto insurance than drivers with "similar risk" living in zip codes that were primarily white. In less-regulated states like Missouri and Illinois, drivers living in primarily minority zip codes paid as much as 30 percent more for insurance than drivers residing in majority-white zip codes.[10]

These kinds of inequalities are deeply imbedded in insurance practice and have been intensified by partnerships with government that prioritize corporate interests over both consumer rights and the social good. As numerous failed efforts to combat insurance discrimination have shown, rampant inequalities in private insurance provision cannot be eliminated by state-level regulation alone. Federal regulation that addresses insurance as a social issue, and not simply a consumer one, is needed in order to eradicate systemic inequalities historically baked into insurance marketing, underwriting, pricing, and classification structures. Attempts to repeal McCarran–Fergusson have achieved little success over the past half century, however, despite calls for reform from consumer rights groups and professional organizations in other industries.[11] These efforts led the United States House of Representatives to pass a bill that would repeal McCarran–Fergusson in 2017. After aggressive lobbying by the insurance industry, the bill failed to pass in the Senate—a pattern insurance critics have witnessed repeatedly over the past forty years. If future reformers hope to change the regulatory structure that governs the industry, they will need to develop tools capable of restraining the insurance lobby, while also attracting support from a public that remains largely ignorant of insurance law and its impact on the lives of most Americans.

Efforts to educate the public about insurance practice and regulation over the past half century have achieved the most success in the highly contested field of health insurance, where calls to nationalize the industry and expand public programs have survived despite ongoing assaults from insurers and critics of government social programs. The 2010 passage of the Patient Protection and Affordable Care Act (ACA) marked a turning point in public discourse surrounding both healthcare and insurance provision in the United States. In the months leading up to the act's passage, Americans encountered detailed discussions of premium rating structures, exclusions based on preexisting conditions, financing of long-term care coverage, and other aspects of insurance practice and policy rarely examined in mainstream, public venues. Though the final version of the act failed to secure single-payer, universal health coverage (a primary goal of many proponents), it succeeded in significantly reducing the uninsured population in the United States. This reduction was made possible by the ACA's expansion of Medicaid to cover more low-income Americans; by the creation of market exchanges through which qualifying individuals and businesses could purchase subsidized insurance plans; and through regulations preventing private insurers from charging higher premiums or denying coverage to individuals with preexisting conditions. Under the ACA, the number of uninsured Americans under age sixty-five decreased from more than forty-four million in 2013 (the year before most of its requirements went into effect) to just below twenty-seven million in 2016.[12]

Despite these gains, the ACA has thus far failed to produce lasting reforms capable of providing universal access to health insurance for all Americans. Though the number of uninsured Americans has decreased significantly since implementation of the ACA, millions still lack coverage or struggle to pay high premiums and copays required in order to receive medical care and prescriptions. This is true especially in states that have opted out of federal funding provided by the ACA for Medicaid expansion. Though the expansion was intended to be national, a 2012 Supreme Court ruling made it optional for states, leading many Republican-controlled state legislatures to reject adoption, largely for ideological reasons.[13] Between 2016 and 2018, these states—many of which are located in the American South and are home to large numbers of low-income people of color—witnessed a significant increase in uninsured residents, while states that accepted expansion saw a decrease.[14] Though some nonparticipant states may switch course and accept federal funding for Medicaid expansion in the future, the ACA has thus far served to aggravate long-standing geographic and racial disparities in access to healthcare and insurance coverage in the United States.

These disparities, and many of the ACA's basic features, represent a continuation of established historical trends, not the departure from the past claimed by proponents hesitant to embrace more sweeping change. The enthusiasm of ACA architects for "market-based solutions," exemplified by the creation of online insurance "exchanges," is not new. This enthusiasm grew out of a deep-seated belief that private competition and consumer choice can solve insurance access problems in the United States. This belief represents an extension, not a disruption, of decades-old industry efforts to expand private markets and limit public options. Joel Ario, director of the Office of Health Insurance Exchanges under President Barack Obama, for example, argued that one of the key goals of the ACA was to replace the "welfare model" of healthcare provision with an industry-based "insurance model."[15] Ezekiel Emanuel, Obama's special adviser on healthcare reform during the years the ACA was developed, shared this sentiment, arguing in 2014 that market exchanges would eventually produce an "Amazon-like" shopping experience that would generate "positive branding" and ultimately replace both public insurance and employer group plans.[16] Add to this zeal for marketization a

doubling down on individual responsibility to manage risk, ardently embraced by officials like Ario, Ezekiel, and Obama himself, and the ACA's historical roots in industry logic become clear.

Despite these limitations, since passage of the ACA many Americans
have welcomed the act's ban on preexisting conditions in insurance provision
decisions and accepted the notion that access to healthcare should not be
restricted to those with favorable risk ratings. As of 2018, six in ten Americans polled by the Pew Research Center believed that "it is the government's
responsibility" to provide health coverage for all Americans.[17] A reinvigorated and growing belief that healthcare is a human right—one that should
not be contingent on the ability of corporations to make profits—stands to
fundamentally reshape the relationship between private insurance and the
state. Insurance companies have fought for nearly a century to limit competition from government via expansion of public insurance programs and to
cut short efforts to impose federal regulation on the industry. That fight will
likely continue. If a truly new relationship between private insurance and the
state is to develop, historians and others who specialize in the field will need
to do more to educate the public about basic aspects of insurance practice and
the continuing ability of corporations to keep security out of reach for those
Americans who need it most.

Historians of the United States working on the post-1945 era have done
much to reveal the immense power of government in shaping American life.[18]
More work is needed now to uncover how that power has been contested and
coopted by private industry. This project need not be framed in either/or terms.
Collaborations and partnerships between the state and private institutions have
always been a part of liberal governance. Increased focus on insurance and
other critical industries that govern in partnership with and beyond the state
need not entail a reduced focus on government. We must, however, take seriously the real power that has been exercised by private corporations in influencing politics, the economy, and the state itself. Historians have a major role
to play in educating Americans about the ability of corporations to shape their
lives, and about citizens' potential power to limit that influence through democratic political participation. A growing movement to depict the state as a risk
to the people and the rise of corporate control of big data make historical education more crucial than ever as we move further into the twenty-first century.

INSURANCE AND BIG DATA

The collection and management of data about individuals and groups has
long been a central component of insurance practice. Well before the period

covered in this book, insurers of all stripes relied on information about populations in order to determine who was considered an acceptable risk, how much insurance to sell them, and at what price. Life insurers led this process, drawing on historical group, class, and racial characteristics, as well as medical information and mortality data, to manage and price policies held by hundreds of thousands of Americans before the turn of the twentieth century.[19] These efforts only intensified during the postwar years, as life insurance companies turned to public service initiatives, new surveillance techniques, and other tools to refine their risk classification structures and more efficiently pool risk.

As is often the case in insurance history, other fields of insurance followed the lead of the life insurance sector. Property and casualty insurers, for example, also turned to public service initiatives to shape consumer behavior and gather data. Companies used information collected in postwar driver education classes, for example, to set rates and sell policies. Aetna's Drivotrainer course represented a particularly successful effort to systemize and quantify driving while also offering a means of gathering data on driver behavior. Notably, the Drivotrainer simulator served as an early model for the development of telematic devices, which became popular data collection tools for the auto insurance industry in the early 2000s. These devices, installed voluntarily in the vehicles of insurance consumers, gather data about braking behavior, driving speed, mileage, distance driven, and the time of day when a vehicle is in use. Premium discounts for consumers who install such devices have helped boost their popularity, despite concerns surrounding privacy—and the fact that insurers admit to selling recorded data to third parties.[20] Like wearable fitness trackers and wellness apps, telematic devices are widely advertised by the insurance industry as evidence that insurance rate setting is fair and based on an individual's ability to responsibly manage their own risks.

Not all data used by insurers to price and classify risk is based on behavior individuals can easily control, however. Most insurance companies have relied for decades on broad group characteristics like sex, age, and geographical location in underwriting. By the 1960s, property and casualty insurers had developed rating structures that priced policies differently for older women and younger men, urban and suburban residents, divorcees, widows, unmarried cohabitating couples, and married couples with and without children. In the twenty-first century, insurers continue to seek out new data sets on which to base underwriting decisions. The use of credit scores to price auto and home insurance, for example, is widespread within the industry. Insurance companies regularly charge consumers with low credit scores two, three, or even four times as much for coverage than consumers with higher credit scores and "equal risk."[21] Though consumer advocates argue that credit-based insurance rating is unfair because such data has little relation to the risks associated with driving or homeownership, the industry has successfully evaded regulation of the practice in all but a handful of states.[22]

Technological change and a growing willingness on the part of Americans to surrender personal data is currently in the process of reshaping the insurance industry and insurance practice. Life insurers, for example, began drawing on data gathered through wearable fitness trackers like Apple watches and Fitbits in the early 2010s. These devices record a wide variety of data—including heart rate, the number of steps one walks each day, and even the length and quality of one's sleep. Though insurance consumer use of these devices began on a voluntary basis, some life and health insurers have recently moved to make fitness trackers compulsory for policyholders. The life insurance giant John Hancock, for example, made waves in 2018 when the company announced that it would stop selling traditional life policies, as it had for more than 150 years. Instead, all future consumers insured by the company will be required to purchase "interactive policies" that include use of fitness trackers and wellness aps designed to ensure that policyholders actively maintain healthy lifestyles.

Though Hancock and the companies who manufacture these devices tout their ability to incentivize healthy habits and reward individual responsibility, the potential for discrimination and abuse of data collected by fitness trackers is great. In 2018, the state of West Virginia announced plans to revise its public workers health program, requiring all employees to use a fitness tracking app or pay an annual $500 fee. As several employees complained, these requirements represented a violation of privacy and stood to unjustly punish workers incapable of meeting fitness and wellness metrics measured by the app. A historic nine-day strike launched by the state's teachers' union, which opposed the new health plan, scuttled the program.[23] Without further resistance, however, others like it will no doubt become widespread in coming years. In 2019, Fitbit announced a new product: a wearable tracking device called Inspire HR that will be made available only to participating corporate employees and health insurance plan members.[24] For workers employed by companies that adopt Fitbit-based health plans, the use of these devices will not likely be voluntary.

Attempts to regulate insurance classification practices and the industry's collection and use of personal data have achieved only limited success over the past half century. As the "big data revolution" continues, however, resistance to these practices is likely to increase. The growing availability of genomic data, for example, has set off warning bells for consumers and regulators

fearful that genetic testing will be used by insurance companies to discriminate against otherwise healthy individuals with high genetic risk indicators.[25]
The sense that no one is safe from this looming threat has grown in recent
years. As the insurance law scholar Tom Baker notes, "While some 'low risk'
individuals may believe that they are benefited by risk classification, any particular individual is only one technological innovation away from losing his
or her privileged status."[26] Fears like these spurred the passage of the Genetic
Information Nondiscrimination Act (GINA) in 2008. GINA forbids health
insurers from using genetic information for risk classification and pricing
but does not apply to those who receive health insurance through military
service, the Veterans Health Administration, or the Indian Health Service.
GINA also does not protect against genetic discrimination in life, disability,
or long-term care insurance.[27] Crucially, "employee wellness" programs like
the ones discussed above are also exempt from GINA regulation, a loophole
that allows employers to use genetic tests to identify employee health risks—
and charge those who refuse testing hundreds or thousands of dollars more
per year than other workers for insurance benefits.[28]

Will future attempts to combat discriminatory use of genetic and other
data by the insurance industry meet the same fate as attempts by twentieth-
century civil rights and feminist activists, who failed to abolish risk classifications based on sex and place of residence? Political will is often identified as a
crucial factor in advancing regulation, but the success or failure of future battles
with the industry will depend on more than the willingness of regulators to act.
To attract widespread public support for change, insurance critics will need
to challenge industry justifications for surveillance and risk classification that
have circulated for decades. Understanding the complex historical contexts
in which these practices developed—and the various strategies insurers have
used to defend them—will prove valuable in coming fights with the industry. A
growing number of historians and sociologists have begun recently to study the
history of the "quantified self" and the processes through which populations
and individuals have been surveilled, surveyed, counted, and classified.[29] Few,
however, have addressed the formative role played by the insurance industry in
launching and perpetuating these developments.[30] We need more histories that
address the role of private industry in driving the rise of quantification, surveillance, data collection, and risk classification in the United States.

A New Insurance Era?

By the mid-1990s, sociologists of risk and insurance had identified a large-
scale shift in capitalist societies in the liberal West, away from compensatory

"insurantial logics" and toward the "embrace of risk." This concept, popularized by the legal scholar Tom Baker and the sociologist Jonathan Simon,
sought to highlight the celebration of risk taking, particularly among elites,
that became prevalent in the United States and other nations during the 1980s
and 1990s.[31] Baker and Simon's work on this topic remains relevant well into
the twenty-first century. It largely overlooks, however, the negative impacts of
the privatization of risk and security in the United States during the second
half of the twentieth century. The term *embrace of risk* suggests a choice, but
many Americans never had one. Forced to seek security via the private market, they were exposed to its whims, seeing the values of their homes plum-
met and the disintegration of their pensions and retirement savings during
the financial crisis of 2008 and the Great Recession that followed.[32] The risk-
taking behaviors of elites working in finance caused these disasters and the
widespread human suffering created by a distressed global economy. A privatized security system designed to shift the burden of risk toward individuals
and away from corporations and government—a process the political scientist Jacob Hacker calls the "Great Risk Shift"—deepened the consequences of
the economic crisis.[33]

To claim that Americans embraced these changes would be misleading.
They have been given no alternatives. The security system that developed in
the United States over the period covered in this book did not protect Americans from the risks of the market—it exposed them. The "embrace of risk" by
elites over the past thirty years has harmed most middle- and working-class
Americans, who have been forced to take on the heavy burden of achieving
security on their own, distanced and divorced from the collectives that might
have offered a base to stand on. Is it any wonder that Americans who came
of age in the twenty-first century, the generational cohort known as millennials, have been shown to forgo marriage, child rearing, and home ownership? They lack the security to pursue these commitments, despite cultural
traditions that encourage them to do so.[34] Not finding it elsewhere, they have
sought community online, in social media outlets controlled by private corporations. Relationships formed on these platforms may be less shallow than
their critics often imply, but they do not offer material security of the sort
necessary to gain a solid footing in the world, or as the sociologist Jennifer
Silva has argued, to "grow up."[35]

Increasing precarity and exposure to risk, however, has led to resistance—
particularly among younger Americans. Since the Great Recession, calls to
regulate the insurance industry and politicize risk classification, to remove
profit from the pursuit of security, and to build and expand public insurance programs have multiplied. Health insurance, as noted above, emerged

as a major site of activism and policy discussions in the national elections of 2016 and 2018. This activism differed from earlier efforts in its willingness to directly challenge the profit motives of insurance companies, and crucially, in its calls to abolish private health insurance as an industry. Will the fears of Wallace Stevens and other midcentury insurance executives concerning the nationalization of private insurance be realized in the twenty-first century? Perhaps. Gallup polling shows a steady and significant uptick since 2010 in American support for replacement of private health insurance with a government-run system—support that has reached levels unseen since the 1940s.[36] As the enduring popularity of programs like Social Security and Medicare has illustrated, access to security once granted is very difficult to take away. Nationalization of health insurance in the United States may very well lead to calls for expansion of other public insurance programs and the nationalization, or significant reform, of other insurance fields.

Two decades into the twenty-first century, Americans continue to rely on private insurance institutions launched in the nineteenth and early twentieth centuries for security and protection from life's uncertainties. Though these institutions have transformed significantly over time, the fundamental basis of insurance—the sharing of risk across populations—remains unchanged. Private insurers have fought for nearly a century to downplay and contain the fact that insurable security is achieved through collectives. During the second half of the twentieth century, these efforts helped shift public sentiment away from New Deal–era faith in collective risk sharing and toward the individualization of risk and the privatization of security. Future attempts to reform insurance in the United States—particularly those that seek to separate security from profit and create more egalitarian and inclusive insurance systems—will need to understand this history. Calls to expand public insurance programs, for example, will need to do more than address questions of cost. They will also need to dissect and dismantle decades-old narratives about risk and responsibility created and disseminated by private industry.

How might we bring about a new insurance era? The first step will be understanding the basic workings of insurance and the often hidden role it plays in our lives. Insurance has long served as a reminder of the pervasiveness of uncertainty and our helplessness in the face of chance. But it also emboldens us as agents with the power to care for one another and to compensate for misfortune through collective means. What we do with that power will depend on our willingness to imagine futures that look different from our present—futures less like Pohl's vision of a society infinitely divided, and more like Royce's dream of a human community that rises or falls together.

Acknowledgments

Many people have helped make this book possible, and it is a pleasure to thank them here.

This project began at the History Department at the University of Minnesota and has benefited over the years from Elaine Tyler May's guidance and unwavering generosity. My debt to Elaine is enormous, and I am lucky to count her as a mentor and friend. I am grateful as well for the other lasting intellectual friendships I formed while studying at Minnesota. Barbara Welke energetically supported this project for years. Andrew Urban and Nate Holdren provided essential camaraderie, advice, and ideas. Daniel LaChance read and commented on every draft—his brilliance made this book better. Jay Kim left for another world before she could complete her own manuscript and made me promise I would complete mine. I dedicate this book to her.

I have been fortunate to receive assistance from a number of other individuals and institutions while working on this project. The staff at the Rubenstein Library at Duke University helped tremendously as I conducted research at the John W. Hartman Center for Sales, Advertising, and Marketing History. Joshua Rowley, Hope Ketcham-Geeting, and Amanda Lazarus were especially helpful during my time at Duke. I am grateful as well to Doris Singleton, who helped me navigate the Prudential archives, and to Tom Carey, who oversaw my research at the San Francisco Public Library's San Francisco History Center. Ken Sargeant and the directors of the Harlem Cultural Archives kindly provided access to clips from the excellent documentary project "Down by the Riverside, a Place to Be Free" and answered my questions about the Riverton housing development and its history. The postwar insurance industry was a prolific producer of printed material, and I am indebted to Princeton's ReCAP staff and the interlibrary loan workers at many institutions for processing hundreds of requests for obscure insurance textbooks, investment manuals, and industry reports and newsletters.

The University of Chicago Press has supported this project for many years. I was lucky to work with Doug Mitchell before his passing and am grateful to have briefly encountered his vivacious spirit. Timothy Mennel generously took on this project midstream and has patiently seen it through numerous stages of development. I am grateful to Tim, Susannah Engstrom, and Johanna Rosenbohm for their kindness, hard work, and assistance. I would also like to thank the anonymous readers of the manuscript, who provided constructive comments that helped me revise and expand the project.

The History Department at Princeton University offered vital resources and intellectual community during my time there, between 2011 and 2015. I am grateful to the staff at the Princeton University Library for their help and to Margot Canaday and Kevin Kruse for their mentorship. Bill Jordan, Rosina Lozano, Emily Thompson, Alison Isenberg, Keith Wailoo, Joseph Fronczak, and Paul Miles also deserve thanks for supporting me and my work. I am thankful as well to Matthew Karp, Alden Young, and Ronny Regev for their companionship, and for conversations packed with ideas. A good deal of research for this project was completed in 2016–2017, during my year as a fellow at the Shelby Cullom Davis Center for Historical Studies at Princeton. I am thankful to Angela Creager and Jennifer Houle Goldman for creating a vibrant and intellectually stimulating environment at the center. Conversations with other fellows, and particularly Vanessa Ogle and Shennette Garrett-Scott, helped me develop this project at a crucial stage.

I feel lucky to have found an academic home at the Massachusetts Institute of Technology. This project has benefited from the dedication of MIT's administrative and library staffs, and from the creativity and curiosity of its students. My wonderful colleagues in History and the HASTS program have done much to move this book toward completion. Sana Aiyar, Deborah Fitzgerald, Malick Ghachem, Kenda Mutongi, Harriet Ritvo, and Elizabeth Wood deserve special thanks for their mentorship and advising. I am grateful as well for the support of the MIT School of Humanities, Arts, and Social Sciences, and to Craig Wilder, Jeff Ravel, and Chris Capozzola for their patient guidance and help in securing promotions and research leaves that proved crucial in advancing my work.

Many other intellectual comrades helped shape this project. Jamie Pietruska offered wisdom and advice. Dan Bouk served as a reader of the manuscript on multiple occasions and offered creativity, patience, and kindness at every stage. Jonathan Levy made me a better thinker and seamlessly took on the roles of mentor, interlocutor, and friend—sometimes in the same conversation. I am thankful to Jamie, Dan, and Jon for their friendship, and for paving the way for my research with their excellent scholarship. Joseph Haker, William Deringer, Bettina Stoetzer, Pouya Alimagham, Alison Lefkovitz, William San Martín, Katherine Hill, Christy Wampole, Kristen Koenig, Matthew Thompson, Olivia Solis, Kevin Holden, and James Melching have all contributed to this book in meaningful ways. I thank them and the many workshop participants, acquaintances, and strangers who engaged in thoughtful conversations about risk and insurance in cafés and conference halls over the years.

The most important contributors to this manuscript were the people who loved and supported me in spite of it. My parents, Beege and Darrel Horan, have always offered unconditional love. Matthew Backes lived with this project for nearly a decade and shaped it in countless ways. For his help, and for the fullness of the life we share, I will always be grateful.

Notes

Introduction

1. Wallace Stevens, "Insurance and Social Change," *Wallace Stevens Journal* 4, no. 3 (Fall 1980): 37.

2. Stevens, "Insurance and Social Change," 37–39. Several literary scholars have analyzed Stevens's poetic works in connection with the politics of the US Social Security program. Joseph Harrington, for example, argues that Stevens believed nationalized, universal insurance programs would "eliminate the need for imagination and so the conditions necessary for the imagination's functioning." Joseph Harrington, "Wallace Stevens and the Poetics of National Insurance," *American Literature* 67, no. 1 (March 1995): 100. See also Michael Szalay, *New Deal Modernism: American Literature and the Invention of the Welfare State* (Durham, NC: Duke University Press, 2000).

3. Stevens, "Insurance and Social Change," 37. On the resistance of business leaders to the New Deal, see Kim Phillips-Fein, *Invisible Hands: The Making of the Conservative Movement from the New Deal to Reagan* (New York: Norton, 2009).

4. Stevens, "Insurance and Social Change," 39.

5. James Gilbert, *Designing the Industrial State: The Intellectual Pursuit of Collectivism in America* (Chicago: Quadrangle Books, 1972). On industrial accidents and the socialization of risk, see Nate Holdren, *Injury Impoverished: Workplace Accidents, Capitalism, and Law in the Progressive Era* (New York: Cambridge University Press, 2020); and David Moss, *Socializing Security: Progressive-Era Economists and the Origins of American Social Policy* (Cambridge, MA: Harvard University Press, 1995). On pragmatists and risk, see Jonathan Levy, *Freaks of Fortune: The Emerging World of Capitalism and Risk in America* (Cambridge, MA: Harvard University Press, 2012); and Ian Hacking, *The Taming of Chance* (New York: Cambridge University Press, 1990). On the socialization of risk as a pragmatist solution to war, see Jonathan Simon, "Peace and Insurance: Recovering the Utopian Vision of Insurance in Royce's War and Insurance," *Connecticut Insurance Law Journal* 10, no. 1 (2003): 51–72.

6. Simon, "Peace and Insurance," 52; and Jonathan Simon, "Driving Governmentality: Automobile Accidents, Insurance, and the Challenge to Social Order in the Inter-war Years, 1919 to 1941," *Connecticut Insurance Law Journal* 4, no. 2 (1997): 524.

7. See François Ewald, *L'État providence* (Paris: Grasset, 1986); François Ewald, "Norms, Discipline, and the Law," *Representations* 30 (1990): 138–61; and François Ewald, "Insurance and

Risk," in *The Foucault Effect: Studies in Governmentality*, ed. G. Burchell, C. Gordon, and P. Miller (Chicago: University of Chicago Press, 1991), 197–210.

8. See Mary Douglas and Aaron Wildavsky, *Risk and Culture: An Essay on the Selection of Technological and Environmental Dangers* (Berkeley: University of California Press, 1983); Mary Douglas, *Risk and Blame: Essays in Cultural Theory* (London: Routledge, 1992); Mary Douglas, "Risk as a Forensic Resource," in E. J. Burger, ed., *Risk* (Ann Arbor: University of Michigan Press, 1993); and Ulrich Beck, *Risk Society: Towards a New Modernity*, trans. Mark Ritter (Los Angeles: Sage, 1992). Over the past three decades, an interdisciplinary subfield dedicated to the theoretical importance of insurance institutions has emerged. For influential studies in this field, see G. Burchell, C. Gordon, and P. Miller, eds., *The Foucault Effect: Studies in Governmentality* (Chicago: University of Chicago Press, 1991); Tom Baker and Jonathan Simon, eds., *Embracing Risk: The Changing Culture of Insurance and Responsibility* (Chicago: University of Chicago Press, 2002); Richard V. Ericson and Aaron Doyle, eds., *Risk and Morality* (Toronto: University of Toronto Press, 2003); Richard V. Ericson, Aaron Doyle, and Dean Barry, *Insurance as Governance* (Toronto: University of Toronto Press, 2003); Richard V. Ericson and Aaron Doyle, *Uncertain Business: Risk, Insurance, and the Limits of Knowledge* (Toronto: University of Toronto Press, 2004); Michael Dillon, "Underwriting Security," *Security Dialogue* 39, no. 2 (2008): 309–32; Mitchell Dean, *Governmentality: Power and Rule in Modern Society* (London: Sage, 1999); and Pat O'Malley, *Risk, Uncertainty and Government* (London: Cavendish, 2004). Much of this scholarship was influenced by the thought of Michel Foucault, particularly his late work on governmentality developed during his lectures at the Collège de France. For risk and insurance scholars, the most important of Foucault's lectures include *Society Must Be Defended: Lectures at the Collège de France, 1975–1976*, trans. David Macey (New York: Picador, 2003); *Security, Territory, Population: Lectures at the Collège de France, 1977–1978*, trans. Graham Burchell (New York: Picador, 2007); and *The Birth of Biopolitics: Lectures at the Collège de France, 1978–1979*, trans. Graham Burchell (New York: Picador, 2010).

9. The "risk society" literature, launched by Ulrich Beck in the 1980s, focuses specifically on the "uninsurability" of manmade risks under the conditions of late modernity. See Beck, *Risk Society*. As Ericson, Doyle, and Barry argue, however, the claim promoted by risk society scholars, that "more and more risks are uninsurable" in late modernity, fails to address the actual functioning of insurance as an industry. "Not having studied the insurance industry," they argue, "[risk society scholars] fail to appreciate that it will insure just about everything." Ericson, Doyle, and Barry, *Insurance as Governance*, 9.

10. Ewald, "Insurance and Risk," 197–210.

11. Ewald, 198.

12. On Ewald's importance in shaping scholarship on the European welfare state, see Michael Behrent, "Accidents Happen: François Ewald, the 'Antirevolutionary' Foucault, and the Intellectual Politics of the French Welfare State," *Journal of Modern History* 82 (September 2010): 585–624. See also George Steinmetz, *Regulating the Social: The Welfare State and Local Politics in Imperial Germany* (Princeton, NJ: Princeton University Press, 1993) 1–12, 37–40.

13. Levy, *Freaks of Fortune*. For another account of insurance in the nineteenth-century United States, see Sharon Ann Murphy, *Investing in Life: Insurance in Antebellum America* (Baltimore: Johns Hopkins University Press, 2010).

14. David Beito, *From Mutual Aid to the Welfare State: Fraternal Societies and Social Services, 1890–1967* (Chapel Hill: University of North Carolina Press, 2000); Theda Skocpol, Ariane Liazos, and Marshall Ganz, *What a Mighty Power Can Be: African American Fraternal Groups and the Struggle for Racial Equality* (Princeton, NJ: Princeton University Press, 2016).

15. Beito, *From Mutual Aid to the Welfare State*, 18.

16. For a study of the importance of fraternal organizations to Black communities in the United States and the prominent leadership Black women played in their organization and management, see Shennette Garrett-Scott, *Banking on Freedom: Black Women in U.S. Finance before the New Deal* (New York: Columbia University Press, 2019).

17. Competition from large industrial insurers, whose leaders claimed that fraternal organizations were inefficient and prone to corruption, undoubtedly contributed to the decline of voluntary mutual aid organizations.

18. Bruce Lewenstein, "Industrial Life Insurance, Public Health Campaigns, and Public Communication of Science, 1908–1951," *Public Understanding of Science* 1, no. 4 (October 1992): 349. For an extended discussion of industrial insurance and its impact on commercial insurance practices, see Dan Bouk, *How Our Days Became Numbered: Risk and the Rise of the Statistical Individual* (Chicago: University of Chicago Press, 2015).

19. Jennifer Klein, *For All These Rights: Business, Labor, and the Shaping of America's Public-Private Welfare State* (Princeton, NJ: Princeton University Press, 2003).

20. Jennifer Klein, "The Politics of Economic Security: Employee Benefits and the Privatization of New Deal Liberalism," *Journal of Policy History* 12, no. 1 (2004): 48.

21. Colin Gordon, "Why No National Health Insurance in the U.S.? The Limits of Social Provision in War and Peace, 1941–1948," *Journal of Policy History* 9, no. 3 (1997): 277–310. See also Klein, *For All These Rights*.

22. Klein, *For All These Rights*.

23. Karen Orren, *Corporate Power and Social Change: The Politics of the Life Insurance Industry* (Baltimore: Johns Hopkins University Press, 1974).

24. Decades of conservative planning had protected the assets of most of the largest insurers during the stock market crash of 1929 and the ensuing Great Depression. For many life insurance companies, the crash accelerated growth, as investors who had lost heavily attempted to supplement losses to their estates by increasing their life insurance. See Thomas Derdak, ed., *International Directory of Company Histories* (Chicago: St. James Press, 1988), 3:292–93.

25. Holgar J. Johnson, *Speaking with One Voice* (New York: Appleton-Croft, 1967). Throughout this book I examine private insurance as both a general idea and a unified industry. When necessary, I make distinctions between life, health, property, and casualty insurance, and between group and individual coverage. The distinction between private and public insurance is a central focus of this study, though even here blurring occurs when discussing private contractors who were employed by the state to manage public programs, as so often happened during the postwar years (see, for example, Medicare and Medicaid).

26. Marsha Levick, "Pro and Con: Women vs. The Insurance Industry—Sex, Risk, and the Actuarial Equation," *New York Times*, August 16, 1987, 26.

27. Robert Aronowitz, *Risky Medicine: Our Quest to Cure Fear and Uncertainty* (Chicago: University of Chicago Press, 2015).

28. See Michael A. Peters, "The New Prudentialism in Education: Actuarial Rationality and the Entrepreneurial Self," *Educational Theory* 55, no. 2 (2005): 123–37.

29. See Bernard Harcourt, *Against Prediction: Profiling, Policing, and Punishing in an Actuarial Age* (Chicago: University of Chicago Press, 2007).

30. Zsuzsanna Vargha, "Insurance after Markets," *Economic Sociology—the European Newsletter* 17, no. 1 (November 2015): 2. See also David Knights and Theo Vurdubakis, "Calculations of Risk: Towards an Understanding of Insurance as a Moral and Political Technology,"

Accounting Organizations and Society 18, no. 7/8 (1993): 729–64; Ericson, Doyle, and Barry, *Insurance as Governance*; Ericson and Doyle, *Uncertain Business*; and O'Malley, *Risk, Uncertainty and Government*.

31. See esp. Baker and Simon, eds., *Embracing Risk*; Ericson, Doyle, and Barry, *Insurance as Governance*; and Ericson and Doyle, *Uncertain Business*.

32. Deborah Stone, "Beyond Moral Hazard: Insurance as Moral Opportunity," in Baker and Simon, *Embracing Risk*, 4.

Chapter One

1. Holgar J. Johnson, *Speaking with One Voice* (New York: Appleton-Century-Crofts, 1967), 167.

2. Johnson, *Speaking with One Voice*, 143.

3. Johnson, 18.

4. Johnson, 147.

5. Johnson, 26.

6. Franklin Delano Roosevelt, "Annual Message to the Congress," in *The Court Disapproves, 1935*, vol. 4, *Public Papers and Addresses of Franklin D. Roosevelt* (13 vols.; New York: Russell and Russell, 1938–50), 17.

7. The comparative literature on the welfare state is extensive. For introductory accounts, see Gøsta Esping-Andersen, *The Three Worlds of Welfare Capitalism* (Princeton, NJ: Princeton University Press, 1990); Peter Baldwin, "The Welfare State for Historians: A Review Article," *Comparative Studies in Society and History* 34, no. 4 (October 1992): 695–707; Jacob Hacker, *The Divided Welfare State: The Battle over Public and Private Social Benefits in the United States* (Cambridge: Cambridge University Press, 2002); and Julia Lynch, "A Cross-national Perspective on the American Welfare State," in D. Béland, C. Howard, and K. J. Moran, eds., *Oxford Handbook of U.S. Social Policy* (New York: Oxford University Press, 2014).

8. The most important exception to this trend remains Jennifer Klein's *For All These Rights: Business, Labor, and the Shaping of America's Public-Private Welfare State* (Princeton, NJ: Princeton University Press, 2003).

9. For a study of the early history of advertising in the United States, see Roland Marchand, *Advertising the American Dream: Making Way for Modernity, 1920–1940* (Berkeley: University of California Press, 1986). See also Jackson Lears, *Fables of Abundance: A Cultural History of Advertising in America* (New York: Basic Books, 1994).

10. A. H. Thiemann, *Life Insurance Advertising: What It Is and How It Works* (New York: Life Insurance Advertisers Association, 1963), 11.

11. Quoted in Thiemann, *Life Insurance Advertising*, 10.

12. Roland Marchand, *Creating the Corporate Soul: The Rise of Public Relations and Corporate Imagery in American Big Business* (Berkeley: University of California Press, 1998) 43.

13. Marchand, *Creating the Corporate Soul*, 43.

14. Prudential Life Insurance Company of America, "Two Widows," 1924, Baden Collection, Hartman Center for Sales, Advertising, and Marketing History, Rare Book, Manuscript, and Special Collections Library, Duke University.

15. Richard Farmer, "The Long-Term Crisis in Life Insurance," *Journal of Risk and Insurance* 33, no. 4 (December 1966): 623–34.

16. For analysis of the limited scope of insurance advertising in the early twentieth century, see Life Insurance Advertisers Association, *Life Insurance Advertising: The Techniques of*

Reaching the Public through Mass Media (New York: Life Insurance Advertises Association, 1958); and Thiemann, *Life Insurance Advertising*.

17. Thiemann, 10.

18. Thiemann, 15.

19. Life Insurance Advertisers Association, *Life Insurance Advertising*, 1.

20. Life Insurance Advertisers Association, 1.

21. Viviana A. Rotman Zelizer, *Morals and Markets: The Development of Life Insurance in the United States* (New York: Columbia University Press, 1979).

22. In 1959, State Farm Insurance vice president Thomas Morrill urged companies to multiply coverage through multiline selling: "The agent who can supply all of [the insurance buyer's] basic insurance needs can make the contact worth his time, whereas the single-line agent would find it impossible to do so. . . . The warm feelings of security that people seek in their relations with their insurance agent are not tied to a particular type of protection." Thomas C. Morrill, "Creative Marketing of Life Insurance," *Journal of Marketing* 24, no. 2 (October 1959): 15.

23. Simkin, *Life Insurance Advertising*, iii.

24. Arthur Daniels, "The Research Facilities of the Institute of Life Insurance," *Journal of Risk and Insurance* 25, no. 1 (July 1958): 32.

25. Johnson, *Speaking with One Voice*, 2.

26. Holgar Johnson discusses the many challenges faced by the industry during the 1930s in *Speaking with One Voice*, 7-9.

27. Richard B. Johnson, "The Cost of Legal Reserve Life Insurance," *Southern Economic Journal* 8, no. 3 (January 1942): 351.

28. For a contemporary discussion of the TNEC investigations, see Norman Kogan and Arthur Michaelson, "Cost and Coverage of Industrial Insurance," *Yale Law Journal* 16, no. 1 (January 1952): 46-74.

29. Johnson, "Cost of Legal Reserve Life Insurance," 354.

30. Johnson, *Speaking with One Voice*, 19. See also *Final Report and Recommendations of the Temporary National Economic Committee*, S. Doc. No. 35 (1941).

31. *Final Report and Recommendations of the Temporary National Economic Committee*, 43.

32. Johnson, "Cost of Legal Reserve Life Insurance," 353.

33. Johnson, 351.

34. Albert Linton, "Life Insurance and the Democratic State: The Warning Signals Are Up," Barbara Weinstock Lecture on the Morals of Trade, University of California, Berkeley, April 22, 1941, published in *Vital Speeches of the Day* 7, no. 15 (1941): 465-67.

35. This was one of the first corporate uses of polling services. For a compelling history of organizations like Roper and the rise of public polling, see Sarah Igo, *The Averaged American: Surveys, Citizens, and the Making of a Mass Public* (Cambridge, MA: Harvard University Press, 2007).

36. Johnson, *Speaking with One Voice*, 17.

37. Johnson, 19.

38. Linton, "Life Insurance and the Democratic State," 467.

39. Linton, 467.

40. Johnson, *Speaking with One Voice*, 107.

41. Johnson, 92.

42. Numerous scholars have examined the influence of Cold War political culture on social life. See Elaine Tyler May, *Homeward Bound: American Families in the Cold War Era*, 20th anniversary ed. (New York: Basic Books, 2008); Robert Griffith, "The Cultural Turn in Cold War

Studies," *Reviews in American History* 29 (2001): 150–57; and Stephen Whitfield, *The Culture of the Cold War* (Baltimore: Johns Hopkins University Press, 1996).

43. Johnson, *Speaking with One Voice*, 93, 109.

44. Johnson, 141.

45. *J.W.T. News* 4, no. 39 (September 26, 1949), J. Walter Thompson Company Newsletter Collection, 1910–2005, David M. Rubenstein Rare Book & Manuscript Library, Duke University.

46. ILI, "The Only Real Security Is Self-Made!," "Creating His <u>Own</u> Security!," and "Why These Americans Believe in Self-Made Security," 1950, J. Walter Thompson Company, Domestic Advertisements Collection, David M. Rubenstein Rare Book & Manuscript Library, Duke University.

47. ILI, "More Folks Making Their <u>Own</u> Security!," 1950, J. Walter Thompson Company, Domestic Advertisements Collection, David M. Rubenstein Rare Book & Manuscript Library, Duke University.

48. *J.W.T. News* 5, no. 15 (April 10, 1950), J. Walter Thompson Company, Newsletter Collection, David M. Rubenstein Rare Book & Manuscript Library, Duke University.

49. "Insurance—John Hancock," Gary P. and Sandra G. Baden Collection of Print Advertisements, David M. Rubenstein Rare Book & Manuscript Library, Duke University.

50. North America Insurance Company, "Free Enterprise at Work," *Better Homes and Gardens*, July 1950, 32.

51. National Board of Fire Underwriters, "Protection," *Saturday Evening Post*, September 19, 1953, 5 (emphasis in the original).

52. Quoted in Richard Hooker, *Aetna Life Insurance Company: Its First 100 Years* (Hartford, CT: Aetna Life Insurance Company, 1965), 192.

53. Thiemann, *Life Insurance Advertising*, 50.

54. Thiemann, 27.

55. Johnson, *Speaking with One Voice*, 55–56.

56. ILI, "Why Your Life Insurance Companies Urge You to Keep Up the Fight against Rising Prices," 1944, J. Walter Thompson Company, Domestic Advertisements Collection, David M. Rubenstein Rare Book & Manuscript Library, Duke University.

57. ILI, "Who's to *Blame* if the Cost of Living Gets Out of Hand," 1950, and "Keeping America Strong Is <u>Everybody's</u> Job!," 1945, J. Walter Thompson Company, Domestic Advertisements Collection, David M. Rubenstein Rare Book & Manuscript Library, Duke University.

58. ILI, "What <u>You</u> Can Do to Prevent Runaway Prices," 1944, J. Walter Thompson Company, Domestic Advertisements Collection, David M. Rubenstein Rare Book & Manuscript Library, Duke University.

59. Johnson, *Speaking with One Voice*, 110.

60. Johnson, 55.

61. Thiemann, *Life Insurance Advertising*, 29.

62. For a contemporary study of the impacts of inflation on insurance companies, see David Houston, "The Effects of Inflation on Life Insurance," *California Management Review* 2, no. 2 (Winter 1960): 76–79.

63. ILI, "32 Cents Lost from Your Dollar Just since the War," 1959, J. Walter Thompson Company, Domestic Advertisements Collection, David M. Rubenstein Rare Book & Manuscript Library, Duke University.

64. ILI, "You Can Plan Your Future with Confidence Only When the Lid Is on Inflation," 1959, J. Walter Thompson Company, Domestic Advertisements Collection, David M. Rubenstein Rare Book & Manuscript Library, Duke University.

65. Thiemann, *Life Insurance Advertising*, 29.

66. Minutes, ILI meeting, June 26, 1958, J. Walter Thompson Company Review Board Records, J. Walter Thompson Company, Domestic Advertisements Collection, David M. Rubenstein Rare Book & Manuscript Library, Duke University.

67. Minutes, ILI meeting, July 1, 1958, J. Walter Thompson Company Review Board Records, J. Walter Thompson Company, Domestic Advertisements Collection, David M. Rubenstein Rare Book & Manuscript Library, Duke University.

68. Minutes, ILI meeting, June 26, 1958.

69. Minutes, ILI meeting, June 26, 1958.

70. Minutes, ILI meeting, June 26, 1958.

71. Minutes, ILI meeting, July 1, 1958.

72. Minutes, ILI meeting, July 1, 1958. Insurance industry investments in commercial real estate, and particularly shopping centers, intensified during the 1950s; see chapter 4.

73. JWT representatives warned that these approaches would have "an indirect effect on favorable tax and regulation conditions, but only that." Minutes, ILI meeting, July 1, 1958.

74. ILI, "How Do Life Insurance Companies Figure Premiums?," 1955, J. Walter Thompson Company, Domestic Advertisements Collection, David M. Rubenstein Rare Book & Manuscript Library, Duke University.

75. ILI, "What Standards Govern the Life Insurance Companies in Investing Your Money?," 1953, J. Walter Thompson Company, Domestic Advertisements Collection, David M. Rubenstein Rare Book & Manuscript Library, Duke University.

76. ILI, "How Does the Money People Put into Life Insurance Benefit All of Us?," 1953, J. Walter Thompson Company, Domestic Advertisements Collection, David M. Rubenstein Rare Book & Manuscript Library, Duke University.

77. ILI, "Is America a Better Place Because You Own Life Insurance?," 1953, J. Walter Thompson Company, Domestic Advertisements Collection, David M. Rubenstein Rare Book & Manuscript Library, Duke University.

78. On the corporate funding of think tanks and research institutes, see Kim Phillips-Fein, *Invisible Hands: The Businessmen's Crusade against the New Deal* (New York: Norton, 2010); and Jason Stahl, *Right Moves: The Conservative Think Tank in American Political Culture since 1945* (Chapel Hill: University of North Carolina Press, 2016).

Chapter Two

1. Lyman Bryson, ed., *Facing the Future's Risks: Studies toward Predicting the Unforeseen* (New York: Harper and Brothers, 1953), 1 (emphasis added).

2. See Kim Phillips-Fein, *Invisible Hands: The Making of the Conservative Movement from the New Deal to Reagan* (New York: Norton, 2009).

3. For a representative example of this argument, see Bruce Lewenstein, "Industrial Life Insurance, Public Health Campaigns, and Public Communication of Science, 1908–1951," *Public Understanding of Science* 1, no. 4 (1992): 347–66.

4. Louis Dublin, *A Family of Thirty Million: The Story of the Metropolitan Life Insurance Company* (New York: Metropolitan Life Insurance Company, 1943), 423.

5. Clarence Myers, "The Wider Role of Business in the Community," address, Rotary Club of New York, May 28, 1959, in *The Life Insurance Business: A Selection from Talks on Various Subjects Relating to Business, Given from 1954 to 1962* (New York: New York Life Insurance Company, 1963), 9–10.

6. Eugene Thore, "Current Developments and Problems in Life Insurance," *Journal of Risk and Insurance* 27, no. 1 (March 1960): 32.

7. Thore, "Current Developments and Problems in Life Insurance," 32.

8. Carl Carmer, *A Tower of Strength: The Story of the Health and Welfare Program of the Metropolitan Life Insurance Company* (New York: The Metropolitan Life Insurance Company, 1959), 27.

9. Dan Bouk, *How Our Days Became Numbered: Risk and the Rise of the Statistical Individual* (Chicago: University of Chicago Press, 2015), 55–88.

10. Daniel Hawthorne, *The Hartford of Hartford: An Insurance Company's Part in a Century and a Half of American History* (New York: Random House, 1960). See also Bouk, *How Our Days Became Numbered*, 128.

11. On insurance, immorality, and gambling, see Viviana A. Rotman Zelizer, *Morals and Markets: The Development of Life Insurance in the United States* (New York: Columbia University Press, 1979). See also Sharon Murphy, *Investing in Life: Insurance in Antebellum America* (Baltimore: Johns Hopkins University Press, 2013).

12. On Armstrong as a factor leading to insurance public health work, see Bouk, *How Our Days Became Numbered*, 89–111; and William Rothstein, *Public Health and the Risk Factor: A History of an Uneven Medical Revolution* (Rochester: University of Rochester Press, 2003), 156–64.

13. On the Life Extension Institute, see Bouk, *How Our Days Became Numbered*, 134–47.

14. Metropolitan Life Insurance Company, *Syphilis*, 1927, Roy Lightner Collection of Antique Advertisements, David M. Rubenstein Rare Book & Manuscript Library, Duke University.

15. Metropolitan Life Insurance Company, *Curbstone Medical Advice*, 1940, Roy Lightner Collection of Antique Advertisements, David M. Rubenstein Rare Book & Manuscript Library, Duke University.

16. Diane Hamilton, "Metropolitan Life Insurance Company Visiting Nurse Service: 1909–1953" (PhD diss., University of Virginia, 1987).

17. Dublin, *A Family of Thirty Million*, 87–92.

18. Dublin, 424.

19. On debates over cost and ability to assess the success of the visiting nurse program, see Bouk, *How Our Days Became Numbered*, 128–32; Diane Hamilton, "The Cost of Caring: The Metropolitan Life Insurance Company's Visiting Nurse Service: 1909–1953," *Bulletin of the History of Medicine* 63, no. 3 (Fall 1989): 414–34; and Rothstein, *Public Health and the Risk Factor*, 156–64.

20. Rothstein, 175.

21. Haley Fiske, "Manager's Annual Banquet," *Addresses Delivered at the Triennial Conventions III*: 34–45, cited in Rothstein, *Public Health and the Risk Factor*, 171.

22. Donald Armstrong and Alma Haupt, "A Forty-Year Demonstration of Public Health Nursing by the Metropolitan Life Insurance Company," *Public Health Nursing* 43 (1951): 41–42.

23. Rothstein, *Public Health and the Risk Factor*, 163.

24. Hamilton, "The Cost of Caring," 414–34.

25. Rothstein, *Public Health and the Risk Factor*, 160.

26. Hamilton, "The Cost of Caring," 414–34.

27. Hamilton, 424–25.

28. Haley Fiske, "Business Convention Address," *Addresses Delivered at the Triennial Conventions* (New York: 1924), 2:26.

29. See Irving Fisher and Eugene Lyman Fiske, *How to Live: Rules for Healthful Living Based on Modern Science* (1915; New York: Funk and Wagnalls, 1920).

30. I am grateful to Dan Bouk for his insights on the question of change over time in Metropolitan's health messaging.

31. Metropolitan Life Insurance Company, "It Pays to Know When to *Relax!*," 1946, Roy Lightner Collection of Antique Advertisements, David M. Rubenstein Rare Book & Manuscript Library, Duke University.

32. Metropolitan Life Insurance Company, "Most Likely to Succeed . . . in Getting Over a Stomach Ulcer," 1956, Roy Lightner Collection of Antique Advertisements, David M. Rubenstein Rare Book & Manuscript Library, Duke University.

33. Bouk, *How Our Days Became Numbered*, 122. See also Amanda M. Czerniawski, "From Average to Ideal: The Evolution of the Height and Weight Table in the United States, 1836–1943," *Social Science History* 31, no. 2 (Summer 2007): 273–96. Czerniawski notes that medical reference books throughout the twentieth century relied heavily on height and weight tables developed and revised by insurance companies, particularly Metropolitan.

34. Ian Hacking, "Making Up People," in Thomas Heller, ed., *Reconstructing Individualism: Autonomy, Individuality, and the Self in Western Thought* (Stanford: Stanford University Press, 1986), 222–36.

35. Roland Marchand, *Creating the Corporate Soul: The Rise of Public Relations and Corporate Imagery in American Big Business* (Berkeley: University of California Press, 1998), 187.

36. Metropolitan Life Insurance Company, *An Epoch in Life Insurance: A Third of a Century of Achievement* (New York: Metropolitan Life Insurance Company, 1924), 271.

37. Holgar J. Johnson, *Speaking with One Voice* (New York: Appleton-Century-Crofts, 1967), 116.

38. Johnson, *Speaking with One Voice*, 116.

39. Johnson, 84.

40. ILI, Education Division, *Arithmetic in Action* (New York: ILI, 1954), J. Walter Thompson Company, Domestic Advertisements Collection, David M. Rubenstein Rare Book & Manuscript Library, Duke University.

41. ILI, Education Division, *Arithmetic in Action*.

42. ILI, "Young People Do Want to Know the Facts of Life Insurance," 1953, J. Walter Thompson Company, Domestic Advertisements Collection, David M. Rubenstein Rare Book & Manuscript Library, Duke University. See also H. G. Enterline and Kennard Goodman, eds., *Blueprint for Tomorrow: A Life Insurance Workbook for Business Education* (New York: ILI, 1953), J. Walter Thompson Company, Domestic Advertisements Collection, David M. Rubenstein Rare Book & Manuscript Library, Duke University.

43. ILI, "Young People Do Want to Know."

44. Johnson, *Speaking with One Voice*, 84.

45. Enterline and Goodman, *Blueprint for Tomorrow*, 3.

46. Johnson, *Speaking with One Voice*, 60.

47. Johnson, 86.

48. Johnson, 61.

49. Johnson, 71.

50. On the history of polling in the United States, see Sarah Igo, *The Averaged American: Surveys, Citizens, and the Making of a Mass Public* (Cambridge, MA: Harvard University Press, 2007).

51. Johnson, *Speaking with One Voice*, 70.

52. Johnson, 107.

53. Arnold Brown, "How to Get the Jump on Your Future: The Life Insurance Industry Has Developed an 'Early Warning System' to Keep Its Members Alert to What's Ahead in Business and Society," *Management Review* (June 1977): 44–45.

54. Johnson, *Speaking with One Voice*, 106.

55. Johnson, 139.

56. Johnson, 58.

57. Johnson, 128.

58. Johnson, 132.

59. On the popularity of psychology and its appeal to business leaders during the postwar years, see John Burnham, *After Freud Left: A Century of Psychoanalysis in America* (Chicago: University of Chicago Press, 2012).

60. Johnson, *Speaking with One Voice*, 69–78.

61. Johnson, 72.

62. Johnson, 71.

63. The question of "how to live" was raised regularly in school curricula and advice literature produced by the ILI. For one example, see "ILI, "Young People Do Want to Know." See also Johnson, *Speaking with One Voice*, 82.

64. ILI, "Remember, Dear, Happiness Doesn't Just *Happen!*," 1947, J. Walter Thompson Company, Domestic Advertisements Collection, David M. Rubenstein Rare Book & Manuscript Library, Duke University.

65. ILI, "Why Is Marriage Like a Canoe?," 1947, J. Walter Thompson Company, Domestic Advertisements Collection, David M. Rubenstein Rare Book & Manuscript Library, Duke University.

66. ILI, "How Young Should People Marry?," 1948, J. Walter Thompson Company, Domestic Advertisements Collection, David M. Rubenstein Rare Book & Manuscript Library, Duke University.

67. On expertise and postwar culture, see Elaine Tyler May, *Homeward Bound: American Families in the Cold War Era*, 20th anniversary ed. (New York: Basic Books, 2008); and Igo, *The Averaged American*.

68. ILI, "Does the Extra Paycheck Always PAY?," 1947, J. Walter Thompson Company, Domestic Advertisements Collection, David M. Rubenstein Rare Book & Manuscript Library, Duke University.

69. ILI, "Should Wives Work Too?," 1948, J. Walter Thompson Company, Domestic Advertisements Collection, David M. Rubenstein Rare Book & Manuscript Library, Duke University.

70. ILI, "The Birthday Tommy Tried to FORGET!," 1952, J. Walter Thompson Company, Domestic Advertisements Collection, David M. Rubenstein Rare Book & Manuscript Library, Duke University.

71. ILI, "The *Real* Culprit Was Never Tried!," 1947, J. Walter Thompson Company, Domestic Advertisements Collection, David M. Rubenstein Rare Book & Manuscript Library, Duke University.

72. Metropolitan Life Insurance Company, "The Restless Years: 9–12," 1959, Roy Lightner Collection of Antique Advertisements, David M. Rubenstein Rare Book & Manuscript Library, Duke University.

73. Johnson, *Speaking with One Voice*, 83.

74. ILI, "I Pray the Lord My Soul to Keep," 1952, J. Walter Thompson Company, Domestic Advertisements Collection, David M. Rubenstein Rare Book & Manuscript Library, Duke University.

75. For a history of the American safety movement, see Arwen Mohun, *Risk: Negotiating Safety in American Society* (Baltimore: Johns Hopkins University Press, 2012).

76. Jonathan Simon, "Driving Governmentality: Automobile Accidents, Insurance, and the Challenge to Social Order in the Inter-war Years, 1919 to 1941," *Connecticut Insurance Law Journal* 4 (1997): 521.

77. Auto insurers resisted efforts by the states to pass compulsory coverage laws well into the 1960s. The Association of Casualty and Surety Companies, a professional organization representing some of the nation's largest auto insurance providers, hired JWT in 1954 to produce a series of advertisements designed to discourage New Yorkers from passing a compulsory coverage law, for example. See Association of Casualty and Surety Companies, "Why Compulsory Automobile Insurance Is Bad for You," "Is Compulsory Automobile Insurance in Your Best Interest?," and "Compulsory Automobile Insurance Won't Stop Killings on Our Highways!," 1954, J. Walter Thompson Company, Domestic Advertisements Collection, David M. Rubenstein Rare Book and Manuscript Library, Duke University.

78. Saskatchewan's socialist government adopted the Columbia plan in 1947. Unfortunately, little scholarship exists on the province's experience with no-fault insurance.

79. "Kemper Group in Auto Safety More Than Half Century," *National Underwriter*, September 22, 1967.

80. The first driver training class was offered in State College, Pennsylvania, in 1932, the same year the Columbia plan was published. Driver education didn't receive national attention, however, until the war years, when military officials discovered that many recruits lacked sound driving skills. See "Kemper Group in Auto Safety."

81. Hearings before Subcommittee of the Committee on Interstate and Foreign Commerce, House of Representatives, 85th Congress, H. R. 5416, *A Bill to Promote Safety in Transportation by Motor Vehicle in Interstates Commerce by Assisting the States to Establish Programs for Driver Education*," 1957, 11 (statement of Stanley Withe).

82. See Association of Automobile Mutual Insurance Companies, *Caution at the Crossroads*, 1950, video, 11:24, https://archive.org/details/6251_Caution_at_the_Crossroads_01_21_17_13; Liberty Mutual Insurance Company, Teenage Road-e-o, 1955, video, 14:51, https://archive.org/details/0776_Teenage_Road-e-o_03_39_02_00; Aetna Casualty and Surety Company, Live and Let Live, 1947, video, 10:15, https://archive.org/details/LiveandL1947.

83. On the development of the Steerometer, see Lee Vinsel, "'Safe Driving Depends on the Man at the Wheel': Psychologists and the Subject of Auto Safety, 1920–55," *Osiris* 33 (2018): 191.

84. Richard Hooker, *Aetna Life Insurance Company: Its First Hundred Years* (Hartford, CT: Aetna Life Insurance Company, 1956), 211.

85. "Drivotrainer Is Effective, Reaches Nearly 1.5 Million," *National Underwriter* 71, no. 23 (June 9, 1967): 1, 18.

86. Dean Cook, "Realism without Risk: The Story of the Aetna Drivotrainer," *Insurance Red Book* 69 (1968): 74.

87. "Traffic Safety Men Meet at Aetna Home Office," *Eastern Underwriter* 58 (1957): 42.

88. "Cullen Believes Young Drivers Offer New Hope," *Weekly Underwriter—Accident and Health* 168 (1953): 1764.

89. "Cullen Believes Young Drivers Offer New Hope," 1764.

90. "Drivotrainer Is Effective," 18.

91. "Cullen Believes Young Drivers Offer New Hope," 1764.

92. Cook, "Realism without Risk," 75.

93. "Traffic Safety Men Meet at Aetna Home Office," *Eastern Underwriter* 58 (April 12, 1957): 42.

94. *Driver Education: Hearings before a Subcommittee of the Committee on Interstate and Foreign Commerce, House of Representatives, Eighty-Fifth Congress, First Session, on H.R. 5416,* June 10, 17, and 24, 1957, 10.

95. *Driver Education: Hearings,* 10.

96. *Driver Education: Hearings,* 11.

97. *Driver Education: Hearings,* 44.

98. "Drivotrainer Is Effective," 1.

99. "Drivotrainer Is Effective," 18.

100. "Aetna Drivotrainer," *Journal of Data Management* 5 (1967): 52.

101. "Aetna Drivotrainer," 52.

102. Cook, "Realism without Risk," 75.

103. Cook, 75.

104. Cook, 75.

105. Cook, 75.

106. Cook, 74–75.

107. Cecil Zuan and Melvin Schroeder, "The Drivotrainer: A Teaching Machine," *Journal of Secondary Education* 37, no. 2 (February 1967): 112–16.

108. L. I. Bernoff, *An Experimental Study of Teaching Efficiency of the Aetna Drivotrainer System* (Hartford: Aetna Life and Casualty Company, 1958); T. Seals, *An Evaluation of Selected Driver and Traffic Safety Education Courses* (Hartford, CT: Aetna Life and Casualty Company, 1966).

109. H. Bowman, "An Evaluation of the Teaching Effectiveness of the Aetna Drive-Trainer," *Traffic Safety Research Review* (September 1959); Charles B. Stoke and Phillip Harris, *A Performance Report for Use in Driver Education Evaluation* (Charlottesville: Virginia Highway and Transportation Research Council, 1984).

110. Walter Gray, "Space Age Driver Education," *Contemporary Education* 41 (1970): 162–65.

111. Edward A. Tenney, *The Highway Jungle: The Story of the Public Safety Movement and of the Failure of Driver Education in Public Schools* (New York: Exposition Press, 1962), 132.

112. Tenney, *The Highway Jungle,* 84.

113. Tenney, 93.

114. Tenney, 79.

115. The ILI released a series of issue ads on the problems affecting America's cities and what the industry was doing to solve them, in 1969. See ILI, "When You Invest a Billion Dollars to Help the Cities, You Learn Some Things. Like Hope," "What Can a Billion Dollars Do for the Cities These Days?," and "A Lot That Is Said about Urban Problems Is Pure Myth," 1969, J. Walter Thompson Company, Domestic Advertisements Collection, David M. Rubenstein Rare Book & Manuscript Library, Duke University.

Chapter Three

1. Corinne Demas, *Eleven Stories High: Growing Up in Stuyvesant Town, 1948–1968* (Albany: State University of New York Press, 2002), 8.

2. Demas, *Eleven Stories High,* 4.

3. Demas, 6.

4. Demas, 7.

NOTES TO PAGES 73-77

5. Demas, 5.

6. Demas, 5.

7. Demas, 6.

8. See Arthur Simon, *Stuyvesant Town, U.S.A.: Pattern for Two Americas* (New York: New York University Press, 1970); Arnold Hirsch, *Making the Second Ghetto: Race and Housing in Chicago, 1940–1960* (Chicago: University of Chicago Press, 1983); Roberta Moudry, "Architecture as Cultural Design: The Architecture and Urbanism of the Metropolitan Life Insurance Company" (PhD diss., Cornell University, 1995). More recent studies include my own dissertation, which identified life insurance housing developments as a national phenomenon; see Caley Horan, "Actuarial Age: Insurance and the Emergence of Neoliberalism in the Post-WWII United States" (PhD diss., University of Minnesota, 2010). See also Samuel Zipp, *Manhattan Projects: The Rise and Fall of Urban Renewal in Cold War New York* (New York: Oxford University Press, 2010); Elihu Rubin, *Insuring the City: The Prudential Center and the Postwar Urban Landscape* (New Haven, CT: Yale University Press, 2012); Sara Stevens, *Developing Expertise: Architecture and Real Estate in Metropolitan America* (New Haven, CT: Yale University Press, 2016); and Adam Tanaka, "Fiduciary Landlords: Life Insurers and Large-Scale Housing in New York City" (working paper, Harvard Joint Center for Housing Studies, April 2017).

9. Tanaka, "Fiduciary Landlords," 58.

10. Interview with Frederick H. Ecker, quoted in Robert E. Schultz, *Life Insurance Housing Projects* (Philadelphia: S. S. Huebner Foundation for Insurance Education, 1956), 95.

11. Moudry, "Architecture as Cultural Design," 305.

12. "Chicago Redevelops: Slums Yield to Low-Density Skyscraper Housing Financed with Insurance Company Money," *Architectural Forum*, August 1950, 99.

13. Schultz, *Life Insurance Housing Projects*, 3.

14. Zipp, *Manhattan Projects*, 76.

15. Charles Abrams, "Stuyvesant Town's Threat to Our Liberties: Government Waives the Constitution for Private Enterprise," *Commentary*, November 1, 1949, https://www.commentary magazine.com/articles/charles-abrams/stuyvesant-towns-threat-to-our-libertiesgovernment -waives-the-constitution-for-private-enterprise/.

16. Most state statutes allowed insurers to hold foreclosed properties for a limited period, typically under ten years. After that period, states required companies to dispose of properties. See Harold Wayne Snider, *Life Insurance Investment in Commercial Real Estate* (Philadelphia: S. S. Huebner Foundation for Insurance Education, 1956); and Schultz, *Life Insurance Housing Projects*, 25.

17. Viviana A. Rotman Zelizer, *Morals and Markets: The Development of Life Insurance in the United States* (New York: Columbia University Press, 1979); JoAnne Yates, *Structuring the Information Age: Life Insurance and Technology in the Twentieth Century* (Baltimore: Johns Hopkins University Press, 2005).

18. Schultz, *Life Insurance Housing Projects*.

19. Thomas Derdak, ed., *International Directory of Company Histories* (Chicago: St. James Press, 1988), 3:292–93.

20. Federal Deposit Insurance Corporation, "Historical Timeline," 2014, https://www.fdic .gov/about/history/timeline/1930s.html.

21. "History of New York Life Insurance Company," *Reference for Business: Encyclopedia of Businesses*, n.d., accessed February 12, 2020, http://www.referenceforbusiness.com/history2/64 /New-York-Life-Insurance-Company.html.

22. Schultz, *Life Insurance Housing Projects*, 25–26.

23. Unlike the 1922 emergency amendment passed by the state, this law contained no provision for tax exemption.

24. Schultz, *Life Insurance Housing Projects*, 30.

25. The literature on the midcentury housing shortage—created by a combination of decreased home building during the Great Depression and World War II, as well as the return of large numbers of veterans after the war—is extensive. For a general introduction to the housing shortage, see Kenneth T. Jackson, *Crabgrass Frontier: The Suburbanization of the United States* (New York: Oxford University Press, 1987). On attempts to solve the crisis through public rather than private means, see Jackson, *Crabgrass Frontier*; see also Richard Rothstein, *The Color of Law: The Forgotten History of How Our Government Segregated America* (Newark: Liverlight, 2017).

26. For a comprehensive list of the statutory provisions of insurance codes and state constitutions pertaining to real estate investment by life insurance companies in the United States through 1952, see Schultz, *Life Insurance Housing Projects*, 103–33. For an extended discussion of the New York legislation passed in the 1940s, see Moudry, "Architecture as Cultural Design."

27. Exceptions included Alabama, Florida, Kentucky, Montana, South Carolina, South Dakota, and Texas. Schultz, *Life Insurance Housing Projects*, 96. For accessible treatments of changes in insurance investment law from the 1930s through the 1960s, see Snider, *Life Insurance Investment in Commercial Real Estate*; David Cummins, ed., *Investment Activities of Life Insurance Companies* (Homewood: Richard Irwin, 1977); and Bertrand Fox and Eli Shapiro, eds., *Life Insurance Companies as Financial Institutions* (Englewood Cliffs, NJ: Prentice-Hall, 1962).

28. Schultz, 2.

29. "15,000 Persons Now Living in Life Insurance Companies' Housing Projects," *Eastern Underwriter* 50 (October 7, 1949): 16–17.

30. "Life Insurance Companies Plan Post-war Housing Projects," *Weekly Underwriter* 150 (May 13, 1944): 24.

31. "How to Order a City: Metropolitan Life Makes Housing Pay," *Fortune* 33, no. 4 (1946): 133.

32. "Metropolitan's Parkchester," *Architectural Forum* 71 (December 1939): 412–26; "Chicago Redevelops."

33. See Lewis Mumford, "Prefabricated Blight," in *From the Ground Up: Observations on Contemporary Architecture, Housing, Highway Building, and Civic Design* (New York: Harvest Books, 1956), 108–14; Lewis Mumford, "From Utopia Parkway, Turn East," in *From the Ground Up*, 3–10; and Lewis Mumford, "Fresh Meadows, Fresh Plans," in *From the Ground Up*, 11–19.

34. Mumford, "Fresh Meadows, Fresh Plans," 19.

35. Schultz, *Life Insurance Housing Projects*, 30.

36. "120-Acre Housing Will Rise in Bronx as Private Project," *New York Times*, April 8, 1938, cited in Moudry, "Architecture as Cultural Design," 347.

37. Moudry, "Architecture as Cultural Design," 374.

38. "Metropolitan's Parkchester," 412.

39. "How to Order a City," 136.

40. Schultz, *Life Insurance Housing Projects*, 32.

41. "How to Order a City," 136.

42. "How to Order a City," 136.

43. Moudry, "Architecture as Cultural Design," 360, 368.

44. On "lore," see Jeffrey S. Gurock, "'Getting Along' in Parkchester: A New Era in Jewish–Irish Relations in New York City, 1940–1970," *Religions* 9, (2018): 181. Numerous online blogs and social media sites organized by former residents of Parkchester also discuss the tenant selection process.

45. Moudry, "Architecture as Cultural Design," 376.

46. "How to Order a City," 212.

47. Quoted in Gurock, "'Getting Along' in Parkchester," 181; and Morris Markey, "40,000 Neighbors," *Saturday Evening Post*, May 18, 1940, 44.

48. "Metropolitan's Parkchester," 16.

49. Gurock, "'Getting Along' in Parkchester," 181.

50. "Parkchester Boys Not as Docile as Statistics Actually Find," *New York Herald Tribune*, October 14, 1944, 13, cited in Gurock, "'Getting Along' in Parkchester," 181.

51. Moudry, "Architecture as Cultural Design," 335–36.

52. Moudry, 335–36.

53. "How to Order a City," 216.

54. Jo Chamberlin, "Showing Uncle Sam the Way," *American Magazine* 28, no. 6 (December 1939): 116.

55. Gretta Palmer, "Middletown-on-the-Subway," *Christian Science Monitor*, November 1, 1941, cited in Moudry, "Architecture as Cultural Design," 379.

56. "How to Order a City," 136.

57. "How to Order a City," 216. The subway stop at East 177th Street was later renamed Parkchester station.

58. On the total cost of the development, see Schultz, *Life Insurance Housing Projects*, 32.

59. Schultz, 37.

60. Paul Goldberger, "To Utopia by Bus and Subway," *New York Times*, April 17, 1981, C1.

61. Goldberger, "To Utopia by Bus and Subway," C1.

62. For an in-depth account of the eviction and the protest it provoked at Parkchester, see Elihu S. Hicks, "The Battle of Parkchester," *Jewish Life* (July 1953): 17–19.

63. See Moudry, "Architecture as Cultural Design"; and Schultz, *Life Insurance Housing Projects*.

64. Zipp, *Manhattan Projects*, 79.

65. Zipp, 85.

66. For a detailed account of the neighborhood replaced by Stuyvesant Town and the efforts of residents to resist relocation, see Zipp, 83–99.

67. Zipp, 99.

68. Charles Gotthart, "Speed Vast New Homes Project in New York City: Slums Make Way for Huge Apartments," *Chicago Daily Tribune*, February 21, 1946.

69. Zipp, *Manhattan Projects*, 103.

70. Scott Henderson, *Housing and the Democratic Ideal: The Life and Thought of Charles Abrams* (New York: Columbia University Press, 2000), 127.

71. Moudry, "Architecture as Cultural Design," 406–7.

72. "They Live in Stuyvesant Town," *House and Garden* (September 1948): 94. See also Moudry, "Architecture as Cultural Design," 543.

73. Mumford, "Prefabricated Blight," 109.

74. Mumford, 109.

75. Mumford, 110-111.

76. For a meditation on the Social Security number as an aspect of the quantified self that grew out of insurance industry practice, see Bouk, *How Our Days Became Numbered*.

77. Zipp offers an extended discussion of criticism of Metropolitan's segregation policy at Stuyvesant in *Manhattan Projects*, 118.

78. Joseph B. Robison, "The Story of Stuyvesant Town," *Nation* 17, no. 22 (June 2, 1951): 514–17.

79. Schultz, *Life Insurance Housing Projects*, 90.

80. "Housing Project Will Bar Negro Tenants," *New York Post*, April 18, 1943.

81. Charles G. Spellman, "The Black Press: Setting the Political Agenda during World War II," *Negro History Bulletin* 51, no. 12 (December 1993): 38–42.

82. "Mayor Signs Contract for Riverton Housing Project," *New York Amsterdam News*, November 25, 1944, A1–2.

83. Martha Biondi, *To Stand and Fight: The Struggle for Civil Rights in Postwar New York City* (Cambridge, MA: Harvard University Press, 2003), 129.

84. *Dorsey v. Stuyvesant Corp.* For extended discussions of the Stuyvesant lawsuit, see Simon, *Stuyvesant Town, U.S.A.*; Zipp, *Manhattan Projects*; and Henderson, *Housing and the Democratic Ideal*, 122–46. Local and national coverage of the case was extensive. For one representative account from the Black press outside New York, see "Judge Rules Stuyvesant Project Bias Is O.K.," *Atlanta Daily World*, August 3, 1947.

85. Marquis James, *The Metropolitan Life* (New York: Viking Press, 1947), 386.

86. James, *The Metropolitan Life*, 386.

87. Abrams, "Stuyvesant Town's Threat to Our Liberties."

88. Abrams, "Stuyvesant Town's Threat to Our Liberties."

89. Biondi, *To Stand and Fight*, 123.

90. The first privately financed housing for Black tenants in the United States was the Prudential Life Insurance Company's Douglass–Harrison complex, built by the company in Newark following a temporary amendment to New Jersey's insurance code in 1929. The complex was completed in 1935. Little research has been conducted on this or other developments built by Prudential in the 1930s. For brief treatments, see Schultz, *Life Insurance Housing Projects*, 29–31, 43–44; and Roberta Moudry, "Prudential Insurance and Housing Development," in David Goldfield, ed., *Encyclopedia of American Urban History* (Thousand Oaks, CA: Sage, 2007).

91. "Stuyvesant Town to Admit Negroes after a Controversy of Seven Years," *New York Times*, August 25, 1950.

92. Gotthart, "Speed Vast New Homes Project in New York City," 3.

93. The number of people living in the area covered by the 1949 plan may have been higher than Moses reported, as residents of boardinghouses were counted, but residents of hotels were not. Moses was also notorious for misrepresenting and undercounting populations in areas he targeted for clearance and redevelopment. See New York City Committee on Slum Clearance Plans, *Harlem Slum Clearance Plan under Title I of the Housing Act of 1949*, January 1951, 52 pp., https://www.huduser.gov/portal/publications/Harlem-Slum-Clearance-Plan.html.

94. Schultz, *Life Insurance Housing Projects*, 55.

95. "Highest NY Court Backs Housing Bias: Riverton's Doors Open to New Tenants," *New York Amsterdam News*, August 2, 1947, 1, 20.

96. Ken Sargeant, Keith Hunter, and Glenn Hunter, dirs., "Down by the Riverside, a Place to Be Free" (documentary project in progress, 2007), clips via email to the author, courtesy of Sargeant and the Harlem Cultural Archives, New York.

97. Sargeant, Hunter, and Hunter, "Down by the Riverside."

98. "Ex Tenants Fondly Recall a Haven in Harlem," *New York Times*, March 15, 1986, 1.

99. "Highest NY Court Backs Housing Bias," 20.

100. Sargeant, Hunter, and Hunter, "Down by the Riverside."

101. Sargeant, Hunter, and Hunter.

102. "Luxury Housing Opens in Harlem," *New York Times*, October 17, 1958, 16.

103. Sargeant, Hunter, and Hunter, "Down by the Riverside."

104. "*Ebony, Glamour* on Magazine Rack at Home: Commutes between White World of Wall Street, Black World of Harlem," *Globe and Mail*, August 20, 1968, 4.

105. James Baldwin, "Fifth Avenue, Uptown," *Esquire*, July 1960, https://www.esquire.com/news-politics/a3638/fifth-avenue-uptown/.

106. Baldwin, "Fifth Avenue, Uptown."

107. Baldwin.

108. Baldwin.

109. Crime at Riverton was a recurring problem well into the late 1960s and was covered extensively by both the *New York Times* and the *New Amsterdam News*.

110. Baldwin, "Fifth Avenue, Uptown."

111. Baldwin.

112. Baldwin.

113. "*Esquire* Calls Riverton a 'Slum,'" *New York Amsterdam News*, June 18, 1960, 1.

114. "Riverton Article Draws Some Comment," *New York Amsterdam News*, June 25, 1960, 1.

115. "Riverton Article Draws Some Comment," 1.

116. Joe Darden, *Detroit: Race and Uneven Development* (Philadelphia: Temple University Press, 1987), 121–22; David Freund, *Colored Property: State Policy and White Racial Politics in Suburban America* (Chicago: University of Chicago Press, 2010), 307–16.

117. Hirsch, *Making the Second Ghetto*, 18.

118. Hirsch, 23.

119. Hirsch, 20.

120. Hirsch, 4.

121. Hirsch, 18–22.

122. Hirsch, 117.

123. Edward Schreiber, "Two Insurance Firms May Ask Housing Sites: Consider Investing in Chicago," *Chicago Daily Tribune*, December 7, 1945, 39.

124. Schreiber, "Two Insurance Firms May Ask Housing Sites," 39.

125. Philip Hampson, "N. Y. Gets Big Housing Units; Midwest Pays: Chicago Ignored by Insurance Firms," *Chicago Daily Tribune*, May 3, 1947, 1.

126. "Manufacturers Urge Probe of Housing Slight: Ask Why Big Insurance Firms Ignore City," *Chicago Daily Tribune*, May 4, 1947, 7.

127. Hampson, "N. Y. Gets Big Housing Units," 1.

128. "Manufacturers Urge Probe of Housing Slight," 7.

129. Thomas Buck, "Urge Seeking of Insurance Housing Cash: Council Advises Chicago to Act," *Chicago Daily Tribune*, September 5, 1948, A7.

130. Quoted in Buck, "Urge Seeking of Insurance Housing Cash," A7.

131. Buck, A7.

132. Buck, A7.

133. Hampson, "N. Y. Gets Big Housing Units," 1.

134. Hampson, 1.

135. Metropolitan undertook three projects in 1941: Parkfairfax in Alexandria, Virginia; Parkmerced in San Francisco; and Park La Brea in Los Angeles. Park Fairfax was solicited by the federal government with the goal of providing housing for Pentagon personnel. See Schultz, *Life Insurance Housing Projects*, 33.

136. Hirsch, *Making the Second Ghetto*, 116.

137. "Manufacturers Urge Probe of Housing Slight," 7.

138. Schultz, *Life Insurance Housing Projects*, 59–61.

139. On existing structures, see Schultz, *Life Insurance Housing Projects*, 60. On families relocated by Lake Meadows, see Digital Scholarship Lab, "Renewing Inequality," ed. Robert K. Nelson and Edward L. Ayers, *American Panorama*, accessed February 20, 2020, http://dsl.richmond.edu/panorama/renewal/#view=0/0/1&viz=cartogram&city=chicagoIL&loc=11/41.8730/-87.6340&project=2468.

140. Schultz, *Life Insurance Housing Projects*, 60.

141. Hirsch, *Making the Second Ghetto*, 120.

142. Wendell E. Pritchett, "The 'Public Menace' of Blight: Urban Renewal and the Private Uses of Eminent Domain," *Yale Law and Policy Review* 21, no. 1 (2003): 34.

143. Pritchett, "The 'Public Menace' of Blight," 34.

144. Pritchett, 34.

145. "Citizens Hold Huge Rally to Block Land Grab," *Pittsburgh Courier*, June 25, 1949, cited in Pritchett, "The 'Public Menace' of Blight," 34.

146. Pritchett, 35. The phrase "Negro clearance" was popularized years later, when James Baldwin used it to describe urban renewal's impacts on Black communities in a 1963 televised interview with Kenneth Clark on WNDT-TV, New York City. See "Conversation with James Baldwin, A; James Baldwin Interview," June 24, 1963, WGBH Media Library & Archives, http://openvault.wgbh.org/catalog/V_C03ED1927DCF46B5A8C82275DF4239F9.

147. See Hirsch, *Making the Second Ghetto*; Pritchett, "The 'Public Menace' of Blight"; and Andrew Diamond, *Chicago On the Make: Power and Inequality in a Modern City* (Oakland: University of California Press, 2017), 128–64.

148. Hirsch, *Making the Second Ghetto*, 125.

149. "Chicago Redevelops."

150. Arnold Hirsch, "Urban Renewal," *Encyclopedia of Chicago*, 2004–5, http://www.encyclopedia.chicagohistory.org/pages/1295.html.

151. Digital Scholarship Lab, "Renewing Inequality"; Jane Jacobs, *The Death and Life of Great American Cities* (New York: Vintage, 1992), 45.

152. Hirsch, "Urban Renewal."

153. Hirsch, *Making the Second Ghetto*, 118.

154. Hirsch, 119.

155. "Homes Project Held a Leader for Many More," *Chicago Daily Tribune*, July 23, 1948, 12.

156. Schultz, *Life Insurance Housing Projects*, 89.

157. Schultz provides the most through study of the industry's turn away from urban housing. See also Louis Winnick, *Rental Housing: Opportunities for Private Investment* (New York: McGraw-Hill, 1958).

158. Hicks, "The Battle of Parkchester," 17, 19.

159. "Harlem Project Asks Rise of 79%," *New York Times*, April 9, 1954.

160. "Tenants at Riverton Assail Parking Lot," *New York Amsterdam News*, September 29, 1951, 1, 14.

161. Zipp, *Manhattan Projects*, 123–29.

162. "Hidden Rent Boost Claimed at Parkmerced by Tenants," *San Francisco Examiner*, February 5, 1951, and "Clothesline Battle Ended: Outdoor Facilities at Parkmerced to Stay," *San Francisco Examiner*, February 6, 1951, Parkmerced Clippings File, San Francisco History Center, San Francisco Public Library.

163. "Pickett Ban at Parkmerced," no publication listed, August 9, 1953, Parkmerced Clippings File, San Francisco History Center, San Francisco Public Library.

164. Bill Van Niekerken, "How SF State's Bloody Strikes Changed Academia and the Nation 50 Years Ago," *San Francisco Chronicle*, November 7, 2018, https://www.sfchronicle.com/chronicle_vault/article/How-SF-State-s-bloody-strikes-changed-academia-13362709.php.

165. Niekerken, "How SF State's Bloody Strikes Changed Academia and the Nation."

166. "Parkmerced Tenant: Ouster Laid to Strike Aid," no publication listed, June 1, 1969, Parkmerced Clippings File, San Francisco History Center, San Francisco Public Library.

167. "Parkmerced Won't Toss Out Tenant," no publication listed, July 3, 1969, Parkmerced Clippings File, San Francisco History Center, San Francisco Public Library.

168. *Trafficante v. Metropolitan Life Insurance Company*, 409 U.S. 205 (1972)

169. *Trafficante v. Metropolitan Life Insurance Company*. See also Mark Stephen Davis, "Standing to Challenge Housing Discrimination: The Limits of *Trafficante v. Metropolitan Life*," *Urban Law Annual* 31 (1974): 311–18.

170. Davis, "Standing to Challenge Housing Discrimination," 311.

171. J. Linn Allen, "A Second Transformation Awaits Lake Meadows," *Chicago Tribune*, March 23, 1997, https://www.chicagotribune.com/news/ct-xpm-1997-03-23-9703270074-story.html.

172. "Black Builder Buys Complex in Harlem," *New York Times*, February 29, 1976, 226.

173. "Black Builder Buys Complex in Harlem," 226.

174. Snider, *Life Insurance Investment in Commercial Real Estate*, 15.

Chapter Four

1. Robert Sheehan, "That Mighty Pump, Prudential," *Fortune* 69, no. 1 (January 1964), 99.

2. Sheehan, "Mighty Pump," 99.

3. "Chip Off the Old Rock," *Time*, March 18, 1957, 93.

4. James Walter, *The Investment Process as Characterized by Leading Life Insurance Companies* (Cambridge, MA: Harvard University Press, 1962), 253.

5. "Chip Off the Old Rock," 92.

6. The literature on postwar suburbanization in the United States is extensive. For definitive accounts, see Robert Fishman, *Bourgeois Utopias: The Rise and Fall of Suburbia* (New York: Basic Books 1987); Kenneth T. Jackson, *Crabgrass Frontier: The Suburbanization of the United States* (New York: Oxford University Press, 1985); and Thomas Sugrue, *The Origins of the Urban Crisis: Race and Inequality in Postwar Detroit* (Princeton, NJ: Princeton University Press, 1996). Scholars have only recently begun to examine private industry's role in shaping suburbanization. For recent studies focused on real estate, see Adrienne Brown and Valerie Smith, eds., *Race and Real Estate* (New York: Oxford University Press, 2016); and Keeanga-Yamahtta Taylor, *Race for Profit: How Banks and the Real Estate Industry Undermined Black Homeownership* (Chapel Hill: University of North Carolina Press, 2019). Thomas Hanchett, the only historian to focus specifically on insurance and suburbanization, first identified Prudential as an important financier of

suburban ventures, in "Financing Suburbia: Prudential Insurance and the Post–World War II Transformation of the American City," *Journal of Urban History* 26, no. 3 (2000): 312–28.

7. For early, essential accounts of this process, see Fishman, *Bourgeois Utopias*; Jackson, *Crabgrass Frontier*; and Sugrue, *Origins of the Urban Crisis*. For a more recent discussion, see David Freund, "Marketing the Free Market: State Intervention and the Politics of Prosperity in Metropolitan America," in *The New Suburban History*, ed. Kevin Kruse and Thomas Sugrue (Chicago: University of Chicago Press, 2006).

8. For a representative account of this argument, see Kathleen Tobin, "The Reduction of Urban Vulnerability: Revisiting 1950s American Suburbanization as Civil Defense," *Cold War History* 2, no. 2 (2010): 1–32. See also Jennifer Light, *From Welfare to Warfare: Defense Intellectuals and Urban Problems in Cold War America* (Baltimore: Johns Hopkins University Press, 2005).

9. Elaine Tyler May's classic study of suburban family life remains the definitive text on Cold War–era ideological commitments to suburbanization and the nuclear family. See Elaine Tyler May, *Homeward Bound: American Families in the Cold War Era* (New York: Basic Books, 1988). See also Joanne Meyerowitz, ed., *Not June Cleaver: Women and Gender in Postwar America, 1945–1960* (Philadelphia: Temple University Press, 1994).

10. Haughton Bell and Harold G. Fraine, "Legal Framework, Trends, and Developments in Investment Practices of Life Insurance Companies," *Law and Contemporary Problems* 17, no. 1 (Winter 1952): 45.

11. Bell and Fraine, "Legal Framework," 45.

12. Bell and Fraine, 63.

13. Walter, *The Investment Process*, 247–51.

14. Bell and Fraine, "Legal Framework," 70.

15. Bell and Fraine, 69–70.

16. "Chip Off the Old Rock," 92.

17. "Chip Off the Old Rock," 92.

18. "Chip Off the Old Rock," 92.

19. "Chip Off the Old Rock," 98.

20. "Chip Off the Old Rock," 98.

21. During the early 1940s, the industry invested heavily in government bonds. This patriotic commitment during wartime offered a good look for the industry, but a bad return on investment dollars. See Bell and Fraine, "Legal Framework," 50.

22. "Chip Off the Old Rock," 97–98.

23. "Chip Off the Old Rock," 98.

24. George A. Bishop, *Capital Formation through Life Insurance: A Study in the Growth of Life Insurance Services and Investment Activities* (Homewood, IL: Richard D. Irwin, 1976), 3–24, 113.

25. Bishop, *Capital Formation*, 120.

26. Hanchett, "Financing Suburbia," 314.

27. Hanchett, 318.

28. Sheehan, "Mighty Pump," 102.

29. Sheehan, 102.

30. Walter, *The Investment Process*, 114–18.

31. Walter, 247–51.

32. Hanchett, "Financing Suburbia," 314.

33. Jack Guttentag and Morris Beck, *New Series of Home Mortgage Yields since 1951* (New York: Columbia University Press, 1970), 101–3, cited in Bishop, *Capital Formation*, 118.

34. Bishop, 117–18.

35. The literature on racial discrimination and federal housing policy is large and growing. For recent accounts, see Robert Self, *American Babylon: Race and the Struggle for Postwar Oakland* (Princeton, NJ: Princeton University Press, 2003); Richard Rothstein, *The Color of Law: The Forgotten History of How Our Government Segregated America* (New York: Liveright, 2017); and Taylor, *Race for Profit*. For an analysis of the discriminatory impact of the VA housing program on lesbian and gay Americans, see Margot Canaday, *The Straight State: Sexuality and Citizenship in Twentieth-Century America* (Princeton, NJ: Princeton University Press, 2009).

36. Rothstein, *The Color of Law*, 66.

37. This quote, from Metropolitan president Frederick Ecker, was citied widely during debates over racial segregation at the company's Stuyvesant Town housing development. It first appeared in "Housing Project Will Bar Negro Tenants," *New York Post*, April 18, 1943.

38. On the long history of racial discrimination in insurance underwriting, see Mary L. Heen, "Ending Jim Crow Life Insurance Rates," *Northwestern Journal of Law and Social Policy* 4, no. 2 (2009): 360-99.

39. Karen Orren, *Corporate Power and Social Change: The Politics of the Life Insurance Industry* (Baltimore: Johns Hopkins University Press, 1974), 126.

40. Harold Wayne Snider, *Life Insurance Investments in Commercial Real Estate* (Philadelphia: S. S. Huebner Foundation for Insurance Education, 1956), 17.

41. Bishop, *Capital Formation*, 129.

42. William Cahn, *A Matter of Life and Death: The Connecticut Mutual Story* (New York: Random House, 1970), 205. On pipelines, see Richard W. Hooley, *Financing the Natural Gas Industry: The Role of Life Insurance Investment Policies* (New York: Columbia University Press, 1961). Individual companies eagerly publicized their nation-building capacities by citing their commitments to infrastructure financing, and industry-penned company histories are awash with references to these projects. On turnpikes, see Richard Hooker, *Aetna Life Insurance Company: Its First 100 Years* (Hartford, CT: Aetna Life Insurance Company, 1965), 209. For an overview of postwar insurance infrastructure investments, see Bishop, *Capital Formation*, 153-55.

43. Snider, *Life Insurance Investment in Commercial Real Estate*, 121. Shopping centers play a key role in the historiography of the postwar United States. For an overview of the literature, see Kenneth T. Jackson, "All the World's a Mall: Reflections on the Social and Economic Consequences of the American Shopping Center," *American Historical Review* 101, no. 4 (October 1996). See also William Severini Kowinski, *The Malling of America: An Inside Look at the Great Consumer Paradise* (New York: William Morrow, 1985); Margaret Crawford, "The World in a Shopping Mall," in Michael Sorkin, ed., *Variations on a Theme Park: The New American City and the End of Public Space* (New York: Hill and Wang, 1992); and the work of Richard Longstreth, esp. *City Center to Regional Mall: Architecture, the Automobile, and Retailing in Los Angeles, 1920-1950* (Cambridge, MA: MIT Press, 1998), and *The American Department Store Transformed, 1920-1960* (New Haven, CT: Yale University Press, 2010). The definitive account of postwar American consumerism, Lizabeth Cohen's *A Consumers' Republic: The Politics of Mass Consumption in Postwar America* (New York: Vintage, 2003), provides a detailed study of shopping center design, construction, and management, as well as the impacts of these spaces on postwar culture and politics. While Cohen and others address shopping center developers at length, they pay little attention to the financing of centers or the oversized role of the insurance industry in that process. Thomas Hanchett offers a rare exception to this rule. See Hanchett, "Financing Suburbia"; and Thomas Hanchett, "U.S. Tax Policy and the Shopping-Center Boom of the 1950s and 1960s," *American Historical Review* 101, no. 4 (October 1996): 1082-110.

44. Bishop, *Capital Formation*, 129-30.

45. Robert Foster, "The Effect of Shopping Center Financing on the Opportunity for Occupancy in Independent Retailers" (PhD diss., Graduate School of Business, Indiana University, 1966), 16.

46. "Shopping Center Investment Popular with Insurance Firms," *Boston Globe*, March 11, 1962, A32.

47. Kowinski popularized this phrase in *The Malling of America*.

48. "How to Order a City: Metropolitan Makes Housing Pay," *Fortune* 33, no. 4 (1946): 210.

49. Foster, "The Effect of Shopping Center Financing," 15.

50. "Work Started on Big Norwalk Store Center," *Los Angeles Times*, May 12, 1951, 19.

51. "Vast Commercial Tract Sold in Norwalk Area," *Los Angeles Times*, December 15, 1950, 5.

52. Pacific Life Insurance Company, "Pacific Mutual: A Careful Investor," Pacific Life 150th Anniversary: Vision and Promise, n.d., accessed January 29, 2020, http://pl150years.com /vision-and-promise/careful-investing-pacific-mutual.

53. "New Market Center Plans Made Public: Norwalk Shopping Area Project to Cost $1,500,000," *Los Angeles Times*, December 22, 1950, B6.

54. "Store Center Expansion Set," *Los Angeles Times*, August 24, 1952, 9.

55. Snider, *Life Insurance Investments in Commercial Real Estate*, 125.

56. Michael Kindig, "Norwalk Square," Historical Marker Database, accessed March 1, 2020, https://www.hmdb.org/m.asp?m=65827.

57. Pacific Mutual Insurance Company, "Enterprise to Match the Vision of the West," *Los Angeles Times*, January 2, 1957, 29.

58. "Chip Off the Old Rock," 95.

59. "Short Hills Gets New Luxury Homes," *New York Times*, June 3, 1951, 217.

60. See Philip Roth, *Goodbye, Columbus* (1959; New York: Vintage, 1993).

61. "Millburn Rezones Turnpike Site for Shopping Center: Pru's $15,000,000 Project Set," undated clipping, no publication listed, Properties Files, Prudential Insurance Company of America Archives; Alexander Milch, "Fifth Ave of New Jersey," *Newark Evening News*, November 6, 1959, Properties Files, Prudential Insurance Company of America Archives.

62. Prudential Life Insurance Company of America, *Millburn Plaza at Short Hills*, promotional brochure, 1959, Properties Files, Prudential Insurance Company of America Archives.

63. Prudential, *Millburn Plaza at Short Hills*.

64. Prudential.

65. "Short Hills Mall: Elegance and Restraint for 'Class' Tenants," *Architectural Record* 131 (June 1962): 171.

66. "Short Hills Mall: Elegance and Restraint," 171.

67. "Short Hills Mall: Elegance and Restraint," 171.

68. "At Issue in Town: The Mall at Short Hills," May 5, 1977, no publication listed, Properties Files, Prudential Insurance Company of America Archives; "David Wins Again," April 19, 1979, no publication listed, Properties Files, Prudential Insurance Company of America Archives.

69. "At Issue in Town."

70. On the importance of shopping centers as privatized "community centers," see Cohen, *A Consumer's Republic*. Cohen argues that the quasi-public nature of shopping center space discouraged public life and community-building, and that the privatization of public meeting spaces in malls posed a threat to democratic life.

71. In his study of Prudential's postwar suburban investments, Thomas Hanchett lists a number of malls financed by the company, including Shoppers' World in Framingham,

Massachusetts (1951); Bishops Corner Mall outside Hartford, Connecticut (1955); Normandale Shopping Center in Montgomery, Alabama (1954); Kenwood Plaza in Cincinnati (1957); Park Central in Phoenix (1958); Waterbury Plaza in Waterbury, Connecticut (1958); Northshore Mall in Boston (1958); Prince George's Plaza in Washington, DC (1959); and Lloyd Center in Portland (1960). See Hanchett, "Financing Suburbia," 320.

72. Victor Gruen and Larry Smith, *Shopping Towns USA: The Planning of Shopping Centers* (New York: Reinhold, 1960), 28.

73. W. W. Bodine, "The 'New Look' on Investments," *Best's Insurance News, Life Edition,* September 1948; Foster, "The Effect of Shopping Center Financing," 22.

74. Foster, 31.

75. Foster, 24.

76. Foster, 24.

77. Hanchett, "Financing Suburbia," 320.

78. Snider, *Life Insurance* Investments in Commercial Real Estate, 125.

79. Snider, 124.

80. U.S. Senate, *Shopping Centers, 1959: Hearings before a Subcommittee of the Select Committee on Small Business, United States Senate, Eighty-Sixth Congress, First Session . . . April 28 and 29, 1959* (Washington, DC: US Government Printing Office, 1959), 62–63.

81. Select Committee on Small Business (hereafter cited as SCSB), *The Impact of Suburban Shopping Centers on Independent Retailers*, Report No. 106, 86th Cong., 1st Sess. 10–11 (1960).

82. SCSB, *The Impact of Suburban Shopping Centers*, 21.

83. US Senate, *Shopping Centers, 1959: Hearings* 137.

84. SCSB, *The Impact of Suburban Shopping Centers*, 22.

85. SCSB, 36, 20.

86. *11th Annual Report of the Select Committee on Small Business US Senate, Together with Supplemental Views* (Washington, DC: US Government Printing Office, 1961), 43.

87. *11th Annual Report of the Select Committee*, 43.

88. Foster, "The Effect of Shopping Center Financing," 72.

89. The building belonged to the Chicago Home Insurance Company. For an introduction to the building and its history, see "Father of All Skyscrapers: Home Insurance Building, Chicago," *Scientific American* 146 (1932): 290.

90. For a discussion of the Metropolitan home office and its role in turn-of-the-century speculative fiction, see Nick Yablon, "The Metropolitan Life in Ruins: Architectural and Fictional Speculations in New York, 1909–19," *American Quarterly* 56, no. 2 (June 2004): 308–47.

91. Leased space in home office buildings offered one of the rare exceptions to prohibitions against ownership of income-producing real estate before state insurance laws changed in the 1940s.

92. Louise Mozingo, *Pastoral Capitalism: A History of Suburban Corporate Landscapes* (Cambridge, MA: MIT Press, 2000), 23.

93. William Carr, *From Three Cents a Week: The Story of the Prudential Insurance Company of America* (Englewood Cliffs, NJ: Prentice Hall, 1975), 125–30; "Chip Off the Old Rock," 92; Sheehan, "Mighty Pump," 102. For a detailed study of the construction of the Prudential Center, see Elihu Rubin, *Insuring the City: The Prudential Center and the Postwar Urban Landscape* (New Haven, CT: Yale University Press, 2012).

94. Sheehan, "Mighty Pump," 102.

95. For a history of the insurance industry's early adoption of computing technology, including brief discussions of changes to office structure in the wake of computerization, see JoAnne

Yates, *Structuring the Information Age: Life Insurance and Technology in the Twentieth Century* (Baltimore: Johns Hopkins University Press, 2009).

96. "Eugene Branch Is Housed in Modernistic Office Building," *New York Life Insurance Company Review*, August 1952, 17; "Capital Branch Housed in New Quarters in Madison," *New York Life Insurance Company Review*, October 1952, 21.

97. "Designed to Be Functional in Plan, Quiet in Expression: Home Office Building for Phoenix Insurance Company," *Architectural Record* 112 (December 1952): 126–35.

98. Manufacturers made the move to the suburbs a few years earlier than insurers, relocating headquarters out of cities beginning in the late 1940s and early 1950s. The General Motors Technical Center, designed by the architect Eero Saarinen for a site in the suburbs of Detroit, is typically credited with the distinction of launching the movement of corporations to the suburbs. That facility opened one year before Connecticut General's suburban facility. For a study of the GM Technical Center, see Mozingo, *Pastoral Capitalism*.

99. Frazar Wilde, *Time Out of Mind: Address Delivered at Newcomen Society in North America* (Princeton, NJ: Newcomen, 1959), 7.

100. Frazar Wilde, "Welcome," in *The New Highways: Challenge to the Metropolitan Region* (Hartford: Connecticut General Life Insurance Corporation, 1958), 1–2, cited in Mozingo, *Pastoral Capitalism*, 112.

101. Wilde, *Time Out of Mind*, 7.

102. Carol Herselle Krinsky, *Gordon Bunshaft of Skidmore, Owings and Merrill* (Cambridge, MA: MIT Press, 1988), 61.

103. Krinsky, *Gordon Bunshaft*, 61.

104. Krinsky, 55–56.

105. "A Dramatic New Office Building," *Fortune* 56, no. 3 (September 1957): 233.

106. Mozingo, *Pastoral Capitalism*, 188–89.

107. Anthony Bailey, "Moving Out," in *Through the Great City* (New York: MacMillan, 1967), 99.

108. "Insurance Sets a Pattern" *Architectural Forum* 107, no. 3 (September 1957): 113, 114.

109. "Dramatic New Office Building," 164.

110. "Insurance Sets a Pattern," 113.

111. Bailey, "Moving Out," 99.

112. "It's Nice to Work in the Countryside," *Saturday Evening Post*, July 5, 1958, 21.

113. "Dramatic New Office Building," 233.

114. Quoted in Bailey, "Moving Out," 96.

115. "Dramatic New Office Building," 233.

116. Krinsky, *Gordon Bunshaft*, 59.

117. Bailey, "Moving Out," 96.

118. Bailey, 96.

119. Krinsky, *Gordon Bunshaft*, 59.

120. Bailey, "Moving Out," 95.

121. Bailey, 95.

122. "It's Nice to Work in the Countryside," 70.

123. "It's Nice to Work in the Countryside," 70.

124. Krinsky, *Gordon Bunshaft*, 58.

125. "It's Nice to Work in the Countryside," 72.

126. "It's Nice to Work in the Countryside," 72.

127. For a meditation on human relations theory and its embrace by corporate executives in the postwar era, see Reinhold Martin, *The Organizational Complex: Architecture, Media, and Corporate Space* (Cambridge, MA: MIT Press, 2005).

128. Bailey, "Moving Out," 96; "It's Nice to Work in the Countryside," 70.

129. "It's Nice to Work in the Countryside," 70.

130. "It's Nice to Work in the Countryside," 70.

131. Postwar corporations engaged in "human resource" management adopted personality tests widely. By 1956 they had become so widespread that William Whyte included a section describing how to cheat on the tests in his best-selling critique of corporate culture, *The Organization Man* (Philadelphia: University of Pennsylvania Press, 2002), 405–10.

132. "It's Nice to Work in the Countryside," 72.

133. Bailey, "Moving Out," 96.

134. "It's Nice to Work in the Countryside," 70.

135. Bailey, "Moving Out," 96.

136. "It's Nice to Work in the Countryside," 70.

137. "It's Nice to Work in the Countryside," 71.

138. "It's Nice to Work in the Countryside," 71.

139. "It's Nice to Work in the Countryside," 71.

140. "It's Nice to Work in the Countryside," 71.

141. Bailey, "Moving Out," 93-94.

142. "Insurance Sets a Pattern," 125.

143. "Insurance Sets a Pattern," 125.

144. Krinsky, *Gordon Bunshaft*, 147.

145. *An Uncommon Vision: The Des Moines Art Center* (Des Moines, IA: Des Moines Art Center, 1998), 279.

146. Krinsky, *Gordon Bunshaft*, 149.

147. Jennifer P. James, "American Republic Insurance Company Headquarters Building," nomination form, National Register of Historic Places, US Department of the Interior, National Park Service, Polk County, Iowa, November 6, 2015, 30.

148. James, "American Republic Headquarters Building," 30.

149. Watson Powell Jr., preface to *Collection of the American Republic Insurance Company* (Des Moines, IA: American Republic Insurance Company, 1970).

150. Chris Welles, "Total Design on a Grand Scale," *Life Magazine*, April 29, 1966, 59.

151. Welles, "Total Design," 59.

152. Welles, 56.

153. William Marlin, "The Scale of Things," in Yukio Futagawa, ed., *Global Architecture: Kevin Roche and John Dinkeloo and Associates* (Tokyo: A. D. A. Edita, 1974), 6.

154. Marlin, "The Scale of Things," 6.

155. Mozingo, *Pastoral Capitalism*, 8.

156. See "Insurance Sets a Pattern."

157. Bishop, *Capital Formation*, 129–30.

158. Mozingo, *Pastoral Capitalism*, 14.

159. "Pittsburgh Renascent," *Architectural Forum* 91 (November 1949): 62. On the history of Point Park, see Stevens, *Developing Expertise*.

160. For a detailed study of the Prudential Center, see Rubin, *Insuring the City*.

161. *Connecticut General Annual Report, 1968* (Hartford, CT: Connecticut General, 1968), 19.

162. Hanchett, "Financing Suburbia," 321.

163. Prudential Insurance Company of America, *The Prudential Business Campus*, promotional brochure, 1979, Properties Files, Prudential Insurance Company of America Archives.

164. "About Real Estate: Prudential's Projects," *New York Times*, May 11, 1977, Properties Files, Prudential Insurance Company of America Archives.

165. *The Prudential Business Campus*, 1979.

166. Robert E. Lang, "Office Sprawl: The Evolving Geography of Business" (Washington, DC: Brookings Institution, 2000), cited in Mozingo, *Pastoral Capitalism*, 17.

167. "Chip Off the Old Rock," 94.

168. "Chip Off the Old Rock," 92.

Chapter Five

1. National Advisory Commission on Civil Disorders, *Report of the National Advisory Commission on Civil Disorders: Summary of Report* (Washington, DC: US Government Printing Office, 1968), https://www.hsdl.org/?abstract&did=35837.

2. *Meeting the Insurance Crisis of Our Cities: A Report by the President's National Advisory Panel on Insurance in Riot-Affected Areas* (Washington, DC: US Government Printing Office, 1968), 126.

3. *Meeting the Insurance Crisis*, 482.

4. The historical literature on redlining has focused almost entirely on federal programs. For a representative example, see Richard Rothstein, *The Color of Law: A Forgotten History of How Our Government Segregated America* (New York: Liveright, 2017). For a recent exception to this trend, see Keeanga-Yamahtta Taylor, *Race for Profit: How Banks and the Real Estate Industry Undermined Black Homeownership* (Chapel Hill: University of North Carolina Press, 2019).

5. Richard Farmer, "The Long-Term Crisis in Life Insurance," *Journal of Risk and Insurance* 33, no. 4 (December 1966): 624.

6. On the boycott, part of King's "Chicago campaign," see Karen Orren, *Corporate Power and Social Change: The Politics of the Life Insurance Industry* (Baltimore: Johns Hopkins University Press, 1974), 148.

7. Quoted in Orren, *Corporate Power and Social Change*, 149.

8. Quoted in Orren, 149.

9. Orren, 150–51.

10. On Beal's encounter with the uprising in Newark, see Clearinghouse on Corporate Social Responsibility (hereafter cited as CCSR), *A Report on the $2 Billion Urban Investment Program of the Life Insurance Business, 1967–1972* (New York: Institute of Life Insurance, 1973), 10.

11. Charles Moeller, "Economic Implications of the Life Insurance Industry's Investment Program in the Central Cities," *Journal of Risk and Insurance* 36, no. 1 (March 1969), 97.

12. Orren, *Corporate Power and Social Change*, 148.

13. CCSR, *Report on the UIP*, 11. On the president's announcement, see also Moeller, "Economic Implications," 97.

14. "The Cities: A Big First Step," *Time*, September 22, 1967, 24.

15. "The Cities," 24.

16. John Fey, "Insurance in the Public Interest," *Journal of Risk and Insurance* 38, no. 4 (December 1971): 523; Moeller, "Economic Implications," 97.

17. Moeller, 95.

18. Moeller, 95.

19. Moeller, 97.

20. Orren, *Corporate Power and Social Change*, 152.

21. CCSR, *Report on the UIP*, 15.

22. CCSR, 15.

23. CCSR, 15.

24. Moeller, "Economic Implications," 99.

25. CCSR, *Report on the UIP*, 15.

26. Eugene Epstein, "The Insurance Industry's Quiet Retreat," *Business and Society Review* 2 (1972): 41.

27. Epstein, "The Insurance Industry's Quiet Retreat," 41.

28. ILI, "What Can a Billion Dollars Do," 1969, J. Walter Thompson Company, Domestic Advertisements Collection, David M. Rubenstein Rare Book & Manuscript Library, Duke University.

29. ILI, "When You Invest a Billion Dollars to Help the Cities," "What Can a Billion Dollars Do," and "A Lot That Is Said about Urban Problems."

30. See ILI, *Whose Crisis? . . . Yours* and *The Cities . . . Your Challenge Too*, 1969, J. Walter Thompson Company, Domestic Advertisements Collection, David M. Rubenstein Rare Book and Manuscript Library, Duke University.

31. CCSR, *Report on the UIP*, 29.

32. CCSR, 12.

33. CCSR, 12.

34. Orren, *Corporate Power and Social Change*, 171.

35. Orren, 171.

36. Orren, 168.

37. CCSR, *Report on the UIP*, 18.

38. Select Committee on Small Business, *The Impact of Suburban Shopping Centers on Independent Retailers*, Report No. 106, 86th Congress, 1st Sess. (Washington, DC: US Government Printing Office, 1960), 36. See chapter 4 for a discussion of these hearings.

39. CCSR, *Report on the UIP*, 12.

40. CCSR, 19.

41. Moeller, "Economic Implications," 101.

42. Orren, *Corporate Power and Social Change*, 168.

43. Abram Collier, *A Capital Ship: New England Life, a History of America's First Chartered Mutual Insurance Company, 1835–1985* (Boston: New England Life Mutual Insurance Company, 1985), 143–44. On defaults and delinquencies, see CCSR, *Report on the UIP*, 20.

44. Orren, *Corporate Power and Social Change*, 161.

45. Orren, 177.

46. Both examples of community resistance to the UIP come from Orren's study of the program in Chicago. Orren, *Corporate Power and Social Change*, 181.

47. Orren, 175.

48. Epstein, "The Insurance Industry's Quiet Retreat," 40.

49. Epstein, 41.

50. For Karson's denial, see Stanley Karson, "The Insurance Industry Responds," *Business and Society Review* 4 (1972): 72.

51. CCSR, *Report on the UIP*, 34.

234 NOTES TO PAGES 154-160

52. Orren, *Corporate Power and Social Change*, 161.

53. CCSR, *Report on the UIP*, 3.

54. CCSR, 3. On "retained" jobs, see Orren, *Corporate Power and Social Change*, 171.

55. Orren, 147.

56. Allan Gordon, "Putting Premium Dollars to Work: Fostering Community Investing by the Insurance Industry" (California Senate Office of Research, July 1995), 15.

57. Moeller, "Economic Implications," 97.

58. CCSR, *Report on the UIP*, 18.

59. Mary Heen, "Ending Jim Crow Life Insurance Rates," *Northwestern Journal of Law and Social Policy* 4, no. 2 (Fall 2009): 391–92. See also Julia Angwin et al., "Minority Neighborhoods Pay Higher Car Insurance Premiums Than White Areas with the Same Risk," *ProPublica*, April 5, 2017, https://www.propublica.org/article/minority-neighborhoods-higher-car-insurance-premiums -white-areas-same-risk.

60. Heen, "Ending Jim Crow Life Insurance Rates," 392.

61. John Hugh Gilmore, "Insurance Redlining and the Fair Housing Act: The Lost Opportunity of *Mackey v. Nationwide Insurance Companies*," *Catholic University Law Review* 34, no. 2 (Winter 1985): 567–68.

62. It was not until 2013 that the US Department of Housing and Urban Development conclusively ruled that the Fair Housing Act applies to insurance. See Ronen Avraham, Kyle D. Logue, and Daniel Benjamin Schwarcz, "Understanding Insurance Anti-discrimination Laws," *Law & Economics Working Papers* 52 (2013): 1–15.

63. Unlike industries that dealt in more static "goods," such as natural resources, insurance companies were mobile and could move operations to new territories at relatively low costs.

64. Orren, *Corporate Power and Social Change*, 36.

65. Orren, 36.

66. Quoted in Orren, 52.

67. Gerald Keenan, "No Escape from Insurance Redlining," *Business and Society Review* (Fall 1979): 53.

68. C. Robert Hall, statement, Subcommittee on Citizens and Shareholders Rights and Remedies, January 18, 1978, quoted in Gregory Squires, ed., *Insurance Redlining: Disinvestment, Reinvestment, and the Evolving Role of Financial Institutions* (Washington, DC: Urban Institute Press, 1997), 1.

69. Robert Yaspan, "Property Insurance and the American Ghetto: A Study in Social Irresponsibility," *Southern California Law Review* 44 (Fall 1970): 233.

70. Gregory D. Squires, Ruthanne Dewolfe, and Alan S. Dewolfe, "Urban Decline or Disinvestment: Uneven Development, Redlining and the Role of the Insurance Industry," *Social Problems* 27, no. 1 (October 1979): 80.

71. Well into the twenty-first century, anti-redlining activists continue to produce detailed exposés, based on empirical research, disclosing subjective practices underlying supposedly objective risk measurements in property and casualty insurance. For a recent example, see Angwin et al., "Minority Neighborhoods Pay Higher Car Insurance Premiums."

72. Gregory Squires, "Insurance Redlining: Still Fact, Not Fiction," *Shelterforce* 79 (January/February 1995), http://www.nhi.org/online/issues/79/isurred.html.

73. Squires, "Insurance Redlining: Still Fact, Not Fiction."

74. Quoted in Keenan, "No Escape from Insurance Redlining," 54.

75. Midwestern Regional Advisory Committees to the US Commission on Civil Rights, *Insurance Redlining: Fact, Not Fiction* (Washington, DC: US Government Printing Office, 1979), 7.

76. Squires, "Insurance Redlining: Still Fact, Not Fiction."

77. Squires.

78. Joanne Dwyer, "Fair Plans: History, Holtzman and the Arson-for-Profit Hazard," *Fordham Urban Law Journal* 7, no. 3, (1978): 617–48.

79. Squires, Dewolfe, and Dewolfe, "Urban Decline or Disinvestment," 85.

80. See George Knight, "What's Working: Insurance as a Link to Neighborhood Revitalization," in Gregory Squires, ed., *Insurance Redlining: Disinvestment, Reinvestment, and the Evolving Role of Financial Institutions* (Washington, DC: Urban Institute Press, 1997), 215–33.

81. "Darden Gets Senior Allstate Post," *Washington Informer* 19, no. 47 (September 14, 1983): 28.

82. Squires, *Insurance Redlining: Fact, Not Fiction*, 9.

83. Federal riot reinsurance was discontinued by the second Reagan administration.

84. "High Risk Urban Insurance Is Under Attack in State," *New York Times*, April 24, 1977, R1, 8.

85. "High Risk Urban Insurance Is Under Attack," R1.

86. Regina Austin, "The Insurance Classification Controversy," *University of Pennsylvania Law Review* 131, no. 3 (January 1983): 521.

87. Insurance bodies in California, Indiana, Iowa, Kansas, Louisiana, Minnesota, Missouri, New York, Oregon, Puerto Rico, and Virginia all elected to forgo federal riot reinsurance rather than comply with the amendment. See Austin, "Insurance Classification Controversy," 527.

88. "High Risk Urban Insurance Is Under Attack," 8.

89. Ralph Blumenthal, "Insurance Redlining Rises as Homeowners' Hurdle," *New York Times*, January 24, 1979, B1.

90. Blumenthal, "Insurance Redlining Rises," B1.

91. Blumenthal, B1. See also "Insuring a Fair Deal for Homeowners," *New York Times*, June 16, 1978, A26; and E. J. Dionne Jr., "Insurance Redlining and FAIR Rate Revisions," *New York Times*, June 4, 1979, B8.

92. Austin, "Insurance Classification Controversy," 532.

93. Austin, 552.

94. Austin, 552.

Chapter Six

1. Naomi Naierman, Ruth Brannon, and Beverly Wahl, *Sex Discrimination in Insurance: A Guide for Women* (Washington, DC: Women's Equity Action League, 1977), ii.

2. Insurance companies used the term *sex* to refer to biological sex at birth for most of the twentieth century. Though insurance underwriters drew on data related to both biological differences and socially mediated behavioral differences between male and female insureds, the term *gender* was rarely used within the industry before the twenty-first century.

3. Most scholarly accounts of the late twentieth-century insurance discrimination debates have emerged out of the critical legal studies movement and governmentality scholarship. See Jonathan Simon, "The Ideological Effects of Actuarial Practices," *Law & Society Review* 22 (1988): 771–800; David Knights and Theo Vurdubakis, "Calculations of Risk: Towards an Understanding of Insurance as a Moral and Political Practice," *Accounting Organizations and Society* 18 (1993): 729–64; Regina Austin, "The Insurance Classification Controversy," *University of Pennsylvania Law Review* 131, no. 3 (January 1983): 517–83; Brian Glenn, "The Shifting Rhetoric

of Insurance Denial," *Law and Society Review* 34 (2000): 779–808; and Carol A. Heimer, "Insuring More, Ensuring Less: The Costs and Benefits of Private Regulation through Insurance," in Tom Baker and Jonathan Simon, eds., *Embracing Risk: The Changing Culture of Insurance and Responsibility* (Chicago: University of Chicago Press, 2002), 116–45.

4. H.R. 100 was introduced to the House of Representatives on January 3, 1983, and referred to the House Energy and Commerce Committee. Opponents responding to the public pressure amended the original version to apply unisex treatment only to group employee insurance plans, not to individual automobile, life, and health insurance plans. The cosponsors, Representatives Dingell (D-Mich.), Florio (D-N.J.), and Mikulski (D-Md.), declined to bring the amended and greatly weakened version to a floor vote. S. 372 was introduced to the Senate on February 1, 1983, and referred to the Senate Commerce, Science, and Transportation Committee, which took no action on the bill. See 128 Cong. Rec. 42 (1983); and 129 Cong. Rec. 795 (1983).

5. A large body of literature embraces the notion of "backlash" as a means of understanding the diminished willingness of Americans to support civil rights and feminist objectives during the 1970s and 1980s. See esp. Jane Mansbridge, *Why We Lost the ERA* (Chicago: University of Chicago Press, 1986); and Susan Faludi, *Backlash: The Undeclared War against American Women* (New York: Three Rivers Press, 1991).

6. Life, health, property, and casualty firms insure against different outcomes, but classification data is used in similar ways for most forms of insurance sold on the private market. Categories like marital status, biological sex, place of residence, and type of employment, for example, are used across the industry to classify risk. For a study of the development of risk classification structures in the field of life insurance, see Dan Bouk, "The Science of Difference: Developing Tools for Discrimination in the American Life Insurance Industry, 1830–1930," *Enterprise & Society* 12, no. 4 (December 2011): 771–31; and Dan Bouk, *How Our Days Became Numbered: Risk and the Rise of the Statistical Individual* (Chicago: University of Chicago Press, 2015).

7. Amanda M. Czerniawski, "From Average to Ideal: The Evolution of the Height and Weight Tables in the United States, 1836–1943," *Social Science History* 31 (2007): 273–96.

8. Race-integrated mortality tables had become an industry-wide standard in life insurance by the 1960s, a development enacted voluntarily by insurers fearing impacts of civil rights legislation. Race-blind underwriting was widely embraced in other fields by the end of that decade, but redlining (the use of geographical location as a proxy for race) continues to this day. For a definitive account of the removal of race from insurance underwriting, see Mary Heen, "Ending Jim Crow Life Insurance Rates," *Northwestern Journal of Law and Social Policy* 4, no. 2 (Fall 2009): 391–92.

9. The threat of "overly individualized" classification is mentioned often in discussions surrounding human genomic testing and its potential impacts on insurance practice. These discussions typically reflect popular fears surrounding insurance-industry control of sensitive genetic information and the likelihood that it might lead to "unfair" discrimination. Public discussions of genomic testing rarely note the challenges that widespread availability of this kind of data might pose to the risk-spreading function of private insurance systems. See Antoinette Rouvroy, *Human Genes and Neoliberal Governance: A Foucauldian Critique* (New York: Routledge-Cavendish, 2008).

10. For elaboration on this argument, see Tom Baker, "Containing the Promise of Insurance: Adverse Selection and Risk Classification," *Social Science Research Network*, October 14, 2002, https://ssrn.com/abstract=322581.

11. Of course, categories like sex (or gender)—deemed by insurers to be "easily identifiable"— are not always as natural or obvious as such arguments imply. At the same time, insurers do not

consider many easily identifiable characteristics relevant to actuarial calculations. Hair color, for example, is not considered a useful category by the industry when classifying and calculating risk.

12. The sociological and legal literature on moral hazard is extensive. For historical accounts, see Tom Baker, "On the Genealogy of Moral Hazard," *Texas Law Review* 75 (1996): 237–92; and Carol Heimer, *Reactive Risk and Rational Action: Managing Moral Hazard in Insurance Contracts* (Berkeley: University of California Press, 1985). For a study of rhetorical uses of moral hazard and adverse selection by the insurance industry, see Baker, "Containing the Promise of Insurance."

13. Naierman, Brannon, and Wahl, *Sex Discrimination in Insurance*, 3.

14. *Insurance and Women in North Carolina: Report of the Task Force on Sex Discrimination in Insurance* (Raleigh: State of North Carolina Department of Insurance, 1976), 3.

15. Midwestern Regional Advisory Committees to the US Commission on Civil Rights, *Insurance Redlining: Fact, Not Fiction* (Washington, DC: US Government Printing Office, 1979), 7.

16. Quoted in "Economic Problems of Women," *Hearings Before the Joint Economic Committee*, 92nd Cong., 1st Sess., July 10–12, 1973, 169 (prepared statement of Barbara Shack, assistant director, New York Civil Liberties Union).

17. Quoted in "Economic Problems of Women," 169.

18. For an early example, see Susan Stoiber, "Insured in Case of War, Suicide, and Organs Particular to Females," *Ms.*, May 1973.

19. National Commission on the Observance of International Women's Year (hereafter cited as NCOIWY), *Insurance: A Workshop Guide* (Washington, DC: NCOIWY, 1977), 5–7.

20. NCOIWY, *Insurance: A Workshop Guide*, 7.

21. Barbara J. Lautzenheiser, "Unisex Pricing Is Unfair to Women: Letter to Editor," *New York Times*, November 9, 1983, A26.

22. Quoted in "Pro and Con: Women vs. the Insurance Industry—Sex, Risk, and the Actuarial Equation," *New York Times*, August 16, 1987, E26.

23. Austin, "The Insurance Classification Controversy," 541.

24. Austin, 539.

25. "Pro and Con: Women vs. the Insurance Industry," E26.

26. Quoted in Michael deCourcy Hinds, "Parity in Insurance for Men and Women," *New York Times*, June 10, 1983, B7.

27. NCOIWY, *Insurance: A Workshop Guide*, 4.

28. Nondiscrimination in Insurance Act of 1983, H.R. 100, *Hearings Before the Subcommittee on Commerce, Transportation, and Tourism of the House Committee on Energy and Commerce*, 98th Cong., 1st Sess. (1983), 212.

29. Nick Ravo, "Hartford Weighs Insurance Curbs," *New York Times*, February 28, 1988, 33.

30. Access to insurance for transgender Americans has become a new site of insurance activism in recent years. The impact of transgender activism on sex-based rating structures stands to significantly disrupt insurance practice and offers a promising new field of research for insurance scholars.

31. NCOIWY, *Insurance: A Workshop Guide*, 6.

32. On *Manhart*, see Lea Brilmayer et al., "Sex Discrimination in Employer-Sponsored Insurance Plans: A Legal and Demographic Analysis," *University of Chicago Law Review* 47 (1980): 505; Gordon R. Kanofsky, "The End of Sex Discrimination in Employer-Operated Pension Plans: The Challenge of the *Manhart* Case," *Duke Law Journal* (1979): 682–708; and Harold E. Rainbolt, "Unequal

Contributions to Employee Retirement Plans Determined by Using Sex Segregated Morality Tables Constitute Unlawful Sex Discrimination under Title VII," *University of Arkansas at Little Rock Law Review* 2, no. 2 (1979): 403–18. For a representative response from the insurance industry, see "The Manhart Case," *Actuary: Newsletter of the Society of Actuaries* 12, no. 5 (May 1978): 1–3.

33. *City of Los Angeles Department of Water and Power v. Manhart* (435 U.S. 702), January 18, 1978.

34. *City of Los Angeles Department of Water and Power v. Manhart.*

35. Elinor Langer, "Why Big Business Is Trying to Defeat the ERA: The Economic Implications of Equality," *Ms.*, May 1976, 64–66, 100–108.

36. National Organization of Women, "Will the ERA Be Sacrificed for the Insurance Numbers Game?," *Los Angeles Times*, June 2, 1982, J4.

37. Quoted in John Herberer, "NOW Chief Suggests Corporations Played Major Role in Defeating the Rights Amendment," *New York Times*, June 28, 1982, A1.

38. Quoted in Herberer, "NOW Chief Suggest Corporations Played Major Role," A1.

39. James Kilpatrick, "Unisex Insurance Measure Went the Way of the ERA," *Ocala Star Banner*, May 1, 1984.

40. Common Cause, *Capitol Letters/Invisible Ink: A Common Cause Study of the Insurance Industry's Undisclosed Lobbying Campaign against Unisex Insurance* (Washington DC: Common Cause, 1983), 6. Several prominent Republicans supported the bills, including Senator Robert Packwood of Oregon and, initially, President Ronald Reagan.

41. Hinds, "Parity in Insurance," B7.

42. Peter W. Bernstein, Anna Cifelli, Richard I. Kirkland Jr., and Craig C. Carter, "Getting Tough about Unisex," *Fortune*, July 25, 1983, 21.

43. Common Cause, *Capitol Letters/Invisible Ink*, 6.

44. Historical evidence of corporate lobbying activities is notoriously difficult to find. My figures and evidence come from two sources: a study produced by the consumer rights organization Common Cause in 1983, and materials archived in the Truth Tobacco Industry Documents archive. As part of the Tobacco Master Settlement Agreement, the tobacco industry was required to make a treasure trove of industry documents available to the public. One particular document, an August 27, 1986, memorandum from a field meeting for regional vice presidents and directors of the Tobacco Institute, includes an extended pitch from the Targeted Communications Corporation (TCC), a marketing group geared toward "mobilizing unaffiliated citizens in support of corporate goals." In selling their services to the Tobacco Institute, the TCC emphasized past successes in "comprehensive constituency mobilization programs." The defeat of proposed unisex insurance legislation during the 1983–1984 session of Congress was offered up by the TCC as its crown jewel, a prime example of the company's ability to sway public opinion and impact legislation in favor of its corporate clients. See Common Cause, *Capitol Letters/Invisible Ink*; and Tobacco Institute, memorandum, "Grassroots Seminar at Field Staff Meeting," August 27, 1986, https://www.industrydocuments.ucsf.edu/tobacco/docs/#id=hkgj0051.

45. Common Cause, *Capitol Letters/Invisible Ink*, 8–9 (emphasis in the original).

46. Common Cause, 9.

47. Kilpatrick, "Unisex Insurance Measure."

48. Hinds, "Parity in Insurance," B7.

49. Quoted in Hinds, B7.

50. Clara Germani, "Industry Fights Back against Campaign for 'Unisex' Insurance Rates," *Christian Science Monitor*, June 14, 1983, 6.

51. Germani, "Industry Fights Back," 6; Al Goldsmith, "Unisex Insurance Issue Starts Smoking," *Best's Insurance Management Reports—Life/Health* 27 (August 29, 1983): 1–2.

52. "Be Careful about Unisex Insurance," *New York Times*, April 20, 1983, A26.

53. See Spencer Kimball, "Reverse Sex Discrimination: *Manhart*," *American Bar Foundation Research Journal* 4 (Winter 1979): 83–139.

54. Tamar Lewin, "Insurers' Rates Biased by Sex," *New York Times*, March 23, 1982, D2.

55. Packwood quoted in Hinds, "Parity in Insurance," B7; Barbara Bergmann, "Insurance by Gender, Point Counter Point: Beware the Industry's Logic," *New York Times*, June 26, 1983, F2.

56. "Sexy Premiums: Feminists vs. Insurance Firms," *Time*, June 20, 1983, 62.

57. Kristin L. Nelson, "Is Gender Neutral Dead?," *Best's Review—Property/Casualty* (February 1995): 33–34.

58. Nelson, "Is Gender Neutral Dead?," 34.

59. *Arizona Governing Committee v. Norris*, 103, U.S. Supreme Court 3492 (1983). On *Norris*, see Mary Heen, "Sex Discrimination in Pensions and Retirement Annuity Plans after *Arizona Governing Committee v. Norris*: Recognizing and Remedying Employer Non-compliance," *Women's Rights Law Reporter* 8, no. 3 (1985).

60. Indeed, this argument was taken up by a number of critics of *Manhart*. See Lea Brilmayer et. al., "The Efficient Use of Group Averages as Nondiscrimination: A Rejoinder to Professor Benston," *University of Chicago Law Review* 50 (1983): 222–49; and Simon, "Ideological Effects of Actuarial Practices."

61. See Daniel Rogers, *Age of Fracture* (Cambridge, MA: Belknap Press, 2011); and Lisa Duggan, *The Twilight of Equality: Neoliberalism, Cultural Politics, and the Attack on Democracy* (Boston: Beacon Press, 2003).

62. See esp. Simon, "The Ideological Effects of Actuarial Practices"; Baker, "Risk, Insurance, and the Social Construction of Responsibility"; and Knights and Vurdubakis, "Calculations of Risk." See also Ericson, Doyle, and Barry, *Insurance as Governance*; and Ericson and Doyle, *Risk and Morality*.

63. Baker, "Containing the Promise of Insurance." See also Lorraine Daston, "Life, Chance, and Life Chances," *Daedalus* 137, no. 1 (Winter 2008): 5–14.

64. Baker, "Containing the Promise of Insurance," 3.

65. Baker, 14.

66. Daniel Defert, "Popular Life and Insurance Technology," in Burchell, Gordon, and Miller, *The Foucault Effect*, 213.

67. J. Simon, "Ideological Effects of Actuarial Practices," 798.

68. Deborah Hellman, "Is Actuarially Fair Insurance Pricing Actually Fair? A Case Study in Insuring Battered Women," *Harvard Civil Rights and Civil Liberties Law Review* 21 (1997): 355–411.

69. Deborah Stone, "The Struggle for the Soul of Health Insurance," *Journal of Health Politics, Policy and Law* 18, no. 2 (Summer 1993).

70. For a study of the use of risk classification in education, see Michael A. Peters, "The New Prudentialism in Education: Actuarial Rationality and the Entrepreneurial Self," *Educational Theory* 55, no. 2 (2005): 123–37. For a study of risk aggregation in criminology, see Bernard Harcourt, *Against Prediction: Profiling, Policing, and Punishing in an Actuarial Age* (Chicago: University of Chicago Press, 2007).

71. Kimberly Yuracko and Ronen Avraham, "Valuing Black Lives: A Constitutional Challenge to Race-Based Tables in Calculating Tort Damages," *California Law Review* 106, no. 2 (2018): 325–72.

Epilogue

1. Josiah Royce, *"War and Insurance": An Address Delivered before the Philosophical Union of the University of California, Berkeley* (New York: Macmillan, 1914), 64.

2. Frederik Pohl [Edson McCann, pseud.], *Preferred Risk: A Science Fiction Novel* (New York: Simon & Schuster, 1955).

3. Though many scholars have approached insurance as a form of governance, this notion is explored most explicitly in Richard Ericson, Aaron Doyle and Dean Barry, eds., *Insurance as Governance* (Toronto: University of Toronto Press 2003).

4. Wallace Stevens, "Insurance and Social Change," *Wallace Stevens Journal* 4, no. 3 (Fall 1980): 37–39.

5. Christy Ford Chapin, *Ensuring America's Health: The Public Creation of the Corporate Health Care System* (New York: Cambridge University Press, 2017).

6. In recent years, much attention has been paid to the federal government's historical role in launching and perpetuating discrimination in American housing through government programs like the FHA. Racial bias at the FHA—depicted vividly in redlining maps from the 1930s—is cited often as the cause of long-term racial disparities in home ownership and wealth creation in the United States. A growing literature on housing discrimination perpetrated by banks and real estate corporations has attracted attention to private industry, but more work is needed to understand the impacts of discriminatory practices in insurance and their crucial role in perpetuating inequalities in housing and wealth. See Keeanga-Yamahtta Taylor, *Race for Profit: How Banks and the Real Estate Industry Undermined Black Homeownership* (Chapel Hill: University of North Carolina Press, 2019); Richard Rothstein, *The Color of Law: A Forgotten History of How Our Government Segregated America* (New York: Liveright, 2017); Adrienne Brown and Valerie Smith, eds., *Race and Real Estate* (New York: Oxford University Press, 2015); and Beryl Satter, *Family Properties: How the Struggle over Race and Real Estate Transformed Chicago and Urban America* (New York: Metropolitan, 2009).

7. This exemption allows insurers to collaborate in the setting of prices and engage in other anticompetitive behaviors that increase revenues by raising premiums and limiting coverage and reimbursement.

8. Robert Hunter, Tom Feltner, and Douglas Heller, *What Works: A Review of Auto Insurance Rate Regulation in America and How Best Practices Save Billions of Dollars*, Consumer Federation of America, November 2013, https://consumerfed.org/reports/read-the-entire-report-here-what -works-a-review-of-auto-insurance-rate-regulation-in-america-and-how-best-practices-save-bill ions-of-dollars/. The same report found that Californians spent 0.3 percent less on auto insurance in 2010 than they spent in 1989, while the drivers in the rest of the nation spent 43.3 percent more.

9. An archived memo from 1986, produced during a meeting between top auto insurance executives and the marketing and consulting firm Lord, Geller, Federico, Einstein (a subsidiary of J. Walter Thompson), offers an example of these kinds of efforts. Titled "Top Secret Insurance," the memo calls for insurance industry collaboration with the consulting firm: "Call for insurance companies to band together to mount effort to defeat further legislation, Prop 103 in California. . . . 5 of 6 mayors are in." Memorandum, "Top Secret Insurance," 1986, J. Walter Thompson Company, Domestic Advertisements Collection, David M. Rubenstein Rare Book and Manuscript Library, Duke University.

10. Julia Angwin et al., "Minority Neighborhoods Pay Higher Car Insurance Premiums Than White Areas with the Same Risk," *ProPublica*, April 5, 2019, https://www.propublica.org /article/minority-neighborhoods-higher-car-insurance-premiums-white-areas-same-risk.

11. See, for example, Michael W. Davis, "ADA Lobbies for Repeal of McCarran–Ferguson," *Dentistry Today*, October 17, 2018, https://www.dentistrytoday.com/news/todays-dental-news /item/3932-ada-lobbies-for-repeal-of-mccarran-ferguson.

12. Kaiser Family Foundation, "Key Facts about the Uninsured Population," Henry J. Kaiser Family Foundation, December 7, 2018, https://www.kff.org/uninsured/fact-sheet/key-facts-about -the-uninsured-population/.

13. As of March 2019, fifteen states had not expanded their programs: Alabama, Florida, Georgia, Kansas, Mississippi, Missouri, North Carolina, Oklahoma, South Carolina, North Carolina, South Dakota, Tennessee, Texas, Wisconsin, and Wyoming. See Kaiser Family Foundation, "Key Facts about the Uninsured."

14. Kaiser Family Foundation, "Key Facts about the Uninsured"; and Samantha Artiga, Kendal Orgera, and Anthony Damico, *Changes in Health Coverage by Race and Ethnicity since Implementation of the ACA, 2013–2017* (Washington, DC: Kaiser Family Foundation, 2019), https:// www.kff.org/disparities-policy/issue-brief/changes-in-health-coverage-by-race-and-ethnicity -since-implementation-of-the-aca-2013-2017/.

15. Joel Ario and Tom Baker, "Making Sense of Healthcare Exchanges, and Their Future," March 31, 2015, in *Case in Point Podcasts*, produced by University of Pennsylvania Law School, no. 25 video, 37:06, https://scholarship.law.upenn.edu/podcasts/25.

16. Ezekiel Emanuel, *Reinventing American Health Care: How the Affordable Care Act Will Improve Our Terribly Complex, Blatantly Unjust, Outrageously Expensive, Grossly Inefficient, Error Prone System* (New York: Public Affairs, 2014).

17. Jocelyn Kiley, "60% in US Say Health Care Coverage Is Government's Responsibility," Pew Research Center, October 3, 2018, https://www.pewresearch.org/fact-tank/2018/10/03/most -continue-to-say-ensuring-health-care-coverage-is-governments-responsibility/.

18. The state has been a central cite of inquiry for historical research on the post-1945 period for more than two decades. For a recent study that reflects these efforts, see Brent Cebul, Lily Geismer, and Mason B. Williams, eds., *Shaped by the State: Toward a New Political History of the Twentieth Century* (Chicago: University of Chicago Press, 2019).

19. Dan Bouk, *How Our Days Became Numbered: Risk and the Rise of the Statistical Individual* (Chicago: University of Chicago Press, 2015).

20. The CEO of Allstate Insurance Company, which offers one of the most popular telematics devices, went on record in 2015, claiming that the company plans to "sell this information we get from people driving around to various people and capture some additional profit source." Katie Fitzpatrick, "None of Your Business: The Rise of Surveillance Capitalism," *Nation*, April 30, 2019, https:// www.thenation.com/article/shoshana-zuboff-age-of-surveillance-capitalism-book-review/.

21. Birny Birnbaum, "Credit Scoring in Insurance: An Unfair Practice," United Policy Holders, 2019, https://www.uphelp.org/pubs/credit-scoring-insurance-unfair-practice.

22. As of 2019, credit-based insurance scoring has been prohibited in California, Massachusetts, and Hawaii for auto insurance, and Maryland and Hawaii for homeowners insurance. Birnbaum, "Credit Scoring in Insurance."

23. Jess Bidgood, "'I Live Paycheck to Paycheck': A West Virginia Teacher Explains Why She's on Strike," *New York Times*, March 1, 2018, https://www.nytimes.com/2018/03/01/us/west -virginia-teachers-strike.html.

24. "Fitbit Inspire and Inspire HR," Fitbit, 2019, https://www.fitbit.com/inspire.

25. For focused studies on the relationship between genetics and insurance, see Antoinette Rouvroy, *Human Genes and Neoliberal Governance: A Foucauldian Critique* (New York:

Routledge-Cavendish, 2008); and Mark Rothstein, *Genetics and Life Insurance: Medical Underwriting and Social Policy* (Cambridge, MA: MIT Press, 2009).

26. Tom Baker, "Containing the Promise of Insurance: Adverse Selection and Risk Classification," *Social Science Research Network*, October 14, 2002, https://ssrn.com/abstract=322581.

27. US National Library of Medicine, "What Is Genetic Discrimination?," NIH: Genetics Home Reference, July 9, 2019, https://ghr.nlm.nih.gov/primer/testing/discrimination.

28. Sarah Zhang, "The Loopholes in the Law Prohibiting Genetic Discrimination," *Atlantic*, March 13, 2017, accessed June 12, 2019, https://www.theatlantic.com/health/archive/2017/03/genetic-discrimination-law-gina/519216/.

29. Classic works like Theodore Porter's *Trust in Numbers: The Pursuit of Objectivity in Science and Public Life* (Princeton, NJ: Princeton University Press, 1995) and *The Rise of Statistical Thinking, 1820–1900* (Princeton, NJ: Princeton University Press, 1986) have been joined in recent years by new studies penned by scholars seeking to understand the rise of big data. See Bouk, *How Our Days Became Numbered*; Sarah Igo, *The Averaged American: Surveys, Citizens, and the Making of a Mass Public* (Cambridge, MA: Harvard University Press, 2008); Sarah Igo, *The Known Citizen: A History of Privacy in Modern America* (Cambridge, MA: Harvard University Press, 2018); Bernard Harcourt, *Exposed: Desire and Disobedience in the Digital Age* (Cambridge, MA: Harvard University Press, 2015); Deborah Lupton, *The Quantified Self* (Malden, MA: Polity Press, 2015); and Shoshana Zuboff, *The Age of Surveillance Capitalism: The Fight for a Human Future at the New Frontier of Power* (New York: Public Affairs, 2019).

30. Bouk's *How Our Days Became Numbered* is unique in this regard. Bouk identifies insurance as a crucial site in the development of statistical quantification of individuals and groups in the United States.

31. Tom Baker and Jonathan Simon, eds., *Embracing Risk: The Changing Culture of Insurance and Responsibility* (Chicago: University of Chicago Press, 2002).

32. For an astute analysis of the privatization of pensions that occurred during the final decades of the twentieth century, see Jennifer Klein's epilogue to *For All These Rights: Business, Labor, and the Shaping of America's Public-Private Welfare State* (Princeton, NJ: Princeton University Press, 2006), 258–75.

33. Jacob Hacker, *The Great Risk Shift: The New Economic Insecurity and the Decline of the American Dream* (New York: Oxford University Press, 2006).

34. Jennifer Silva, *Coming Up Short: Working-Class Adulthood in an Age of Uncertainty* (New York: Oxford University Press, 2013). On millennials and homeownership, see Yilan Xu et al., "Homeownership among Millennials: The Deferred American Dream?," *Family and Consumer Science Research Journal*, 44 (2015): 201–12.

35. Silva, *Coming Up Short*.

36. Gallup, "Healthcare System," June 5, 2019, https://news.gallup.com/poll/4708/healthcare-system.aspx.

Index

Black populations (*cont.*)
 clearance and, 97, 98, 99, 133, 224n146; urban
  investment and, 150–51, 152, 154. *See also*
  discriminatory practices; racial discrimination;
  racial discrimination in housing developments;
  racial segregation
Blighted Areas Redevelopment Act of 1947 (IL), 97
Boston, 122, 133
Bouk, Dan, 46, 222n76
Boys Clubs of America, 58
Brooklyn High School of Automotive Trades,
  63, 64
Brown, Arnold, 55
Bruckner, Richard, 164
Bryson, Lyman, 42, 43
Bunshaft, Gordon, 124, 127, 129
Burke, Yvonne Brathwaite, 167–68
Business and Society Review, 153, 155

California Department of Insurance, 193
"C.G. Partition," 129
Chance to Build, A (film; ILI), 149
Chapin, Christy Ford, 193
Chicago: Black populations and, 94–95, 97, 110,
  150–51, 152; insurance home offices and, 121,
  122, 229n89; life insurance housing develop-
  ments and, 76, 94–99; redlining and, 158–59;
  slum clearance and, 95, 97, 98, 99, 152; subur-
  banization and, 134
Chicago Building Congress, 96
Chicago Daily Tribune, 96
Chicago Housing Authority, 95
Christian Science Monitor, 83–84
Cigna Insurance Company, 182
*City of Los Angeles Department of Water and
  Power v. Manhart. See Manhart* decision
Civil Rights Act of 1968: Title VII, 180; Title VIII,
  101
Clearinghouse on Corporate Social Responsibil-
  ity, 153, 154, 232n10
Cold War, 27, 105, 211–12n42, 226n9
College Life Insurance Company, 131–32
Columbia plan, 60, 217n78, 217n80
Columbia University, 60
Commentary Magazine, 89
Committee for Fair Insurance Rates, 176
Committee of Parkmerced Residents, 101
Committee to End Discrimination in Parkchester,
  100
Common Cause, 183
communism, 27, 34
Community Service Society, 85
Connecticut General Life Insurance Company,
  25, 134; shopping centers and, 111, 118; suburban
  home offices and, 120, 123–29, 131, 132, 144,
  230n98

Cook, Dean, 67
crime rates and insurance, 12, 76, 157
Cullen, Paul, 64, 65–66

Dawes, Henry, 125–26
Demas, Corinne, 73, 74, 75
Dinkeloo, John, 132
Directing Your Dollars (filmstrip; ILI), 54
discriminatory practices: actuarial fairness and,
  10–11, 12, 164, 169, 184, 185, 187, 188, 189; auto
  insurance and, 141, 157, 160–61, 193–94; class-
  based, 10, 91, 140–41, 197–98; income-based, 76,
  82, 84, 90; insurance as governance and, 13, 74,
  76, 86; property and casualty insurance and,
  141, 142, 143, 156–59, 163, 176, 234n62, 234n71;
  shopping centers vs. small retailers and, 117–19;
  suburban housing and, 110, 140, 141; urban
  investment and, 147, 148, 152, 155; women and
  insurance and, 11–12, 167–69, 170, 171, 173–79,
  186–88, 235n2, 235–36n3, 236–37n11. *See also*
  racial discrimination; racial discrimination
  in housing developments; racial segregation;
  redlining; risk classification; risk management
"Do-It-Yourself American" campaign, 28–31
Doron Precision Systems, 67
Dorsey, Joseph, 88
Dorsey v. Stuyvesant Town Corporation, 88, 222n84
"Double-V" campaign, 87
Douglas, Mary, 3–4
Dowling, Monroe, 88
Dublin, Louis, 43

Eastern Underwriter, 80
Ebony, 92
Ecker, Frederick, 75, 76, 82, 87, 89, 227n37
educational curriculum, 23, 52–58; "how to live,"
  56–58, 216n63; for women, 54, 55–56. *See also*
  public service programming
Education for Living series, 52–54
Eleven Stories High (Demas), 73, 74
Elmo Roper polling, 25, 27, 55, 211n35
Emanuel, Ezekiel, 195, 196
Epstein, Eugene, 153, 155
Equal Rights Amendment (ERA), 180–81
Equitable Life Assurance Society, 20, 79, 95, 108,
  111–12, 123, 133
Esquire, 92
Ewald, François, 3, 4

Facing the Future's Risks (Bryson), 42
Fair Access to Insurance Requirements (FAIR),
  163–65, 187, 235n87
Fair Housing Act of 1968, 101, 140, 157, 234n62
Family (sculpture; Noguchi), 125
Family Economist (ILI), 55
Farmer, Richard, 142

107, 125–26, 127–28, 174–75, 180. *See also* risk
   classification
Women's Equity Action League (WEAL), 174,
   178, 180
workers: group insurance plans and, 5–7, 8, 59;
   health insurance and, 7, 8; industrial insurance
   and, 6, 46–47, 48; insurance office employees
   and, 125–26, 127–28, 131; public health and safety
   programs and, 46–50, 59; slum clearance and,

85, 88–89, 133; suburbanization and, 134–36;
   women, 57–58, 107, 125–26, 127–28, 174–75, 180
workplace accidents, 3, 59, 60
Wright, Constance, 90

Yale University, 60

Zachary, Jacqueline, 179
Zipp, Samuel, 76